WHERE DEREGULATION WENT WRONG:

A Look at the Causes
Behind Savings and Loan Failures
In the 1980s

Norman Strunk & Fred Case

ontents

Addenda

List of Tables

List of Exhibits

Preface

This book tells a sad story about the many forces that brought hard times to the savings and loan business. What emerges all too clearly is that when the business was "deregulated," the Congress, the administration and the government agencies assigned to supervise and examine these institutions badly misjudged what was happening. In general, the book demonstrates that the savings and loan failures of the 1980s are part of the legacy of deregulation.

As president of the U.S. League of Savings Institutions, the major trade group for the savings and loan business, I asked Norman Strunk to write this book. A great student of the business, he is my predecessor as the chief executive officer of the U.S. League and is a very close friend and associate.

He has served the savings institution business, on both the national and international level, for 50 years. He joined the U.S. League in 1938 as a research assistant, became its executive vice president in 1950, and was elected chief executive officer in 1952. He led the business during its period of great postwar growth, when it grew from $25 billion to nearly $600 billion in assets and the League grew from a staff of 40 to more than 400.

When he retired from the U.S. League in 1980, he became secretary-general of the International Union of Building Societies and Savings Associations, a world-wide organization of thrift and home financing institutions with members in 67 countries. He retired from that position in 1986, but remains affiliated with the U.S. League as senior counselor.

Dr. Fred E. Case, who collaborated with Mr. Strunk on this book, is Professor Emeritus at the Graduate School of Management of the University of California at Los Angeles (UCLA). The author of 18 books, he is widely recognized as an expert on real estate investing, financing, appraising, analysis and forecasting. As a business consultant, his clients have included savings associations, banks and various state agencies in California; and for a time he was an economist for the California Savings League. Like Mr. Strunk, he was also appointed by the Federal Savings and Loan Insurance Corporation to the board of an institution in the FSLIC's management consignment program.

The book these two scholars have produced should prove a valuable source of information to future students of the savings and loan business. As their book shows, from the beginning, the deregulation of savings institutions was characterized by a series of governmental blunders.

It is incredible that Congress undertook to deregulate savings rates during a period of extreme inflation, when interest rates had soared to double-digit levels. In early 1980, for instance, rates on six-month Treasury bills, which had a direct impact on savings costs, touched as high as 15.100% in March. They fell back to single-digit levels for four months beginning in May, but moved back up to double-digit levels again, peaking at 15.548% in August 1981, and not returning to single-digit levels until September 1982.

Despite the fact that at the time most savings institutions had large portfolios of low-yielding, long-term mortgages, savings-rate deregulation began in earnest in 1980 with passage of the Depository Institutions Deregulation and Monetary Control Act. This created the early "spread" problems that found most of these institutions forced to pay more for savings than they were earning on their investment portfolios, setting the stage for many of the problems that followed.

It was a blunder on the part of the regulatory and supervisory authorities not to tighten up as deregulation continued during this difficult period. But the regulatory authorities failed to respond to the need to keep closer watch on these institutions as they began using the new powers suddenly thrust upon them, or to monitor the entry of the so called "high fliers" who moved into the business to take advantage of the situation.

The Bank Board of the early 1980s was not organized or equipped to beef up its regulatory apparatus. It was philosophically inclined to encourage institutions to undertake new kinds of investments that carried risks unfamiliar to them rather than exercising the greater regulatory responsibility it should have assumed in light of these new risks. As a result, it did not take steps that might have enabled regulators to detect problems in their early stages and correct bad situations before they got out of hand.

It is also incredible that the administration opposed bringing the regulatory apparatus up to speed, refusing to give a new Bank Board the manpower and support it needed to cope with the bad asset problems that began developing later in the 1980s. These problems often involved losses suffered by the "high fliers" and newcomers who moved into the business earlier in the decade, when the Bank Board's approach had been to encourage a "wide open" environment despite the many risks that entailed.

As the Strunk case study makes clear, it was a mistake for Congress to delay so long in authorizing adjustable-rate mortgages for the business nationwide, although given the huge portfolios of low-yielding, fixed-rate loans held by savings institutions in the late 1970s, ARM authority a few years earlier would have helped but not made a decisive difference. With ARMs, portfolio yields would have been somewhat higher when the deregulation of savings rates began in earnest but not high enough to avoid the destructive "spread" problems that quickly began eroding the net worth of the business.

Overall, this report is a story of bad judgments at many levels. But while hindsight makes it easy to second-guess what regulatory authorities and financial institutions should have done, this book must also be viewed in the context of the hostile economic environment, which set the stage for the savings and loan failures of the 1980s.

Shortly before deregulation began, the sky-rocketing price of oil had sent the inflation rate soaring to unprecedented levels. Savings associations were forced to operate in an environment in which deposits were lured away by unregulated competitors, primarily money market mutual funds. The money funds could pay higher market rates than the regulated rates savings associations were allowed to pay. As a result, savings associations had little or no money to lend during a period when they could have raised overall portfolio returns by making loans at higher rates. They were also hurt by some unrealistically low state usury ceilings and by "due-on-sale" rulings and laws that, in many states, forced them to assume existing loans at rates less than they were paying for savings, further inhibiting their ability to make new and more profitable loans.

The events documented in this book are not isolated developments. The regional depressions that triggered massive loan defaults and slashed real estate values in many parts of the country after deregulation was well under way have affected other kinds of institutions, too. Many commercial banks located in the Southwest and other depressed areas of the country are now in the same situation many savings associations found themselves in a short time ago.

While the deregulation of savings rates during a period of great inflation and high interest rates was the Achilles heel of the savings and loan business, the sharp drop in oil prices was the major development affecting the commercial banking business. As this report is being published, banking regulators are now trying to determine what to do about the growing major banking problems in the Southwest. The mounting problems of the Federal Deposit Insurance Corporation, which insures deposits in commercial banks, look more and more like those of the Federal Savings and Loan Insurance Corporation, which insures deposits at savings institutions.

A fourth quarter 1987 report by the FDIC found that one-quarter of the nation's banks are unprofitable. It also found that the largest number of unprofitable banks are located in the economically depressed Southwest, where the largest single number of unprofitable savings institutions are concentrated. Like many savings institutions there, banks must also cope with severely depressed regional economies that have resulted in thousands of loan defaults and a sharp decline in real estate values.

This story isn't over—and the deregulation of savings and loan associations is just part of a broad movement that involves all providers of financial services. But it illustrates the risks "deregulators" take when they venture into uncharted waters with an excess of enthusiasm and a lack of appreciation for the consequences of what they are doing.

William B. O'Connell, President
United States League of Savings Institutions
Summer 1988

Introduction ▮

For most of its history, the savings and loan business has been a remarkable success story. Born in the 1830s, it grew from a system of small, mutually owned institutions into the prime supplier of mortgage money for American home buyers.

But in the 1980s, a rash of savings and loan failures has created operating and regulatory problems which some observers believe threaten the system's survival, and with it, of course, the survival of what had often been referred to as the world's most efficient home financing system.

This study, prepared for the United States League of Savings Institutions, was commissioned to analyze the causes of these failures. Hopefully, its findings will contribute toward enabling the business and its regulators and supervisors to avoid more failures in the future. As this report observes, some important corrective measures have already been taken, but more must be done.

This chapter includes a review of how the stage was set for the failures of the 1980s and a summary of their causes. Chapters 2 through 6 focus primarily on the historical background necessary to understand the forces and trends that resulted in these failures. Chapters 7 through 11 explore the causes of failures in detail, and Chapter 12 includes a brief discussion of the choices that now face the business and its supervisors.

In addition to the written record, the research for the report has involved interviews with a number of participants in some of the events described. These include three former chairmen of the Federal Home Loan Board, four district FHLB presidents (whose districts include the three major problem states), a former district FHLB president, three former Bank Board general counsels, three former heads of the Office of Examination and Supervision, two former chief economists, members of the professional staff at the Board and at a number of FHLBs, the present and former California savings and loan commissioner, state league executives, a number of savings and loan executives, a former director of the Division of Bank Supervision at the FDIC and, of course, several members of the staff of the U.S. League. By serving on the boards of failed associations put into the Phoenix and management consignment programs (in Illinois, California and Florida), the authors became intimately familiar with the failure process and result.

As this report will detail, for a long time the savings and loan business was protected from competition and given special advantages by the lawmakers. It was structured to be failure-proof, and supervised with that objective. Then, in the name of "deregulation," almost overnight the business was thrown into the jungle of open competition even though it was not equipped for it by background or temperament, the size of its net worth, or the nature or size of its supervisory and examination establishment.

To their credit, most savings associations and their executives did survive.

SETTING THE STAGE FOR FAILURES

At the heart of the failures of the 1980s has been the inability of the business to find, easily and without great cost, a successful solution to its traditional system of receiving short-term funds and investing them in long-term assets.

In fairness to the managements of savings and loan associations at the time, it must be understood that when the events relating to most of the failures of the 1980s occurred, the business was operating in an extremely hostile political and economic environment unlike anything it had experienced before.

The stage for the failures of the 1980s was set during a period of mounting inflation and rising interest rates, which got progressively worse in the latter years of the 1970s and peaked in 1980-81. It was at the height of this period that savings rates were deregulated, raising savings costs and causing operating losses. At the same time, the higher interest rates were eroding the market value of association loan portfolios, and savings associations were being given new powers without the accompanying tougher supervision their use required.

Certainly another major factor in setting the stage for the savings and loan failures of the 1980s was the political decision, made by Congress in the 1970s, not to allow federally chartered associations to make variable rate home loans. This decision left the business almost totally vulnerable to the period of extremely high interest rates that followed. Moreover, many of the causes of failures identified in this report came together in a hurry. It would be one thing if the business had 10 years or 15 years in which to adjust to the immense pressures playing upon it, but much of the damage that led to these failures occurred in just a year or two.

As the inflation rate began mounting in the late 1960s and into the 1970s, some savings institution executives perceived the need for authority that would allow their institutions to begin protecting themselves against interest rate risk by making adjustable rate loans. Variable rate mortgages were already the standard in most other countries, and these executives reasoned that there was no reason this type of mortgage instrument could not work here too.

As noted later in this report (Chapter 5), two Federal Home Loan Bank Board chairmen of that era at least discussed authorizing variable rate mortgages with the leadership of the House and Senate banking committees, but were discouraged from pursuing the idea. In the late 1970s, another Bank Board chairman formally proposed variable rate mortgage authority for federal associations, but dropped the proposal at the urging of the House and Senate banking committee leaders.

The U.S. League also sought to persuade Congress to accept the concept, at least to the point of allowing the Bank Board to issue permissive regulations. The League also ran into unyielding opposition of banking committee leaders, who were strongly supported in their position by the home builders.

The dangerous rate at which inflation had been rising had been apparent for some time, but few dreamed it would reach the heights that it did. In the first half of the 1960s, the annual increase in the Consumer Price Index was never more than 1.7%, but it moved up to 5.9% by 1970. It first touched double-digit levels (11.0%) in 1974, and after a retreat to 5.8% in 1976 moved back up to peak with three consecutive double-digit years: 11.3% in 1979, 13.5% in 1980 and 10.4% in 1981.

The Federal Reserve acted to throttle this near-runaway inflation by tightening the money supply, which sent interest rates soaring. From an annual average of 9.06% in 1978, the prime rate rose to an 18.87% average in 1981, with a peak of 21.5%.

Ninety-day Treasury bill rates, which had averaged 5.265% in 1977 and 7.221% in 1978, were averaging 14.029% in 1981. Weekly and monthly volatility was even more extreme, with 90-day bill rates moving from a 1980 low of 6.995% in June to an all-time high of 16.295% less than a year later, in May 1981.

As a result, the business in general began suffering huge losses and an erosion of net worth as interest rates continued to rise. Because variable-rate loans were in limited use by state-chartered institutions in only those few states that permitted them, most notably California and Wisconsin, the earnings of the low-yielding, fixed rate mortgages that dominated most association portfolios could not cover the rising savings costs brought on by the deregulation of savings rates. Naturally, the market value of these loans in association portfolios plummeted.

As these difficulties mounted, savings associations were encountering hostility on other fronts. Much of the regulatory focus in the late 1970s, while inflation and interest rates were rising, was on consumer and social issues rather than on helping the business operate in the increasingly volatile economic environment. Meanwhile, the business also had to fight a long battle in the courts and in state legislatures and the Congress before all lenders were permitted to enforce due-on-sale clauses in home mortgages. The major opponents of these clauses, which require that mortgages be paid off when properties are sold, were real estate brokers. These clauses were unenforceable in most states until 1982, and associations remained saddled with many low-interest loans long after the borrowers sold the homes to other parties. New home mortgage yields, for instance, averaged 5.81% in 1965, 8.45% in 1970 and 9.00% in 1975, but had moved up to average 14.70% in 1981 and 15.14% in 1982.

Because these lower-yielding mortgages were not paid off even though the properties had changed hands, associations could not acquire funds they needed to make higher-yielding loans in the late 1970s and early 1980s. This also increased the drag on earnings from low-yielding, older loans, further eroding net worth and making it even more difficult for associations to pay the rising savings rates.

The inability of savings institutions to participate fully in the real estate markets of that era because of the loss of savings funds to other types of financial institutions and to money market mutual funds also left the door open for mortgage banking-type operations in the home mortgage field.

In all the history of the savings and loan business, there had never been an operating environment as complex and hostile as this. It was at this point that deregulation suddenly gave savings associations the opportunity to increase their earnings by making new kinds of loans and investments and using new financial instruments they did not know much about.

In light of this harsh operating environment, what are now seen to be mistakes made by some people in the business are more understandable. When faced with a businesswide earnings squeeze and an inexorable erosion of net worth of these proportions, and in view of the many weak local mortgage loan markets that characterized the early 1980s, it should not be surprising that some savings association managers reached out to make newly authorized investments that later turned sour. In fact, as will be seen, during this extremely dangerous period for the business institutions were actually being encouraged to make what later turned out to be bad loans by a deregulation-minded Bank Board.

THE ENORMOUS COST OF FAILURES

As a result of the failures of the 1980s, savings associations today are forced to pay special assessments levied by the Federal Savings and Loan Insurance Corporation (FSLIC) equal to 1/8 of 1% of deposits, and under the Competitive Equality Banking Act of 1987 (CEBA) the Federal Home Loan Banks are contributing substantial sums from their undivided profits. Since they began in 1985, special assessments through the end of 1987 totaled approximately $3.4 billion. These could continue for five years, although the CEBA legislation urges the Board to phase down the special assessment over five years. The 1987 special assessments will approximate $1.1 billion to $1.2 billion, so the total cost of special assessments will be about $9.5 billion to their scheduled termination date in 1992.

Funds for the recapitalization of FSLIC of up to $3 billion will be funneled to the FSLIC from the Home Loan Banks. This will approximate the total undivided profits account of the Banks as of June 30, 1987, plus much of the expected net earnings for the next few years.

These funds are a direct charge to the business and have been provided basically to pay off future losses, i.e., those losses which have not yet resulted in disbursements from the FSLIC either directly to insure depositors, or by way of contributions to assist supervisory arranged mergers or acquisitions of failed institutions.

From December 31, 1981, through December 31, 1986, the actual cash disbursements from the FSLIC totaled $9.665 billion. Not all of this cash outlay involved actual disbursements in connection with failed institutions. Some involved operating expenses and other disbursements unrelated to failed institutions. In addition to disbursements in dealing with failed institutions prior to the close of 1986, the FSLIC has made commitments to institutions absorbing failed associations to meet a portion of losses in the future. These total several billion dollars for cases handled before mid-1987, not including the institutions placed in the management consignment program. In addition, on December 31, 1986, the FSLIC had issued

$1.710 billion of net worth or income capital certificates to weak institutions to help assure their survival. A considerable portion of this may have to be written off by the FSLIC.

There are major losses in management consignment cases and institutions which are considered near receivership. The extent of the losses from these and institutions that might go into receivership, management consignment or reorganization with FSLIC assistance in the next year or two will depend on the recovery of the real estate market, primarily in the energy states.

Considering the financial position of the management consignment case institutions and others with weak net worth and 1987 earnings, the outlook for losses to the FSLIC is not reassuring. An estimate of $15 billion of losses yet to be recognized is not considered unreasonable. Consider the net worth distribution of FSLIC institutions, not including those in the MCP program, shown in Table 1.

TABLE 1: CURRENT SAVINGS INSTITUTION NET WORTH DISTRIBUTIONS (as of June 30, 1987)

Range of Net Worth as a % of Assets	RAP Net Worth		GAAP Net Worth	
	Number	Assets (in billions)	Number	Assets (in billions)
Less then 0.0	355	$ 95.4	506	$ 143.9
0.0 to 1.0	51	50.5	97	76.0
1.0 to 2.0	92	40.7	152	74.3
2.0 to 3.0	149	76.7	188	106.8
3.0 to 4.0	318	179.9	313	145.4
4.0 to 5.0	375	191.4	350	240.0
5.0 to 6.0	426	240.7	351	165.4
6.0 and over	1,381	376.3	1,190	299.8
All Institutions	3,147	$1,251.6	3,147	$1,251.6

Source: United States League

Also revealing are data showing the financial condition of associations in the management consignment program and those other associations with a negative net worth as measured by regulatory accounting principles (RAP) shown in Table 2.

In addition, associations are paying somewhat higher prices for deposits as a result of publicity surrounding association failures, press reports of the inadequacy of the resources of the FSLIC and the FSLIC's inability to resolve problem cases promptly. Deposit costs are higher for associations competing directly with high rate paying "problem case" institutions than would otherwise be necessary. Some

TABLE 2: FINANCIAL DATA FOR INSTITUTIONS IN MANAGEMENT CONSIGNMENT PROGRAM AND WITH NEGATIVE NET WORTH
(As of June 30, 1987 and First Half 1987 (as a % of Assets))

	MCPs	Negative RAP Net Worth
No. of Institutions	59	249
Total Assets	$ 23.8 Billion	$ 55.2 Billion
RAP Net Worth	$– 6.3 Billion	$– 4.9 Billion
GAAP Net Worth	$– 7.3 Billion	$– 6.0 Billion
Net Operating Income	–5.97%	–3.31%
Net Nonoperating Income	–8.42%	–4.33%
Net Income After Tax	$–1.77 Billion	$–2.03 Billion
ROA	–14.47%	–7.61%

Source: United States League

of these costs might have been avoided if the FSLIC had been given fewer cases to manage and had more resources available to deal promptly and effectively with failures as they occurred.

Savings association failures have involved not only enormous dollar costs, but also concern about the viability of the savings and loan business. Its credibility is being questioned by public opinion makers, business leaders and legislators. The public's acceptance of the business is largely based on the integrity of the FSLIC, which has been subject to question. Further, there has been a psychological cost to the officers and staff of the business and the loss of able people from its managerial ranks. It has brought new, and sometimes unwelcome, types of corporate owners (including commercial bank holding companies) and a breakdown of traditional geographical limits on association operations. The nature of the business has been substantially altered and according to some observers, its very survival threatened. This has important implications in the years ahead as to the availability of credit for American home buyers.

The social and economic cost of savings association failures, both tangible and intangible, thus is enormous. An examination of the causes of these failures is clearly called for.

THE STATISTICAL RECORD OF FAILURES

For purposes of this study, a failure will be defined as one involving supervisory action *and* some type of actual, or anticipated, financial assistance on the part of the FSLIC in order to avoid possible, or probable, losses to insured depositors. Included are institutions which were not necessarily declared insolvent and placed in receivership and closed or merged, but were put into a "Phoenix" or management consignment program.

To be sure, there have been other association failures. These include institutions in Ohio and Maryland involved in the failed state guaranty funds of those states, and those with minimum and deteriorating net worth positions that were merged with supervisory suggestion into others, but without requiring FSLIC assistance. Also included are institutions which voluntarily merged into another institution as a result of deteriorating markets, operating deficits and absence of an interested management or plain discouragement. Confining the record for purposes of this study to failures involving FSLIC financial assistance or Bank Board action of one form or another, however, has the advantage of statistical precision. It also relates, of course, to the costs of failures borne by the entire business through the premiums and assessments on the remaining insured institutions.

Here is the record of failures, year by year (Table 3), and by FHLB districts between 1978 and 1986 (Table 4).

Table 5 shows failures by state.

TABLE 3: FAILURES OF FSLIC-INSURED INSTITUTIONS*

Bank District	1980	1981	1982	1983	1984	1985	1986	1987	TOTAL
Boston	1		3		1	1			6
New York	1	8	14	4	3		3	2	35
Pittsburgh			3	2			1		6
Atlanta	1	7	11	11	2	5	10	9	56
Cincinnati	1		3	5	7	9	7	2	34
Indianapolis	1		2	8	1	1	1		14
Chicago	2	5	12	5	1	3	5	4	37
Des Moines	2	5	5	9	4	2	3	2	32
Dallas	1	2	16	9	6	9	21	23	87
Topeka			1			2	6	11	20
San Francisco			3	2	1	7	23	10	46
Seattle	1	1	1		1	10	5	8	27
TOTAL	11	28	74	55	27	49	85	71	400

Source: Federal Savings and Loan Insurance Corporation

*Includes institutions put into Management Consignment Program.

TABLE 4: ASSETS OF FAILED FSLIC-INSURED INSTITUTIONS*
(In Millions of Dollars)

FHLB District	1980	1981	1982	1983	1984	1985	1986	1987	TOTAL
Boston	$ 24.7	$ —	$ 1,472.3	$ —	$ 138.0	$ 238.0	$ —	$ —	$ 1,873.0
New York	76.3	5,851.1	5,070.0	6,421.9	1,442.5	—	689.3	223.1	19,774.2
Pittsburgh	—	—	162.9	229.9	—	—	136.9	—	529.7
Atlanta	233.6	3,750.7	2,839.5	4,542.9	151.7	1,226.3	4,957.5	3,075.7	20,777.9
Cincinnati	438.8	—	252.1	764.6	1,384.3	936.4	2,663.7	420.5	6,860.4
Indianapolis	128.8	—	860.3	1,222.0	309.8	314.0	361.3	—	3,196.2
Chicago	417.8	404.0	4,485.6	4,212.6	279.0	329.5	400.5	2,744.1	13,273.1
Des Moines	76.6	1,468.0	195.0	1,561.3	392.4	159.0	1,340.0	179.8	5,372.1
Dallas	27.0	38.6	1,845.4	702.7	812.9	2,043.2	13,906.1	7,386.1	26,762.0
Topeka	—	—	N.A.	—	—	181.2	474.7	1,559.8	2,215.7
San Francisco	—	—	2,947.0	83.9	856.8	9,987.5	5,977.8	3,936.3	23,789.3
Seattle	34.0	41.0	72.8	—	233.0	3,026.2	712.7	1,392.7	5,512.4
TOTAL	$1457.6	$11,553.4	$20,202.9	$19,741.8	$6,000.4	$18,441.3	$31,620.5	$20,918.1	$129,936.0

Source: Federal Savings and Loan Insurance Corporation
*Includes institutions placed in Management Consignment Program.

TABLE 5: FAILURES OF FSLIC-INSURED INSTITUTIONS IN PRINCIPAL STATES, 1980-1987

State	Number	Assets (In Million $)
California	42	22,010.0
Illinois	33	12,874.8
Texas	32	14,059.4
Louisiana	29	4,952.0
Florida	21	15,819.9
Ohio	19	5,027.2
New York	18	14,133.7
Missouri	12	3,155.7
New Jersey	12	4,136.5
Virginia	11	1,271.6
Tennessee	9	590.7
Oklahoma	8	1,264.8
Indiana	7	992.9
Maryland	7	1,012.8
Michigan	7	2,203.3
Mississippi	7	660.7
Oregon	7	1,807.1
Washington	7	1.625.3
Iowa	6	544.6
Colorado	5	590.5
Georgia	5	315.5
Kansas	5	212.8
Kentucky	5	832.2
New Mexico	5	303.6
Pennsylvania	5	392.8
South Dakota	5	190.6
Minnesota	4	1,039.6
North Dakota	4	427.9
Puerto Rico	4	1,475.2
Arkansas	3	3,358.6
District of Columbia	3	1,515.4
Massachusetts	3	1,275.3
Utah	3	1,282.1
Alaska	3	93.0
Alabama	2	255.8
Hawaii	2	49.0
Idaho	2	582.1
Montana	2	101.4
North Carolina	2	77.6
Rhode Island	2	162.7
South Carolina	2	177.0
Wisconsin	2	197.3
Arizona	1	1,122.0
Connecticut	1	390.0

(Table 5 continued)

State	Number	Assets (In Million $)
Guam	1	60.0
Nevada	1	55.6
West Virginia	1	136.9
Wyoming	1	72.3
TOTAL	378	124,887.8

Source: Federal Savings and Loan Insurance Corporation

Of interest are data showing the number of failures by state and federal charter and between stock and mutual institutions presented in Table 6. In the early years of the decade—the years of the spread problem—the federals and mutuals substantially outnumbered the state and stock institutions in the number of failures, whereas in the years of failures because of bad assets, the proportion of failures among the state and stock institutions increased substantially.

TABLE 6: SAVINGS AND LOAN FAILURES BY CHARTER AND TYPE

Year	Charter		Type	
	State	Federal	Stock	Mutual
1980	6	5	3	8
1981	8	20	5	23
1982	22	52	16	58
1983	20	35	17	38
1984	12	15	11	16
1985	26	33	28	31
1986	46	39	56	29
1987*	25	14	26	13
TOTAL	165	213	162	216

*As of September 30, 1987.

For purposes of comparison, at the end of 1980 there were 1,985 federal and 2,628 state-chartered associations; 2,752 mutuals and 861 stock associations.

Some indication of the total impact of the economic climate and resulting problems of the 1980s is shown by the decline in total number of institutions. (See Table 7.)

TABLE 7: NUMBER OF SAVINGS AND LOAN ASSOCIATIONS

Year	Federally Chartered	State Chartered		Total
		FSLIC-Insured	Non-Insured*	
1980	1,985	2,017	611	4,613
1981	1,907	1,872	513	4,292
1982	1,727	1,616	482	3,825
1983	1,553	1,487	462	3,502
1984	1,478	1,460	453	3,391
1985	1,419	1,525	253	3,197
1986	1,345	1,466	267	3,078
1987	1,269	1,379	313	2,961

*Includes the assets of institutions insured by state insuring agencies.

This decline in the number of associations should be looked at in the context of the number of new institutions in those same years as follows:

TABLE 8: NUMBER OF NEWLY CHARTERED AND INSURED ASSOCIATIONS*

Year	New State Chartered Assns. Insured by FSLIC	New Federally Chartered Assns.	Total
1980	63	5	68
1981	20	4	24
1982	20	3	23
1983	32	11	43
1984	68	65	133
1985	132	41	173
1986	13	15	28
	348	144	492

Source: Federal Savings and Loan Corporation

*Does not include those existing operating state institutions which became FSLIC-insured during the year. Additionally it does not include thrifts in the management consignment program which are *de novo* institutions, chartered to assume the performing assets of some of the closed thrifts.

Thus, the attrition in institutions existing in 1980 is greater than the decline shown from 4,613 to 3,132.

It is interesting to compare the savings and loan failure record with that for FDIC-insured commercial banks and savings banks, keeping in mind the comparative numbers of institutions at the beginning of 1980. Tables 9 and 10 provide the comparative data.

TABLE 9: NUMBER AND ASSETS OF FAILED INSTITUTIONS
(In Millions of Dollars)

| | FSLIC-Insured S&L Associations | | FDIC-Insured Banks | | | |
| | | | Commercial Banks | | Savings Banks | |
Year	Number	Assets	Number	Assets	Number	Assets
1980	11	$ 1,457.6	10	$ 236.0	—	—
1981	28	11,553.4	7	104.0	3	4,755.0
1982	74	20,202.9	34	2,020.0	8	9,612.0
1983	55	19,741.8	46	4,267.0	2	2,760.0
1984	27	6,000.4	79	42,761.0*	1	515.0
1985	49	18,441.3	118	3,040.0	2	5,701.0
1986	85	31,620.5	138	6,992.0	—	—
1987	71	20,918.1	152	17,627.0**	1	1,180.0
TOTALS	400	129,936.0	584	77,047.0	17	24,523.0

Source: FSLIC and FDIC

*The FDIC reports of failures and insured banks requiring disbursements for some reason does not include the Continental Illinois National Bank and Trust Co. although it is discussed fully in the text of the FDIC's Annual Report for 1984, in the footnotes to the FDICs financial statements and in the 1985 Annual Report under the category of "Assets Acquired in Assistance to an Insured Bank." For purposes of complete reporting of FDIC banks failing or requiring FDIC financial assistance, we have included the Continental Bank in the total for 1984 at $40 billion in assets.
Source: FSLIC and FDIC

**Likewise, the FDIC listing of failed institutions for 1987 does not include the First City Bank Corp. of Texas, with total assets of $12,244 million, even though it is widely recognized that this was a failure. For purposes of complete reporting, we have added that bank to the total failures for the year 1987. It should also be noted that the number of failing banks is understated. For example, the First City Bank Corp. involves 62 banks while in the tabulation it is indicated as only one. The year 1987 also includes the failure of Banctexas Group, Inc., a holding company which involves 11 banks but is included in this tabulation as only one.
Source: United States League

TABLE 10: NUMBER OF INSURED FINANCIAL INSTITUTIONS
(as of 12/31/79)

	Number	Assets (In Millions $)
FSLIC-Insured S&L Associations	4,039	$ 568,107
FDIC-Insured Commercial Banks (State and National)	14,364	1,405,666
FDIC-Insured Mutual Savings Banks	324	147,112

Source: United States League

AN OVERVIEW OF THE CAUSES OF FAILURES

Association failures appear to have occurred in two waves: first, because of the "spread problems," i.e., the costs of funds exceeding the earnings of the assets; and second, because of losses on the asset side of the balance sheet.

Failures for the first reason generally occurred from 1981 through 1984. The second group, far more serious from the standpoint of FSLIC finances, were those in 1985 and 1986, continuing into 1987 and, no doubt, beyond.

A number of factors can be identified as the causes for the failures. The single most important development that precipitated the wave of failures was "deregulation" which first produced operating losses for most institutions and then attracted venturesome entrepreneurs to the business who led savings associations into unfamiliar business activities.

At the same time, supervisory and regulatory staffs were ineffective at supervising the "new" savings and loan business. Unfortunately, the people who worked so hard to deregulate the savings and loan business had failed to realize that there is a basic conflict between deposit insurance and the deregulation of financial institutions—and that by its nature, deregulation requires stronger, not weaker, supervision of the institutions being deregulated. The rate of deregulation required sharp adjustments in regulatory policies and procedures which did not occur. Probably more than anything else, it was this lapse in judgment that brought on the losses now being suffered by the FSLIC.

The following is a detailed summary of the major causes for losses that hurt the business in the 1980s:

1. Lack of net worth for many institutions as they entered the 1980s, and a wholly inadequate net worth regulation.

2. Decline in the effectiveness of Regulation Q in preserving the spread between the cost of money and the rate of return on assets, basically stemming from inflation and the accompanying increase in market interest rates.

3. Absence of an ability to vary the return on assets with increases in the rate of interest required to be paid for deposits.

4. Increased competition on the deposit gathering and mortgage origination sides of the business, with a sudden burst of new technology making possible a whole new way of conducting financial institutions generally and the mortgage business specifically.

5. A rapid increase in investment powers of associations with passage of the Depository Institutions Deregulation and Monetary Control Act (the Garn-St Germain Act), and, more important, through state legislative enactments in a number of important and rapidly growing states. These introduced new risks and speculative opportunities which were difficult to administer. In many instances management lacked the ability or experience to evaluate them, or to administer large volumes of nonresidential construction loans.

6. Elimination of regulations initially designed to prevent lending excesses and minimize failures. Regulatory relaxation permitted lending, directly and through participations, in distant loan markets on the promise of high returns. Lenders, however, were not familiar with these distant markets. It also permitted associations to participate extensively in speculative construction activities with builders and developers who had little or no financial stake in the projects.

7. Fraud and insider transaction abuses were the principal cause for some 20% of savings and loan failures the past three years and a greater percentage of the dollar losses borne by the FSLIC.

8. A new type and generation of opportunistic savings and loan executives and owners—some of whom operated in a fraudulent manner—whose takeover of many institutions was facilitated by a change in FSLIC rules reducing the

minimum number of stockholders of an insured association from 400 to one.

9. Dereliction of duty on the part of the board of directors of some savings associations. This permitted management to make uncontrolled use of some new operating authority, while directors failed to control expenses and prohibit obvious conflict of interest situations.

10. A virtual end of inflation in the American economy, together with overbuilding in multifamily, condominium type residences and in commercial real estate in many cities. In addition, real estate values collapsed in the energy states—Texas, Louisiana, Oklahoma particularly—and weakness occurred in the mining and agricultural sectors of the economy.

11. Pressures felt by the management of many associations to restore net worth ratios. Anxious to improve earnings, they departed from their traditional lending practices into credits and markets involving higher risks, but with which they had little experience.

12. The lack of appropriate, accurate and effective evaluations of the savings and loan business by public accounting firms, security analysts and the financial community.

13. Organizational structure and supervisory laws, adequate for policing and controlling the business in the protected environment of the 1960s and 1970s, resulted in fatal delays and indecision in the examination/supervision process in the 1980s.

14. Federal and state examination and supervisory staffs insufficient in number, experience or ability to deal with the new world of savings and loan operations.

15. The inability or unwillingness of the Bank Board and its legal and supervisory staff to deal with problem institutions in a timely manner. Many institutions, which ultimately closed with big losses, were known problem cases for a year or more. Often, it appeared, political considerations delayed necessary supervisory action.

These items will be dealt with in separate sections of this book, with some comparison made with conditions that generally existed in the business from 1950 to 1975.

The "Historical" Savings and Loan Business

2

Understanding the underlying causes of savings and loan failures in the 1980s requires a brief review of the business' history, and the nature of the climate in which it developed in the postwar years and why that climate changed so abruptly.

The savings and loan business from 1950 onwards developed from early building and loan associations and Depression era legislation. The Federal Home Loan Bank Act (1932), Section 5 of the Home Owners' Loan Act of 1933 which created the Federal Savings and Loan System, and Title IV of the National Housing Act of 1934 which created the Federal Savings and Loan Insurance Corporation with insurance of accounts initially of $5,000 were the basic enactments of Congress that created the modern savings and loan business.

As with New Deal era banking and securities laws, these enactments and subsequent regulations were designed to develop specialization in the country's financial system between housing finance, consumer finance, investment banking, insurance and commercial banking. They also intended to provide a clear separation between finance and banking, on the one hand, and commerce and industry on the other. The overall goal was to prevent abuses and the perceived weakness of the financial system that led to the banking holiday of March 1933 and the emergency legislation of the early presidency of Franklin D. Roosevelt.

Although the federal government intervened in the savings and loan business on a national basis, essentially as a reaction to the Depression-related problems, legislation continued to favor the traditional, "local" neighborhood concept for these institutions. Importantly, it also included legal restrictions designed to protect the business against failure. Thus association lending was restricted for the most part to a 50-mile radius from the home office. Assets were required to be primarily invested in moderate-sized loans on one- to four-family housing, all loans had to be secured by real estate, there was a strict prohibition against second mortgages, maturities on loans were limited to 20 years, and loan-to-value ratios to 80%.

FINANCIAL REFORM LEGISLATION

The Glass-Steagall Act, born during the Depression, is a classic example of legislation designed to protect against alleged abuses and dangers to the commercial and investment banking system. The act creating the Securities and Exchange Commission and the laws administered by it developed from the same point of view. Early laws affecting credit unions were equally restrictive and "protective" against a repetition of the failures that pervaded American finance in the early 1930s.

The leadership of the United States League of Savings Institutions (in the 1930s known as the United States Building and Loan League), looking at Depression-era failures in commercial banking, concluded that many banks closed by the examiners should not have been closed; too much discretion had been given the field examiners to decide the quality of bank assets and hence their solvency, the League believed. In contrast to the bank supervisory apparatus, this led to the separation of the examination and supervision functions in the organization of the Bank Board and a detailed regulatory system for the savings and loan business which was not fundamentally altered until 1986.

STATE AND FEDERAL CHARTERING

Historically, the savings and loan business was created by state and federal legislative bodies to finance homeownership. From its beginning it was considered a thrift and home financing system, and deviated little from that as a legal proposition until the Garn-St. Germain Act of 1982.

Congress began writing laws for the savings and loan business in 1932, and essentially confined it to financing homes and small apartments. The business was kept principally engaged in home mortgage lending, not only by the basic law for federally chartered associations, but by most state laws and by the Internal Revenue Code. By providing a detailed "definition" of a savings and loan association to qualify for a special bad debt deduction, the tax law kept the business engaged almost wholly in home financing.

Over the years, the business tried to secure broader investment and lending authority and a more liberal tax law definition and succeeded to some degree. State legislatures were generally much more inclined to broaden the operating powers of state-chartered associations. Congress broadened the investment powers of the business only slowly and reluctantly, and then essentially in the context of improving the ability of the business to be a viable home financing system. Indeed, the first section of the Garn-St. Germain Act of 1982 states that it is:

> "An Act to revitalize the housing industry by strengthening the financial stability of home mortgage lending institutions and ensuring the availability of home mortgage loans."

The encouragement of homeownership and land tenure by American citizens has long been a fundamental principle of American public policy, dating back to years immediately after the war for American independence. Many legislative enactments have had as their principal objective the promotion of homeownership. These include various provisions of the Internal Revenue Code, the encouragement and protection of the savings and loan system (through Regulation Q, for example), the creation of the Federal Housing Administration and, in more recent years, sponsorship of three federal secondary market operations. Interest in providing special assistance to the home financing system was continued in the Tax Reform Act of 1986 with the creation of the Real Estate Mortgage Investment Conduit (REMIC).

Savings and loan associations developed initially as cooperative, or mutual, organizations. The capital stock form was found only in the system of state charters in Ohio and a dozen western and southwestern states. The Federal Savings and Loan System was wholly a mutual system until 1972. It was not until the 1960s that capital stock associations began to be publicly held and their stock traded on the stock exchanges.

Since the mid-1960s, most newly organized associations were of the capital stock form, but de novo capital stock associations under federal charters were not permitted until 1982. Conversions from mutual form to capital stock form began to take place with some frequency beginning in 1974, but were not actively encouraged by the Bank Board until 1981. Today, of the 200 largest FSLIC-insured savings associations 123 are of the capital stock form. As of March 31, 1987, they held a total of $451 billion in assets, or 79% of the $573 billion assets of the 200 largest.

THE POSTWAR YEARS

Through most of the post-Depression years, the savings and loan business enjoyed an extremely favorable economic and competitive climate. The country suffered a virtual standstill in house construction from 1930 to 1946, causing a sizable shortage of housing. Demand increased significantly, however, when war veterans returned. Their desire for ownership could quickly be satisfied through the Veterans Home Loan Program and a tremendous liberalization of the FHA loan program. In contrast to most commercial banks, savings and loan associations were willing, even eager, to make loans; they had an ideal form of financial institution to gather funds from an increasingly affluent American public for investment in long-term, rather low downpayment, fixed-rate home mortgages. Savings and loan associations became expert in the intermediation of funds for housing finance.

The Housing Act of 1949 gave a boost to the savings and loan business by making the provision of family housing a national priority. It stated that the nation was dedicated to providing an opportunity for every family to acquire safe and sanitary housing within its means.

After 1949, legislation was passed annually to provide substantial financial support for the FHA loan insurance program and the Veterans Administration housing benefits program. At times, these programs were adjusted to provide counter-cyclical support for the national economy.

Through most of the postwar period, the demographics clearly favored an expanding housing finance system, as did the general money and credit markets. A strongly upward sloping yield curve made it profitable to gather funds into payable-on-demand savings deposits for investment in long-term home mortgages. Not only was the investment of funds into mortgages generally safe and profitable, but so was the creation of mortgages (the origination process) and financing and creation of houses (construction lending) and loan servicing. The savings and loan business became proficient in all phases of the residential mortgage business.

POSTWAR SAVINGS AND LOAN BUSINESS

In the first postwar years, savings and loan associations were virtually the only financial institutions interested in developing a savings deposit business. Commercial banks came out of the war years with generally a surplus of funds, interest rates were low and the demand for credit on the part of American business and industry grew slowly. Until 1962, commercial banks were limited by Regulation Q (which until 1966 applied only to FDIC-insured commercial banks) to 3% interest on time and savings deposits. Many banks paid less.

Savings and loan associations were not limited in the rates of interest they paid, or merchandise premiums they could offer as inducements to open new accounts. In some markets, they paid as much as 200 basis points more for savings than commercial banks did. Except for state-chartered associations in some markets, until 1966 associations had only one class of account: the simple savings or passbook account on which interest typically was paid quarterly or semiannually. Except for construction loans, mortgage loans were all 20- to 25-year fixed rate loans; the majority were made at interest rates from 250 to 300 basis points higher than the rate for savings deposits, and on existing single-family homes in suburban locations or stable neighborhoods in cities.

INSURED VERSUS CONVENTIONAL LOANS

Most savings and loan lending was on conventional loans. With some notable exceptions, association executives never really liked the FHA program. In part, this stemmed from the U.S. League executive leadership's dislike of government insurance of home mortgage loans made to private individuals. Also FHA loans required extensive paperwork and government "red tape" with which small associations were ill equipped to cope. It was easier and faster to make a conventional loan with the association doing the loan underwriting and processing and keeping the loan in its own portfolio, instead of selling it to a distant savings bank or insurance company. In such situations, there was little perceived need for government insurance against loss on the loan.

Further, FHA loans usually carried a lower interest rate and associations preferred to put the 1/2 of 1% insurance premium into their own reserves.

The GI loan came at a time when the savings and loan business needed an outlet for its lending energies. It was patriotic, the loans were easily processed and, in contrast to the FHA program, the GI loan program was enthusiastically pushed by the leadership of the U.S. League. In the first two years of that program, associations made some 70% of all GI loans. They gave the business a running start in the housing and home financing boom of the 1950s.

FHLMC IS CREATED

Until the Federal Home Loan Mortgage Corporation was created by the Emergency Home Finance Act of 1970, the savings and loan business never really took part in the so-called secondary market, and it began using Freddie Mac slowly. Those primarily participating in the secondary market were associations on the West Coast which sold conventional and sometimes FHA loans to eastern savings associations or savings banks. Some business was done in whole loans. This activity, however, mostly involved participations in loans with the seller, who was initially required to retain a 50% interest. Little use was made of the Federal National Mortgage Association.

It was not until the early 1970s when demand for mortgage funds began outstripping deposit flows, that the business generally became interested in the secondary market for new loans and as a place to sell, if necessary, some of its seasoned loans. For years associations had been content to keep all the loans they made. Loan payoffs together with strong savings inflows provided all the funds associations needed and produced a respectable net income. In response to this newly-awakened interest in secondary markets, legislation in 1970, supported by both the Bank Board and the U.S. League, created the Federal Home Loan Mortgage Corporation.

THE BUSINESS AND THE FHLB BOARD

While the typical savings and loan executive never really thought so, the Bank Board was friendly to the savings and loan business and its mission of financing homeownership. It was an effective advocate for the business within the administration and before congressional committees. It saw to it that credit flowed from the FHLBanks in virtually unlimited quantities, and at reasonable prices. It was parsimonious in the granting of new charters ("need" had to be shown and no "undue injury" done to existing institutions), and branches were given out with an eye to keeping competitive pressures to a minimum.

One problem was an excessive turnover of Board chairmen and members as well as of department heads, particularly in the Office of the General Counsel, the head of the Office of Examination and Supervision, the Director of the FSLIC and the chief economist. Until recently, however, the repeated appearance of new, inexperienced people at the Board did not seem to present any difficulty. Problems were few, and the staffs of the regional Home Loan Banks were stable. There, the presidents and senior staff were also friendly to the mission of the business and generally furthered a cordial relationship with executives of the member associations.

It should be emphasized, however, that the Bank Board's members were not cheerleaders or patsies of the business, as the commercial banking business accused them of being. The Board was a stern supervisor. It tried to keep the business from making mistakes and confined to making sound home mortgage loans.

FAILURES EMERGE IN THE 1960s

Until the mid-1960s, failures and FSLIC cases were virtually unknown in the savings and loan business. Then, during the Board chairmanship of John Horne (1965 to 1968), there were a number of failures in Illinois, primarily among the state-chartered institutions. In part these arose from some penetration of the home building business by the local mafia and under a state supervisor who later went to prison for the theft of public funds.

In 1968, there was a full blown run on an FSLIC-insured institution in Chicago. Several associations were placed in receivership, and savers were paid up to $15,000, the deposit insurance limit at that time.

In the 1960s, institutions in Nevada embarked on a program of rapid expansion and speculative construction lending. This resulted in a substantial increase in nonearning assets, and most Nevada-based institutions became insolvent. In response, the FSLIC provided a program similar to the management consignment program of the 1980s.

A few rather large associations in California failed and supervisory takeovers occurred in a number of other states. Institution failures, however, were never considered a financial problem to the system, even though there was some blow to the pride of savings and loan executives by being in a business associated with "failure." In addition, the relatively few failures were due largely to poor or excessively greedy management rather than to any weakness in the structure of the business. In any event, subsequent changes in supervisory laws, tightening of Home Loan Bank credit and some regulations seemed to take care of things. By the time Preston Martin became Bank Board chairman in 1969, the economic climate turned more favorable and it was time for a more relaxed supervisory and regulatory atmosphere.

HOUSING, THE SAVINGS AND LOAN BUSINESS AND THE ECONOMY

From the 1960s through the early 1970s, the economic climate was extremely kind to the savings and loan business. (See Table 11.) As noted, yield curves were generally upward sloping, and what little inflation there was generally favored the mortgage lender who might have been somewhat careless in underwriting. Gross National Product had a relatively steady growth and there was general prosperity — no pockets of depression such as exist today in the oil, farm and mineral-producing states, or in older industrial cities. Housing starts and real estate sales were generally strong, with foreclosures at a minimum. Overbuilding occurred during some years and in some cities, generally as a result of lender excesses (as in Las Vegas with four flats in the mid-1960s). These were not markets with large populations, however, nor did overbuilding last long or cast a cloud over the mortgage lending community.

TABLE 11: ECONOMIC INDICATORS FOR THE SAVINGS AND LOAN BUSINESS

Year	GNP ($ Billions)	Inflation Rate*	Housing Starts (Thousands)	Yield on 3-Month Treasury Bill Rate	Yield on 10-Year Treasury Securities
1950	$ 288.3	2.0%	1,951.9	1.218%	n.a.
1955	405.9	3.2	1,646.0	1.753	2.82%
1960	515.3	1.6	1,296.1	2.928	4.12
1965	705.1	2.7	1,509.7	3.954	4.28
1970	1,015.5	5.5	1,469.0	6.458	7.35
1975	1,598.4	9.8	1,171.4	5.838	7.99
1976	1,782.8	6.4	1,547.6	4.989	7.61
1977	1,990.5	6.7	2,001.7	5.265	7.42
1978	2,249.7	7.3	2,036.1	7.221	8.41
1979	2,508.2	8.9	1,760.0	10.041	9.44
1980	2,732.0	9.0	1,312.6	11.506	11.46

*Percent Change in GNP Deflator.

As Table 12 shows, this was the savings and loan business's golden age: limited competition for savings; a high demand for loans; a simple business from an operating standpoint; little risk in underwriting given reasonable care in financing the merchant builder; and a Bank Board that minimized competitive pressures and shaped laws the business needed to keep it moving forward as a sound home

TABLE 12: THE SUCCESSFUL YEARS IN THE SAVINGS AND LOAN BUSINESS

Year	S&L Savings Deposits ($ Billions)	S&L Net Worth ($ Billions)	S&L Mortgage Loans Made ($ Billions)	S&L Scheduled Items as a % of Net Worth
1950	$ 14.0	$ 1.3	$ 5.2	n.a.
1955	32.1	2.6	11.3	n.a.
1960	62.1	5.0	14.3	n.a.
1965	110.4	8.7	24.2	n.a.
1970	146.4	12.4	21.4	n.a.
1975	285.7	19.8	55.0	1.30%
1976	335.9	22.0	78.8	1.18
1977	386.8	25.2	107.4	0.92
1978	431.0	29.1	110.3	0.74
1979	470.0	32.6	100.5	0.69
1980	511.0	33.4	72.5	0.80

financing system. A cooperative relationship existed between the Board and the U.S. League with respect to each other's legislative initiatives. Most legislation passed between 1950 and 1980 came as a result of the Board and the League working out their differences so a common effort could be made in presentations before Congress. There were minority voices in the business, to be sure, and opposition to Board regulatory initiatives and legislative requests. Necessary laws were passed, however, with the joint support of the U.S. League and the Board. Government in the "sunshine" did not exist then, nor did the Freedom of Information Act. Markup sessions of congressional committees were closed to the public.

3 The Net Worth Problem

In 1980, the business entered into a new economic environment, one in which both interest rate and lending risks would increase to a degree far beyond those ever experienced before. It marked a new era for savings and loan executives who came into the business following World War II. The business entered the 1980s without capital adequate to meet the challenges that it faced and, as a result, savings and loans experienced sizable losses.

Before the 1930s, the business thought little about capital reserves. Indeed, the cooperative nature of the business promoted almost a prejudice against retaining earnings for any purpose. Losses were not expected from the lending process as conducted by all but the larger institutions. No interest rate risk existed because associations paid savers only what was earned in the form of dividends.[1]

THE DOMINANCE OF "DEPRESSION" THINKING

Savings and loan executives learned from the Depression that losses could arise from the residential mortgage business, even though the principal Depression problem was cash flow. This is a key reason for the creation of the Federal Home Loan Bank System. Later, the Home Owners' Loan Corporation took most of the defaulted loans off the books of savings associations. The law which created federally chartered savings associations was silent on the subject of reserves,[2] but the act creating the Federal Savings and Loan Insurance Corporation clearly required the building of "reserves for losses." A

---

[1] Until the savings and loan amendments of the Housing Act of 1968, associations were prohibited from offering "deposits" and from promising to pay a certain rate of interest. They offered share accounts and advertised "anticipated" dividends.

[2] For purposes of historical interest and because it was such a model of simplicity in legislative drafting, there is reproduced in Addendum A a copy of the original Federal Savings and Loan Act (Section 5 of the Home Owners' Loan Act of 1933).

minimum 5% of share accounts (deposits), a Federal Insurance Reserve was provided for. Newly chartered institutions were given 10 years to meet this benchmark. A few years later this was extended to 20 years, and in 1972 to 25 years.

The Federal Insurance Reserve was to provide a first line of defense against losses in any one institution. Funds from the reserve were to be used before the resources of the FSLIC had to be called upon to protect the depositors.

The law provided that if an institution failed to meet the required reserve level, dividends could not be paid to depositors and losses could not be charged to the FIR without the permission of a supervisory official. The effect was that it became necessary to build reserves—so-called "free" reserves and undivided profits—above the FIR 5% benchmark. Since mutual institutions were the dominant form in the business, retained earnings were the only source of additional reserves or capital. Given the emphasis on asset growth, which required increasing interest payments to savers, profit margins were not adequate to produce strong net worth ratios.

There were, however, few losses. The business generally felt quite comfortable with reserves of 1% to 2% above the FIR benchmarks. Many associations were organized in the 1950s, and it was not until 20 years after their chartering that the full 5% was required. Therefore, their effective FIR requirement was often considerably less than 5%.

GROWTH AND FEDERAL INSURANCE RESERVES

This requirement for building and maintaining an FIR proved a deterrent to growth. The business tended to measure management success not by the bottom line of the income statement, but by the annual growth rate of assets and the institution's total size. Consequently, the reserve requirement came under increasing attack from institutions in rapidly growing areas of the country, where there was broad and increasing demand for housing credit, and particularly from newly chartered institutions, which had not only to maintain the reserves of a certain ratio but also to improve them.

The problem of building reserves was uneven throughout the country. Institutions in states without interest rate ceilings on mortgage loans (imposed by usury law limitations) and where construction lending and mortgage business was exceptionally profitable (e.g., California, Texas and Arizona) did not find the FIR requirement a great deterrent to a satisfactory rate of asset growth. In the Midwest, East, and in states with low usury ceilings, the reserve requirement's limitation on growth was resented by many, particularly those managing or owning newly chartered institutions. Florida had many new institutions, and while the mortgage business was relatively profitable (although not so much as in California), strong demand for mortgages and significant growth potential fostered a great deal of resentment against the reserve requirement.

Because most institutions were mutuals, there was never any great management urge for, or interest in, building reserves per se. Pressure for reserve accumulation came almost entirely from supervisory authorities.

RESERVES AND FRONT-END FEES

An early response to the constraints of the reserve requirement was to "front end" some portion of the income on mortgage loans. High loan fees (points) were charged at the expense of the loan's interest rate. This practice was particularly prevalent at institutions on the West Coast, anxious to show large per share earnings to investors in the stock. It was also used to stay current on reserve requirements while continuing rapid growth. During this time, some institutions in areas of high mortgage loan profits grew at rapid rates by advertising deposit rates in out-of-state newspapers higher than institutions in those states could afford to pay, and by using brokers to attract deposits from distant markets.[3]

The response of supervisory agencies in January 1964, in collaboration with public accountants, was to permit only a certain number of points as current income, with the balance of the fees credited to a deferred income account. Pressure on Congress from rapidly growing and newly chartered associations brought a change in the law. The Board increased the period of years an institution could take to reach the 5% FIR benchmark.

---

[3] Brokers used in the 1950s and 1960s to attract deposits were not the large security houses used by associations in the 1980s, but rather small organizations engaged exclusively in securing deposits essentially for West Coast institutions. The money obtained proved to be "hot" that "went back home" once parity on deposit rates came to the business after 1966 with the advent of Regulation Q, and particularly after ceiling rates were equalized between California and the eastern states. The liquidity crunch that came with the resulting loss of deposits caused considerable difficulty and some near failures for associations with a higher percentage of out-of-state money.

Pressure by the supervisory establishment with respect to the FIR regulatory requirements was fairly constant. In 1972, the Board published a regulation detailing the consequences of failure to meet the reserve requirement. In effect, this regulation gave the Board authority over a considerable portion of an association's day-to-day operations in the event of failure to meet the reserve or net worth requirement.[4]

Reading this regulation one can readily understand the fear savings and loan executives had of failing to meet the FIR requirements. In the 1980s, this regulation was to have unfortunate consequences in the kinds of loans made by many institutions which fell below the minimums.

When an institution's failure to meet the reserve requirement persisted for a considerable period and portfolio losses contributed to the reserve deficiencies, the Board asked for, and usually received, the institution's board of directors' consent to a Supervisory Agreement. At times, particularly in the 1980s, a Supervisory Directive would be issued under this regulation. Before 1981, few instances occurred in which the Board exercised its authority to control an association's operations as a result of failure to meet the reserve regulation. Still, management lived in constant fear of the regulation. A supervisory "bark" often was enough to bring grudging compliance with supervisory suggestions.

---

[4] (d) Failure to meet statutory or net worth requirements. If an insured institution fails to meet the statutory reserve requirements set forth in paragraph (a) of this section or the net worth requirement set forth in paragraph (b) of this section, the Corporation may, whether through enforcement proceedings or otherwise, require such institution to take any one or more of the following corrective actions:

(1) Increase the amount of its net worth to a specified level or levels;

(2) Convene a meeting or meetings of its board of directors with the Director, Office of Examinations and Supervision, or his designee, for the purpose of accomplishing the objectives of this section;

(3) Reduce the rate of earnings that may be paid on savings accounts;

(4) Limit the receipt of deposits to those made to existing accounts;

(5) Cease or limit the issuance of new accounts of any or all classes or categories, except in exchange for existing accounts;

(6) Cease or limit lending or the making of a particular type or category of loan;

(7) Cease or limit the purchase of loans or the making of specified other investments;

(8) Limit operational expenditures to specified levels;

(9) Increase liquid assets and maintain such increased liquidity at specified levels; or

(10) Take such other action or actions as the Corporation may deem necessary or appropriate for the protection of the Corporation, the insured institution, or depositors or investors in the insured institution.

While supervisory pressure on the reserve regulation was rather persistent, so was the desire for growth on the part of the business, particularly when competitive pressures were reducing operating margins. The supervisory cases that developed from failure, or near failure, to meet the reserve regulation began to increase. Mostly as a result of pressure from Florida institutions the Board promulgated a significant liberalization in the reserve regulation in 1972. It permitted institutions to average year-end savings account balances over five years in computing the savings account base against which the required percentage of reserves had to be determined.

As will be shown, this arrangement had devastating consequences in the 1980s, particularly in the case of some newly organized associations (which, as noted, had 25 years to get to the "regular" FIR minimum) and smaller associations acquired by new owners seeking rapid growth.

RELAXATION OF RESERVES AND GROWTH

A relaxation in reserve requirements in 1972 helped institutions hungry for growth and resulted in a slowdown in the accumulation of net worth. Meanwhile, efforts were made to require the accumulation of reserves based on a mix of assets and judgments about the quality and riskiness of various asset classifications, rather than as a percentage of savings deposits. Precedence, rather than logic, led to computing reserve requirements against savings deposits—with deposits from FHLBank borrowings excluded, even though these borrowings were an alternative to deposit accumulation.

The Board's effort to develop an asset-based reserve requirement was controversial. Resistance came from many institutions which would have been forced to have a higher net worth based on their asset mix rather than as a percentage of savings deposits. The result was a considerable watering down of the percentages of reserves against required assets. Nevertheless, the business had to meet two sets of reserve requirements. In most instances, however, the percent of savings requirement was the most demanding. The Board eliminated the asset-based reserve requirement in 1980.

Addendum B lists the percentages of reserves (or net worth) required for various assets in the Board's short-lived asset-based reserve requirement. It is interesting today to see how investment risk was perceived in the early 1970s.

With hindsight, it is clear that the repeal of this regulation was unfortunate. In fact, it was the forerunner of an asset- or risk-based net worth requirement today. If the 1972 regulation had been retained and revised from time to time, particularly after the enactment of Garn-St Germain and the liberalization of state laws, much of the irresponsible growth and investment of new savings into high risk type assets in 1983, 1984 and 1985 might have been avoided. At the time of its repeal in 1980, however, few people in the business viewed this with regret or alarm.

After the six-month money market certificate of deposit was introduced into the savings market in 1978 and deposit costs escalated, pressures on the reserve regulation intensified. These pressures, however, were not generated by growth rates beyond what institutions could afford, but by market forces which affected even slow-growing institutions. For the first time, the business learned about interest rate risk.

Association executives stood in fear of defaulting on the reserve regulation. Their natural instinct was to ask for a general relaxation of the regulation. The number of "failures" to meet even the lower benchmarks resulting from the moving average formula were beginning to mount. At its Legislative Conference in March 1979, the U.S. League officially asked the Congress to change the law and reduce the 5% FIR requirement to 4%. The Bank Board, under its new chairman, Jay Janis, went even further. It asked Congress to give the Board authority to vary the requirement from 3% to 6%, which was granted in the Depository Institutions Deregulation Act of 1980. In October 1980, the Board reduced the requirement to 4% across the board, with provisions for a somewhat lower requirement for associations with flexible rate mortgages and short-term liquid assets.

The Board, under Chairman Richard Pratt, reduced the requirement to 3%, effective December 1981, while specifically retaining the averaging opportunity. This change was made as many institutions came under pressure to maintain a 4% requirement in the face of sharply declining earnings, and followed a recommendation by the U.S. League to lower the minimum to 3%.

The basic 3% net worth requirement with the five-year averaging made it possible for institutions to grow very rapidly. With the passage of the Garn-St Germain Act and the ability of thrift institutions to use money market accounts to recapture savings deposits from money market mutual funds, the business began to grow at a very rapid rate. Total assets increased $76 billion and $129 billion in 1983 and 1984 respectively.

Spread problems lessened in 1983 and particularly in 1984. By then, however, the business had greatly depleted its net worth, and many institutions were below 3% in regulatory net worth. The general wisdom was that institutions had to grow out of their problems and restructure assets by increasing the proportion of adjustable rate mortgages to total loan portfolio. This meant putting loans on the books at a rapid rate.

By the end of 1983 and through 1984, the business felt that it could not stand still. It needed a program to get back on its feet. To most, this meant rapid growth, which the reserve regulation permitted. With lower interest rates, savings deposits could be attracted at lesser cost. In addition, funds were available through the new money market deposit accounts and interest rate deregulation. The housing market was booming and executives thought they saw a window of opportunity to restructure and put profitable assets on the books. A feeling pervaded that the time for deposit growth was limited and management should take advantage of this opportunity.

The business grew rapidly, and some institutions grew at alarmingly high rates. Data published by the Bank Board's Office of Policy and Economic Research in early 1985 indicated that throughout 1984 institutions holding about one-seventh of the business' assets were growing at a rate that would double its size in two years or less. Institutions growing at a rate where they would double in size in four years or less accounted for 40% of the business' assets. Annual growth rates of several hundred points were no longer uncommon. In some parts of the country such growth became the rule rather than an exception.

The Bank Board noted by late 1983 that a minority of institutions were running wild in deposit growth, principally through the acquisition of deposits from brokers (which is discussed in a later section). The Board felt that it had no way to slow down these institutions except by imposing higher net worth requirements applicable to all associations regardless of the institutions' management record or mix of assets. It spurned, however, the use of cease-and-desist orders or other supervisory means to deal selectively with this problem.

Proposed revisions of the reserve or net worth regulations designed to slow the growth of the business were published on February 15, 1984. Basically, the proposal affirmed the basic 3% minimum but would have eliminated the five-year averaging. This meant that, except for de novo institutions, each $100 million of deposit growth would have to be matched in the same year by an increase in reserves of $3 million, or 3%. However, it permitted a phase-down of the averaging arrangements.

This proposal encountered strong opposition from the business. Institutions believed it would impede restructuring efforts through rapid growth and adding adjustable rate mortgages to portfolios.

Opposition was particularly strong from smaller institutions and those growing rapidly. Policies of the U.S. League and many state leagues reflected this opposition, which was traditional; the business had never accepted a reserve regulation that impeded growth. To many institutions, it was incomprehensible that, while they were struggling to restructure and barely able to meet the existing net worth requirement, the Board would require greater allocations to reserves. Many in the business believed the Board should deal directly with the so-called "high flyers" and those growing at fantastically high rates and not impose new regulatory burdens on the entire business.

Opposition delayed the Board's efforts to put a new reserve regulation into effect for about 10 months. In late 1984, the net worth regulation was reproposed with more demanding terms and adopted in final form January 31, 1985. By year's end, the business generally saw the problems that were developing and approved of stiffer net worth regulations. In retrospect, the Bank Board was probably too responsive to the business' position when initial protests were voiced to its February proposal. The regulations could have been, and should have been, put into effect earlier. With the old, easy net worth regulation staying in effect until 1985, rapid deposit growth was allowed to continue throughout 1984, often accompanied by irresponsible and reckless lending practices.[5]

Until the most recent (1985 and 1986) revisions of the net worth regulations, the Bank Board's reserve and net worth requirements had always affected all institutions equally.[6]

Supervisory inflexibility regarding net worth requirements has always stood in sharp contrast to the commercial banks' supervisory system. Until 1983, no minimum net worth requirements were stated in the banking law or regulations. Examiners and supervisors impose flexible, unwritten requirements, and examiners are authorized to classify loan assets and require additions to reserves, a practice brought to savings and loan examinations for the first time in 1986. This type of supervisory flexibility and discretion would never have been tolerated by savings and loan executives, particularly over a

---

[5] For the record, it is worth noting that savings and loan assets grew from $525 billion at year-end 1981 to $724 billion at year-end 1984, or almost 38%. At the same time, the regulatory net worth of the business increased from $28 billion to $35 billion, or 25%. Loans acquired totaled $76.7 billion in 1982, $178.2 billion in 1983 and $245.4 billion in 1984. The previous highest annual total was $110.3 billion in 1978.

[6] The asset-based requirement, in effect from 1972 to 1980, was not demanding enough to affect the net worth requirement of many associations. The requirement based on a percentage of savings deposits plus 20% of "scheduled assets" (problem loans and assets) was more in most cases than the higher new formula amount.

TABLE 13: NET WORTH AS A PERCENT OF ASSETS BY FHLB DISTRICTS

Year	Boston	N.Y.	Pittsburgh	Atlanta	Cincinnati	Indianapolis
1950	7.15%	5.94%	6.95%	7.20%	8.25%	7.32%
1951	7.29	6.26	7.10	7.26	8.11	7.47
1952	7.07	6.30	7.05	6.97	7.92	7.58
1953	6.94	6.30	6.93	6.82	7.74	7.25
1954	6.78	6.18	6.79	6.63	7.52	7.29
1955	6.67	6.12	6.75	6.59	7.24	7.31
1956	6.86	6.34	6.89	6.74	7.27	7.47
1957	7.01	6.51	7.22	6.91	7.27	7.41
1958	7.06	6.60	7.36	6.92	7.27	7.46
1959	7.09	6.64	7.39	6.83	7.24	7.41
1960	7.05	6.73	7.37	6.94	7.21	7.37
1961	7.00	6.73	7.30	6.92	7.13	7.43
1962	6.84	6.84	7.37	6.89	7.27	7.29
1963	6.47	6.65	7.30	6.69	7.02	6.98
1964	6.37	6.50	7.23	6.56	6.95	6.84
1965	6.44	6.56	7.28	6.69	7.07	7.04
1966	6.56	6.77	7.67	6.98	7.29	7.19
1967	6.34	6.53	7.53	6.81	7.09	6.99
1968	6.31	6.45	7.61	6.84	7.20	7.10
1969	6.35	6.50	7.77	6.99	7.34	7.19
1970	6.23	6.44	7.50	6.87	7.20	7.04
1971	5.86	6.09	6.89	6.21	6.70	6.65
1972	5.68	5.86	6.57	5.74	6.39	6.30
1973	5.66	5.86	6.62	5.86	6.59	6.33
1974	5.58	5.79	6.67	5.92	6.53	6.40
1975	5.33	5.44	6.18	5.55	6.19	6.05
1976	5.16	5.34	5.90	5.36	5.92	5.70
1977	5.04	5.24	5.77	5.22	5.82	5.54
1978	5.08	5.21	5.01	5.25	5.84	5.57
1979	5.25	5.13	5.96	5.35	5.95	5.73
1980	4.97	4.52	5.61	5.06	5.68	5.39

Source: Federal Home Loan Bank Board

matter so sensitive and vital to the competitive standing of institutions in any one market as the reserve or net worth requirements. The result, of course, was that reserve requirements tended to be on the low side and could be met by all reasonably well-operated institutions.

Reserves in the 1960s and early 1970s were probably adequate for a business invested essentially in single-family mortgages, operating in the traditional mode and subject only to traditional risks. But they were not adequate for a business faced with interest rate risks for the first time in 1978 and forced in the early 1980s to cope with deregulation in a changing marketplace.

(Table 13 continued)

Year	Chicago	Des Moines	Little Rock	Topeka	San Francisco	Seattle
1950	6.69%	5.44%	7.30%	7.52%	6.92%	6.98%
1951	6.89	5.63	7.17	7.65	7.24	7.00
1952	6.85	5.72	7.05	7.33	6.47	6.88
1953	6.60	5.70	6.59	7.00	6.59	6.66
1954	6.40	5.60	6.29	6.66	6.63	6.41
1955	6.32	5.58	6.30	6.56	6.80	6.52
1956	6.43	5.92	6.56	6.77	6.75	6.64
1957	6.59	6.26	6.56	6.86	6.89	6.74
1958	6.52	6.15	6.46	6.82	7.04	6.77
1959	6.49	6.20	6.39	6.77	6.86	6.75
1960	6.56	6.34	6.33	6.67	7.04	6.75
1961	6.53	6.34	6.26	6.63	7.14	6.68
1962	6.56	6.57	6.29	6.66	7.07	6.79
1963	6.44	6.51	6.06	6.50	6.49	6.60
1964	6.36	6.43	5.90	6.53	6.56	6.50
1965	6.46	6.60	6.07	6.71	6.62	6.70
1966	6.64	6.83	6.14	6.89	6.77	6.84
1967	6.41	6.66	6.01	6.70	6.27	6.66
1968	6.57	6.65	6.20	6.72	6.49	6.77
1969	6.80	6.73	6.47	6.86	6.78	6.96
1970	6.76	6.55	6.50	6.75	6.58	6.85
1971	6.37	6.15	6.12	6.32	6.39	6.42
1972	6.00	5.80	5.84	6.03	6.13	6.12
1973	6.13	5.68	6.21	6.26	6.78	6.35
1974	6.14	5.52	6.13	6.26	6.67	6.30
1975	5.70	5.18	5.67	5.89	6.23	5.92
1976	5.36	5.07	5.38	5.70	5.97	5.71
1977	5.17	5.03	5.21	5.61	5.84	5.60
1978	5.19	5.07	5.27	5.75	5.97	5.79
1979	5.34	5.24	5.38	5.88	5.95	5.91
1980	4.94	4.87	5.02	5.66	5.62	5.63

Source: Federal Home Loan Bank Board

NET WORTH OF THE BUSINESS 1950 TO 1980

Table 13 shows that the business generally had a good net worth position in the late 1950s and early 1960s. Then it suffered a deterioration of net worth ratios beginning in 1967, with system averages in many parts of the country falling to barely above 5% by 1979. Interestingly, erosion in net worth began with the advent of deposit rate ceilings over savings and loan associations and savings banks, at which point the decision on setting savings rates generally shifted from the individual institutions to the federal agencies. The effect of the moving average formula adopted in 1972 is seen in the falling of net worth ratios in 1973 and subsequent years.

TABLE 14: INTEREST RATES AND THEIR EFFECT ON NET WORTH

Year	6-Month Treasury Bill Rate	Money Market Fund Assets ($ Billion)	Cost of Funds to S&Ls	S&L Portfolio Yield	ROA	Insured Institutions	
						Tangible Net Worth ($ Billion)	Regulatory Net Worth ($ Billion)
1980	11.37%	$ 76.4	8.94%	9.34%	0.13%	$32.2	$32.4
1981	13.78	186.2	10.92	9.91	-0.73	25.5	27.6
1982	11.08	219.8	11.38	10.68	-0.65	3.8	25.4
1983	8.75	179.4	9.83	11.17	0.27	3.9	33.0
1984	9.80	233.6	10.03	11.66	0.13	4.1	37.9
1985	7.66	243.8	9.20	11.53	0.39	9.0	46.6
1986	6.03	292.1	8.06	10.64	0.09	15.5	53.1
1987	6.05	316.1	7.20	9.68	-0.56	n.a.	47.5

Source: United States League of Savings Institutions

Reserves the business had at the beginning of 1980 were soon reduced by high interest rates, competition from money market mutual funds and the phasing out of Regulation Q savings rate controls. The virtual absence of adjustable rate mortgages prevented the business from improving its mortgage portfolio earnings. Data for 1980, 1981 and 1982 in Tables 14 and 15 tell the story.

TABLE 15: THE OPERATING STORY FOR INSURED SAVINGS INSTITUTIONS (In Millions of Dollars)

Year	Operating Income	Operating Expense	Interest on Savings Deposits	Interest on Borrowed Money	After Tax Net Income
1980	$ 56,135	$ 7,920	$41,627	$ 5,801	$ 784
1981	65,152	8,976	54,075	9,206	−4,632
1982	71,509	10,104	58,600	11,653	−4,271
1983	79,983	12,298	58,275	9,380	1,968
1984	100,610	15,326	71,790	12,615	1,101
1985	110,517	19,527	73,471	14,058	3,839
1986	110,987	22,981	68,045	15,437	1,115

Source: United States League of Savings Institutions

The response of the business to its net worth problems in 1982 and 1983 was to ask, in addition to lowering of the net worth requirements to 3%, for forbearance on enforcing even that low benchmark, and net worth assistance in the form of income capital certificates first provided by administrative action of the Board, and later by the Garn-St Germain Act.

The Board responded with a variety of ameliorating provisions. These included the creation of goodwill assets from supervisory-induced mergers, which initially could be amortized up to 40 years;[7] appraised equity capital arising from revaluing the business' fixed assets; and a new regulation permitting the deferral of losses on loan sales. This regulation had the temporary effect of boosting income because associations could sell lower rate loans and reinvest in more profitable assets. But as it turned out, this provision encouraged associations to dump their low rate and lower valued assets at just the wrong time. Hindsight shows that they could have sold these loans at much higher prices. The amortization of the loss deferral is now a drag on earnings for those who took advantage of this authority.

This illustrated a preoccupation of the Bank Board during the chairmanship of Richard Pratt—a focus on net income. This also took

---

[7] The limit is now 25 years as a result of action by the Bank Board and the SEC.

the form of encouraging associations to take on higher yielding assets. Concern about net income, of course, was a natural reaction given the uncertain economic climate and the problems of the business in 1981 and 1982. It is also understandable considering the supervisory cases that came to the Board's attention: institutions with seriously deteriorating net income resulting from portfolios of low rate, fixed rate mortgages supporting competition for savings at escalating rates.

The concept of regulatory net worth (RAP) was introduced. In most cases, this was greater than net worth determined by generally accepted accounting principles (GAAP), accepted by the accounting profession.

By 1983 the business had lost almost all of its net worth. Many associations had regulatory net worth below the rather low regulatory requirements. Some had a negative regulatory net worth and therefore were technically insolvent.

The relatively low levels of net worth in the business as it entered the 1980s made it difficult for many institutions to avoid failure and FSLIC assistance in the resulting mergers or reorganizations. For others, which lost most of their net worth but escaped a supervisory takeover or forced merger, the alternative was a voluntary merger and taking part in a combination of three or more institutions serving the same market. Those that entered the 1980s with strong reserves (6% or better), controlled costs well, had not grown too rapidly with six-month certificates or invested these funds in fixed rate mortgages found the early years of the 1980s worrisome—but far from catastrophic.

Many, if not most, of the association failures might have been avoided if associations had entered the 1980s with much stronger net worth positions. This probably would have resulted only if the Board had instituted much tougher net worth requirements in the mid-1960s or 1970s, such as those the Board proposed in 1968 under chairman John Horne's leadership. In addition, the relationship between net worth requirements and asset mix should have been considered more carefully.

With hindsight, it may now be said that, as persistent as the Board's supervisory staff was in enforcing the reserve regulation, it should have been even tougher. In many cases, forbearance led to bad situations getting worse. For overambitious savings and loan executives, it indicated that the Board's bark was worse than its bite. In other instances, lack of vigorous enforcement of the net worth regulations or other rules indicated that the Board was basically timid. For some in the business, this was the wrong signal to send.

Regulation Q 4

The business had become dependent upon Regulation Q, which controlled savings interest rates at depository institutions. Its demise was probably the principal reason for the first phase of savings and loan failures, those due to the so-called spread problem.

Regulation Q had served the business extremely well. It was a key reason the business developed into a set of significant financial institutions. The regulation first served the business when it applied only to commercial banks by limiting interest on bank time and savings deposits to 3% from 1933 to 1962. To be sure, many banks did not want to pay higher rates, and Regulation Q provided freedom from competition among banks. Nevertheless, it did give the savings and loan business an opportunity to pay higher rates than banks—as much as 200 basis points higher in some markets. This advantage helped overcome the public relations handicap the business suffered from its record during the Depression.

The second phase of Regulation Q came in 1966 with its extension to savings and loan associations and savings banks. It provided stability and permitted thrift institutions to pay rates generally 25 basis points to 50 basis points higher than commercial banks. (See Table 16.)

This savings rate differential was a powerful marketing tool, and the business took full advantage of it. "We pay more than any bank" was a common advertising theme. Equally important, Regulation Q and the differential were also effective in preventing failures.

ADMINISTERING THE REGULATION

Regulation Q was administered in a way that virtually guaranteed an operating profit for all but a small minority of institutions that were grossly inefficient, sustaining mortgage portfolio losses or overcommitted on mortgages for sale at a time of rising interest rates.

TABLE 16: INTEREST RATE CEILINGS ON SAVINGS DEPOSITS*

| Effective Date | Commercial Banks | | Savings & Loan Associations | |
	Savings Deposits	Other Time Deposits*	Savings Deposits	Other Time Deposits*
Sep. 1966	4 %	- 5 %	4¾%	5¼%
Jan. 1970	4½	5½ - 5¾	5	5¾ - 6
Jul. 1973	5	6 - 6½	5¼	6½ - 6¾
Nov. 1973	5	6 - 7¼	5¼	6½ - 7½
Dec. 1974	5	6 - 7½	5¼	6½ - 7¾
Jun. 1978	5	6 - 7¾	5¼	6½ - 8
Jul. 1979	5¼	6 - 7¾	5½	6½ - 8

*Rate on certificates of less than $100,000 with maturities of one year or more.

"What could the business afford" was a key question whenever adjustments in Q ceilings were considered. This kept the business from the cutthroat competition that began to develop in financial markets during the early 1960s.

Economists and Reagan Administration officials who prefer allowing competitive market forces to guide development of the financial system applauded the end of Regulation Q in the 1980s. Clearly, however, it stabilized the American financial system. The end of its usefulness as a stabilizing device contributed to a flood of bank and savings and loan failures.

Regulation Q worked quite satisfactorily as long as interest ceilings stayed reasonably close to market rates, although the business was reluctant to have ceilings increased as market rates rose throughout the 1970s. The collapse of Regulation Q became inevitable, of course, when market rates skyrocketed in the early 1980s.

USURY CEILINGS

While not a factor until the late 1960s and 1970s, associations in most states worked under rather strict usury ceilings applicable to home mortgage loans. These had developed in a much earlier period, imposed by state legislatures (and in Arkansas embodied in the state constitution) whose members were loath to raise or remove them. By the 1970s, the usury ceilings became virtual floors for mortgage rates. With Regulation Q ceilings on deposit interest rates, associations found that one of the principal decisions in conducting the business— product pricing—had been usurped by legislative and regulatory bodies. Some states (such as California and Texas) had no legal restrictions on interest that associations could charge on home loans.

These states became bright spots by originating loans for sale to associations in other states.

MONEY MARKET CERTIFICATES

Regulation Q died not because bank, savings and loan executives or Congress were anxious to get rid of it, or because it failed to achieve its objectives. The regulation was eliminated because it could not cope with inflation and accompanying high market interest rates. Its end began in 1978 with the authorization of the six-month savings certificate, with the initial rate tied to the six-month Treasury bill rate. This was the Carter Administration's answer to the waves of disintermediation that struck the banking system, and especially thrift institutions, from time to time during earlier periods of rising interest rates. This had a devastating effect on home building and the construction industry.

The money market certificate was effective for several years. It permitted banking institutions to keep much of their deposits, but it also increased deposit costs. Many institutions, not anticipating the extent of future interest rate increases, mistakenly invested substantial sums of this money in long-term, fixed rate mortgages at interest rates that proved far too low to pay interest on deposits and operating expenses. More prudent short-term investment of such deposits would have prevented many failures, but association managers had little reason to forecast that interest rates would climb as high as they did. The Bank Board chairman, after all, had told the business that money market certificates would self-destruct.

During this period, powerful competition came from money market mutual funds, managed and promoted by the large security firms and life insurance companies, as well as the traditional mutual fund sponsors. These funds offered a financial instrument that proved devastating to deposit flows at institutions which did not have a product to match its convenience or high interest rate. Not only did the six-month money market certificate increase the business' cost of funds, but it failed to effectively compete with money funds. As a result, the Garn-St Germain Act permitted banks and thrift institutions to offer something roughly similar: the money market deposit account, on which three checks could be written each month. This new account, together with offering interest-bearing checking accounts (NOW accounts), enabled savings associations and banks to keep their deposits. Later, after the phasing out of Q ceilings on all deposit accounts, associations moved aggressively to attract large deposit flows—but, of course, at very high deposit costs.

RISING COSTS OF BORROWED MONEY

Meanwhile, the cost of borrowed money also rose dramatically, adversely affecting association income statements. Many institutions borrowed heavily during the period of disintermediation in the early 1980s.

The effect on savings and loan associations' cost of funds is shown in Tables 14 and 15. Given the extent of fixed rate lending at these institutions, it was virtually impossible to cover their money costs.

With hindsight, it is apparent that the business became too dependent on Regulation Q. When the regulation unraveled, the business had great difficulty adjusting to unregulated markets. It is interesting to speculate on the result if the business had not succeeded in torpedoing the so-called "wild card" initiatives of Arthur Burns and the Board of Governors of the Federal Reserve System in 1973.

On July 5, 1973, the Federal Reserve allowed commercial banks to issue a "ceiling-free," four-year certificate. The law authorizing Regulation Q then did not mandate interest ceilings on time and savings deposits. It merely gave supervisory agencies authority to put ceilings on deposit accounts. The Fed, acting under this generally permissive law, felt that at least an experiment in a market rate deposit instrument would be worth pursuing. Some, but not all, banks responded. Deposit rates as high as 8% began appearing in some markets.[8] Banks everywhere began paying rates substantially higher than savings and loan associations had been authorized under the ceilings imposed by the Bank Board.

The result was a first-class row between the savings and loan business and the Fed, and passage later that year by Congress of a law which, in effect, required the Fed and the Bank Board to impose interest rate ceilings on all types of time and savings deposits under $100,000. If the business had not been successful in that congressional initiative, it gradually might have learned to live with the free market and make wide use of the variable rate mortgage.

---

[8] In New Orleans, banks advertised 9% on their four-year, wild-card certificates. As a result, local associations, with total assets of about $1 billion, lost $35 million in deposits from the time of the wild-card authorization in early July to August 1.

The Fixed Rate Mortgage 5

Short-term mortgages with balloon end payments created great problems in the 1930s for commercial banks and those few savings and loan associations that had used them in the 1920s. Subsequently, in the 1930s the creators of the new Federal Savings and Loan System, looking back and wanting to build a mistake-proof system, wrote into the original regulations the provision that most mortgages must be repaid with equal monthly payments. Interest rates could be varied only if the loan's maturity was increased or decreased. If the loan terms were 15, or even 20 years, this was practical; but not when mortgages had begun, some years later, to be written for 30 years.

This rule was for federally chartered associations. State law proved more flexible, notably in Wisconsin and California. In the 1970s, some state-chartered associations in those states began writing variable rate mortgages, with beneficial effects on the bottom line. During the first wave of the failures of the 1980s, the good record of institutions in those states reflected the effectiveness of variable rate mortgages.

Given the operating environment from the Federal Savings and Loan System's creation in 1933 to approximately 1965, writing fixed rate mortgages based on funds secured from household savings in passbook type accounts seemed reasonable. After 1966, when Regulation Q was applied to the savings and loan business, the savings rate ceilings provided the necessary comfort level. Congress kept putting termination dates on Regulation Q—but that was more for reasons of legislative strategy on the part of the leadership of the congressional banking committees than from doubt about the wisdom of the program.

In fact, the business itself questioned the program's desirability and suggested a termination date in 1966 when Regulation Q was first extended to thrift institutions.

DISINTERMEDIATION AND FLEXIBLE MORTGAGES

Several periods of disintermediation (notably in 1966 and 1969), along with pressures on Regulation Q during those years to increase interest rate ceilings, caused some savings and loan executives to question fixed rate mortgages.

Meanwhile, many managers became better acquainted with the operation of their counterpart institutions in other countries—notably in Great Britain, Australia and South Africa—where interest rate flexibility had long been a feature of the home mortgage loan. Through trips abroad, and particularly to the World Congress of the International Union of Building Societies and Savings Associations in Sydney, Australia, in 1968, American savings and loan executives learned about the advantages of variable rate mortgages.

Following a period of interest rate inflation in Canada, Canadian trust companies, that country's principal mortgage lenders, discarded the fixed rate, long-term mortgage and began to write short-term (three-, four- or five-year) mortgages exclusively. In the early 1960s, the First Federal Savings and Loan Association of Chicago, whose president was a notable internationalist, began to write variable rate mortgages exclusively. These mortgages had a provision in the note that the interest rate could be increased any time at the sole discretion of the association's board of directors.[9] Exercising this authority, of course, would mean lengthening the term of the mortgages.

Writing this type of mortgage in the Chicago market was extremely difficult, but the institution persisted until its management changed in 1966, after which the institution unilaterally canceled the provision in all mortgages. The provision had never been exercised. Efforts were made by one association in Southern California and another in Cleveland to develop a variable rate mortgage program. In both instances, however, a borrower revolt upon the exercise of the clause ended these programs.

Meanwhile, in Wisconsin, a number of associations in smaller cities had been quietly writing these mortgages for years. In northern Michigan, a small state-chartered association began to write five-year mortgages exclusively, but these were isolated examples until the mid-1970s.

During this period, some state-chartered institutions attempted to qualify borrowers on 15-year or 20-year loan terms but with payments

---

[9] This was, and still is, the British system.

related to a 25-year or 30-year maturity. This created the need for a balloon payment. It was an interim, somewhat unsatisfactory, step in search of a better lending instrument.

VARIABLE RATE MORTGAGE EXPERIMENTATION

While the business remained generally complacent about the fixed rate mortgage and the deadline to end Regulation Q was regularly extended, a number of savings and loan executives in California began taking action to develop and write flexible rate mortgages.

Legislation permitting variable rate mortgages was enacted in California in 1970. It prescribed limits on the increase in any one year and the allowable increase over the term of the mortgage. This legislation did not evoke much interest among major state-chartered associations until the 1974 U.S. League convention in San Francisco. At that time, Stuart Davis, chairman of Great Western Savings, California's second largest institution, announced that his institution was preparing to introduce variable rate mortgages in 1975. Great Western's initiative was followed by many of California's other large state-chartered associations.

Preston Martin, who had been Commissioner of Savings and Loans in California from 1967 to 1969 (when he became chairman of the Bank Board) discussed a proposal for variable rate mortgage regulations for all federal associations with the leadership of the House and Senate banking committees. His proposed regulations were somewhat similar to those in California. Martin encountered negative reactions to his idea, however, and dropped this proposal. His successor as Bank Board chairman, Thomas Bomar, tried hard but without success to build support in Congress for the variable rate mortgage. In the late 1970s, under the chairmanship of Robert McKinney, the Bank Board formally proposed a variable rate mortgage authority for federally chartered associations. But the House and Senate banking committees strongly recommended that the Board drop the idea.

LOBBYING FOR THE VARIABLE RATE MORTGAGE

The U.S. League lobbied Congress to win acceptance for variable rate mortgages, so that the Bank Board could go ahead with permissive regulations, but opposition by banking committee chairmen Senator

Proxmire and Representative St Germain was unrelenting. Their opposition was strongly supported by the National Association of Home Builders. Organized consumer groups, led by a corps of retired persons, were also heavily involved.

In view of the tremendous costs to associations and the FSLIC from the inability of associations to have even a portion of their portfolios in variable rate mortgages, it is pertinent to note the following: At any time during the 1960s and 1970s, when interest rate volatility began, the Bank Board could legally, by regulatory action, have authorized the use of such a mortgage. Indeed, it did so in 1981 under Richard Pratt's chairmanship. What retribution might have been levied on the Bank Board or the business if the Board had authorized a variable rate mortgage cannot be known. The Board believed that Congress would overrule any initiative to authorize the variable rate mortgage, although this was unlikely.[10]

Some question how much use the business would have made of the VRM even if it had had this authority. Nevertheless, some of the onus for the first wave of failures occasioned by spread problems must fall on the heads of the Bank Boards of the 1970s and the leadership of the congressional banking committees.

Variable rate mortgages probably would have been used more widely in a number of states (such as Michigan, where the VRM could not be used, but the short-term balloon mortgage was), except that federals could not write this mortgage. This made it virtually unusable by state associations because federally chartered associations dominated most markets (except in California, where most large institutions were state-chartered).

Quicker acceptance of the variable rate mortgage might have been possible if more effort had been made to tie variable payments to variable savings rates. The business generally resisted this idea, however, until the introduction of the money market certificate in 1978. The connection between rates paid for savings and rates charged for mortgage loans is obvious, but too often ignored by legislators even though they were often reminded of it by savings and loan executives.

---

[10] The Bank Board under the chairmanship of Jay Janis did authorize in April 1980 a renegotiable rate mortgage, loans with terms of three, four, or five years secured by a mortgage of up to 30 years. This was the so-called Canadian roll-over mortgage, but it was surrounded by so many restrictions and consumer safeguards that it was seldom used.

PROBLEMS WITH "DUE-ON-SALE" CLAUSE

The problem stemming from the lack of a variable rate mortgage was exacerbated because in many states the courts refused to enforce the so-called "due-on-sale" clause. This permits a lender to demand repayment of the remaining balance on a home loan if the home is sold and the mortgage is assumed by a third party. The clause had been a common feature of savings and loan mortgages for years. It was enforced with little controversy as long as interest rates remained relatively stable. In periods of rising rates, however, homeowners with a relatively low mortgage interest rate found it advantageous to sell their house and have a buyer assume the mortgage and continue paying the original low rate. This added thousands of dollars to a home's potential sales price. Beginning in California and then in 12 important states throughout the country, it became impossible to enforce these clauses as written by federal or state-chartered associations.

Under the chairmanship of Robert McKinney, the Bank Board adopted in July 1976, a regulation applicable to federally chartered associations which preempted state laws by specifically authorizing federal associations to include due-on-sale clauses in mortgage contracts.

In the case of Wellingkamp vs. the Bank of America, brought before the Supreme Court of California, the applicability of the California prohibition against due-on-sale clauses was upheld as to national banks. The issue was decided for federal associations in the federal courts in the case of Fidelity Federal Savings and Loan Association vs. de la Cuesta. The de la Cuesta case went to the Supreme Court of the United States. In 1982, the court affirmed the ability of federally chartered associations to enforce due-on-sale clauses notwithstanding state law. In other words, it supported the Bank Board's preemption regulation and reversed the decision of the California courts.

This left state-chartered institutions unprotected with respect to due-on-sale situations. This was dealt with in the Garn-St Germain Act in late 1982 which permitted all lenders, including state institutions, to enforce due-on-sale clauses except for loans originated or assumed during a period generally before October 15, 1982, and 60 days thereafter.

With due-on-sale clauses unenforceable in most states until late in 1982, savings associations were stuck with portfolios of low interest rate loans. They could not take advantage of the active real estate market in the late 1970s and early 1980s to mature their older mortgages and write a large volume of new, higher rate mortgages.

Real estate brokers were the principal opponents of the due-on-sale clause. Unenforceability of the clause clearly helps explain why associations could not adjust to higher interest rates paid first on money market certificates and then on all deposit accounts, with disastrous results to associations' earnings and net worth.

Increased Competition **6**

As already noted, savings and loan associations faced relatively little competition in the 1950s and much of the 1960s. Indeed, the principal competition faced by any one savings and loan association was that of another association. Not until the mid-1960s did many commercial banks actively seek savings deposits, and they were limited by the ceilings under Regulation Q. Money market funds had not yet been created.

SPECIALIZATION IN HOME LENDING

The specialty of the savings and loan associations, indeed their raison d'être in the eyes of lawmakers and government officials, was all aspects of financing one- to four-family homes—origination, servicing and funding through savings deposits and Home Loan Bank credit. The business provided financing for both existing home or small apartment buyers and small home builders and large merchant builders. Associations provided both the construction funds and the ":take-out" mortgage, although they were often happy to let the take-out go elsewhere. That way, institutions could roll funds over into new construction loans, with higher interest rates and fees.

NO LONGER UNIQUE

As Stuart Greenbaum, a finance professor at Northwestern University, points out, bundled mortgage services at one time were the thrift's hallmark, and they thoroughly dominated residential financing. He observes that "recent thrift industry travail has been accompanied by an unbundling of mortgage services."

Historically, savings and loan associations originated, serviced and funded one- to four-family mortgages. Several factors, however, contributed to the end of this unique role: The rise of the Federal

National Mortgage Association (Fannie Mae); the Government National Mortgage Association (Ginnie Mae); and the thrift industry's own creation, the Federal Home Loan Mortgage Corporation (Freddie Mac). These brought a new system of funding mortgages into play.

Computer applications to mortgage loan servicing enabled competitors to challenge associations in this market. Servicing mortgages is basically a routine bookkeeping, payment and collection service; its stock in trade is the computer processing system, in which economies of scale are considerable. The savings and loan business, of course, brings nothing unique to the servicing function.

In the case of FHA loans and conventional loans sold to Fannie Mae and Freddie Mac and through the use of private mortgage insurance, much of the credit evaluation and risk in originating mortgages was passed on to mortgage insurers and the ultimate buyers of the securities created by the secondary market agencies.

The savings and loan business was expert in arbitraging between the savings deposit and mortgage markets. Profits from this arbitrage function, however, began to narrow in the early 1980s, creating pressures on association earnings.

The securitization of mortgages (currently some 80% of mortgages underwritten are securitized) brought many new participants into the mortgage market and new ways of conducting mortgage finance.

THE SECURITIZATION OF MORTGAGES

The rapid growth of mortgage securitization was a result of computer technology, the standardization of mortgage contracts by Fannie Mae and Freddie Mac, and the involvement of the nation's largest investment banking firms in the market for mortgage-backed bonds. Government agencies and large security firms developed a variety of new mortgage instruments such as pass-throughs, CMOs, REMICs and stripped securities. This has made it possible for savings and loan institutions to concentrate on originating mortgages for sale, basically a mortgage banking function. But it involves different risks than those of the traditional savings association: inventories, or positions, in mortgages not funded by savings deposits can lead to losses if interest rates shift rapidly. Although these positions can be hedged, this involves significant risks if not handled carefully. It also permits institutions to deliberately take certain pricing risks in the hope of added profits.

Under this new system of mortgage finance, associations can buy mortgage-backed securities, and some institutions have chosen to neglect the mortgage origination process in favor of becoming investors in mortgage-backed bonds. The development of repurchase agreements secured by mortgage-backed bonds permits associations to accumulate vast holdings of these securities without developing an extensive deposit base, and to profit from the spread between repos and bonds. In so doing, unusual interest rate risks can be taken. They are usually hedged, but it takes considerable skill to deal in these markets. Difficulties and losses can develop in even the most carefully managed situations, and this has occurred.

Changes in mortgage lending largely became possible because the traditional view of a mortgage as a unique, essentially local financial instrument no longer applied. Basically, the mortgage came to be recognized as a "financial contract" which could be tailored within broadly defined limits to match a lender's and borrower's needs and could also be sold in national financial markets. In this view, the contract was recognized as a bundle of rights—such as payment amounts, term, rate, frequency of payment and distribution of payments between principal and interest—which could be valued as a bundle or as separate investment elements.

Major developments followed the partial privatization of Fannie Mae in 1968 and, more importantly, the organization's move into the conventional mortgage market in 1972. In addition, mortgage banking firms were, after years of successful resistance by the savings and loan business, finally admitted to full participation in the Federal Home Loan Mortgage Corporation's buying program. This substantially increased the scope of its operation. Competition between Fannie Mae and Freddie Mac, together with Wall Street's involvement, radically changed the home finance system. The result has been a reduction in the cost of mortgage finance, but with added risk to savings associations.

Increasingly, savings associations dare making use of options, futures, repos and reverse repos. Most of these transactions are legitimate hedging operations in the mortgage-backed bond and government securities markets.

Other transactions seemingly were entered into primarily for speculative purposes, and major losses were incurred. The collapse of two large securities firms (Bevil, Bressler and Schulman in New Jersey and ESM in Florida) caused major losses to some associations and led to at least one insolvency and a management consignment case. These were instances of associations doing business in "strange waters" seeking to increase profitability. At some associations, losses from mortgage banking operations and the use of new financial instruments led management to take extraordinary risks which often ended with insolvency.

The widespread use of new financial instruments and the new system in mortgage finance—in which the origination of mortgages is the only phase of the business that requires some measure of local information and operation—developed only in the past several years. This development reached its full effect after 1982, just as the savings and loan business was losing its competitive edge in the household savings market because of money market mutual funds, bond funds, a strongly rising stock market and the phasing out of Regulation Q.

The business had enjoyed almost 30 years of prosperity in a favorable competitive environment. Almost overnight the business moved into a competitive market economy. Associations soon lost their marketing advantages on both savings and mortgage products. Protection by the federal government from excessive competition—both from within and without the business to help foster the development of homeownership—abruptly ended. Associations suddenly confronted a world of volatile interest rates, inflation, money

TABLE 17: GUARANTOR OF 1- TO 4-FAMILY MORTGAGE LOANS OUTSTANDING AT YEAR END 1980 AND 1986

	Year-end 1980		Year-end 1986	
Guarantor	Amount (Millions)	% of Total	Amount (Millions)	% of Total
Direct Government:				
(GNFA/FHA and VA)	$114,055	11.56%	$ 281,757	16.8 %
Credit Agencies:				
FHMA	$ 51,775	5.25%	$ 90,718	5.44%
FHMA Pools	—	—	95,791	5.74
FHLMC	3,873	0.39	10,927	0.66
FHLMC Pools	13,471	1.36	165,856	9.94
Subtotal	$ 69,119	7.00%	$ 363,292	21.78%
Private Sector:				
Savings Institutions	$487,252	49.37%	$ 559,263	33.53%
Commercial Banks	160,326	16.24	238,171	14.28
Individuals and Others	156,227	15.83	225,396	13.51
Subtotal	$803,805	81.44%	$1,022,830	61.33%
TOTAL	$986,979	100.0%	$1,667,879	100.0%

Source: Federal Reserve Board and U.S. League of Savings Institutions.

market funds, nonbank banks, mortgage-backed bonds, CMOs, and, most recently, REMICs. The business even faced competition from its former benefactor: the federal government established three government secondary market organizations.

Paradoxically, during the Reagan Administration—with all its emphasis on reducing the federal government's role in American life—the government's role and influence in the residential mortgage market has, in fact, been substantially expanded. Of the one- to four-family mortgage loans outstanding, federal credit agencies accounted for 38.6% of the total at year-end 1986, compared with only 28.5% at year-end 1980. Table 17 tells the story. No wonder many savings and loan associations did not survive this sudden change in their operating environment.

7 Expanded Powers and Relaxed Regulations

With pressure on earnings from the money market certificates and rising costs of money, the Board under Jay Janis began to expand the authority of associations in residential real estate credit. In 1980, it authorized renegotiable rate mortgages, removed geographical limits on real estate lending and authorized loans in excess of 90% of value on one- to four-family properties. In addition, the Board authorized federals to make secured and unsecured loans and to buy, sell and hold commercial paper and corporate debt securities as defined and approved by the Board subject to an overall 20% of assets limit. It also authorized the issuance of credit cards with overdraft privileges, permitted investment of 3% of assets in service corporations (half of the investment that exceeded 1% was allocated to "community" purposes) and raised the maximum maturity of home loans from 30 years to 40 years.

Paralleling the elimination of Regulation Q, and supported by the free market thinking of the Reagan Administration and most of the savings and loan business, the Bank Board under Chairman Pratt moved rather quickly in 1981, 1982 and early 1983 to deregulate the asset side of the balance sheet. This action was undertaken on the theory that because the business must compete for funds with deregulated financial systems and pay higher rates for savings, it should have considerably more flexibility to improve earnings opportunities and shorten the maturity of the institutions' assets.

In the 1960s and throughout the 1970s, many savings and loan executives, particularly those at larger associations, had sought broader investment powers. They primarily wanted authority to invest in land and engage in home building, either directly or through an expanded service corporation program. They also wanted to increase the business' ability to make mortgages on commercial property.

A more limited number of executives sought broader consumer lending powers, and a few wanted power to invest in corporate bonds.

Some expressed interest in making commercial bank type loans. A small minority were outspoken in their desire to become "full service" financial institutions and compete directly with large commercial banks and securities firms.

By the mid-1970s, the business saw the need for authority to write variable rate mortgages. As noted earlier, however, this did not become a high priority until 1978 when California state institutions demonstrated that VRMs were a viable product. The necessity for their use became the theme of U.S. League President Stuart Davis' appearances before savings and loan groups around the country.

As will be seen, a small minority of institution executives greatly abused these new powers. Their actions have accounted for the major part of the FSLIC's losses. Of course, few in the business anticipated that in some states the authority for these investments would be so extensive or that a group of new and irresponsible executives would abuse this authority. Neither did the business foresee that supervisory authorities would be unable to prevent abuses and outright fraud in the use of these powers.

ENTER THE ARM

The Board's first move under Chairman Pratt was to authorize what became known as the Adjustable Rate Mortgage. The regulation to permit ARMs became effective April 30, 1981. It gave the business great freedom to create mortgage products more appropriate for a volatile interest rate environment.

Other initiatives by the Board followed. The Garn-St Germain Act, approved in September 1982, provided the statutory basis for greatly broadened investment opportunities. Following is a list of key regulatory steps taken by the Board to expand lending and investment opportunities for savings associations:

1. **July 1981**   Permitted trading in the futures markets.

2. **July 1981**   Permitted graduated payment adjustable rate mortgages with negative amortization during first 10 years.

3. **August 1981**   Eliminated all maximum loan-to-value ratios.

4. **October 1981**   Permitted balloon loans.

5. **April 1982**   Liberalized loans on manufactured homes.

6. May 1982	Authorized retail repurchase agreements without net worth based limits.
7. August 1982	Permitted financial options.
8. August 1982	Eliminated detailed regulatory limits on mortgage loans, and distinction between home loans based on whether the security property is occupied by the borrower or tenant (in case of investor ownership).
9. October 1982	Authorized consumer loans to 30% of assets.
10. October 1982	Expanded power to invest in loans secured by commercial real estate to 40% of assets.
11. November 1982	Authorized unsecured loans for commercial purposes (commercial bank type loans).
12. August 1983	Eliminated specific loan-to-value ratios for various types of loans.

These changes, the last four of which were authorized by the Garn-St Germain Act, pretty much tore down the regulatory structure that had carefully been built over the years, keeping in mind that the principal objective of laws, regulations and supervision was to avoid institution failures. It should be noted that the Board's regulatory actions often had not given the business the full operating authority provided by Congress. Prior Boards preferred to see how the business would use a new authority before going to full authorization. The Pratt Board, however, immediately gave savings associations permission to use all the new powers authorized by Garn-St Germain.

Particularly significant was the elimination of limits on loan-to-value ratios—thus permitting 100% financing for the first time—and authority to make commercial real estate loans up to 40% of assets.

ACTIONS OF STATE LEGISLATURES

The preceding regulatory and legislative actions of the Board and Congress applied only to federally chartered associations. About half the business had traditionally operated under state charters where the deposit gathering rules were generally set by the Board through FSLIC insurance, but investment side activities were limited only by the laws and regulations of the respective state governments. For years, savings association codes in most states had "tie-in" clauses which gave state associations the same authority Congress provided for federals. Laws and regulations in many states provided more flexible and liberal investment powers than those under which federals operated. This permitted the business to occasionally persuade Congress to liberalize the laws for federals. This was the dual system in operation. State institutions had led the way in authority for consumer lending (Texas, Missouri and Massachusetts, for example) and investment in bonds and common stock (prevalent in the New England states through tie-ins to savings bank laws).

Many states had more liberal rules for investment in loans on multifamily units and commercial real estate. As previously noted, several states (principally California and Wisconsin) allowed their institutions to write variable rate or short-term mortgages.

Based on this precedent, and to keep their state-chartered institutions competitive with federally chartered institutions following the enactment of the Garn-St Germain Act, state legislatures acted promptly to provide similar authority, or even went far beyond it. In some instances, state legislatures or regulatory authorities acted before Congress did. It was apparent what the new law's provisions would be before final congressional action. Aggressive state authorities had always been anxious to give associations under their supervision a reason to remain state chartered. Many believe that the state-chartered system's survival and its separate regulatory structure depended upon more liberal laws and regulations than existed for federally chartered institutions. Political interplay between the two systems of chartering was particularly pronounced in California.

During the administration of California Governor Jerry Brown (1975 to 1983), state-chartered institutions found it increasingly difficult to live with the state administration.

The Brown Administration was exceptionally aggressive in requiring loans to minorities and in older neighborhoods. Branch applications and mergers were held up in exhaustive administrative hearings. To get approval of branches and mergers, institutions were asked to make difficult commitments in their lending programs. Out of frustration, most large California institutions converted to federal charters in 1982 and 1983.

State-chartered associations had dominated the business there. Through 1981, seven of California's 10 largest institutions were state-chartered, including the three largest. By the end of 1983, however, only one of the 10 largest institutions was state-chartered. (In 1987, three of California's 10 largest were state-chartered.)

In California, state corporations may legally make political contributions to candidates for state offices, although not to those seeking federal offices. With the switch by many California institutions to federal charters, an important source of political funding was cut off to candidates for the state legislature. Another result was a substantial reduction of funds for maintaining California's supervisory department. Its staff was cut from 178 in 1978 to a low of 44 on April 3, 1983 (3 in administration, 3 in the Legal Department, 17 examiners, 6 appraisers and 15 clerical people). On that date there were 109 California state-chartered savings and loan associations.

Members of the state legislature, Governor Brown's Administration in Sacramento and Savings and Loan Commissioner Linda Yang thus became interested in rebuilding the state savings and loan system to bring large associations back into the state charter system. The key legislator in this initiative was Assemblyman Pat Nolan, a Republican. He had been friendly with a number of the savings and loan executives, knowledgeable about the business and politically ambitious. He conceived and developed the text for a liberal bill which eventually became law. Enacted in the fall of 1982, effective January 1, 1983, the law's objective was to provide for the complete deregulation of California savings and loan associations, making it advantageous for large institutions to switch back from federal to state charters and for new investors to enter the business.

Provisions of the law succeeded in attracting new investors but not in converting the large institutions back to state charter. By this time, a number of applicants and new associations arrived on the scene supporting broader authority and less regulation. Many of those forming new associations and those newly controlling smaller established associations began to see in Nolan's proposals an opportunity to operate in a way that ultimately led to many association failures in California.

While the law granted far too many powers, it passed with only one dissenting vote in both the state senate and assembly. Responsible savings and loan executives, either through the California League of Savings Associations or individually, did not question the law's provisions or raise a voice against it. The California League gave the bill only moderate support, essentially staying on the sidelines. In retrospect, this was a grave mistake. A major portion of the losses suffered by the FSLIC in recent years occurred in California, second only to Texas. Savings and loan executives in California, who today oppose the use of their institution's resources to recapitalize the FSLIC, are partially to blame for this problem. The business failed to see the pitfalls in combining easy entry, a very liberal law and soft supervision. Losses to the FSLIC resulted that could not be met through its normal funding programs. Apparently savings association leaders thought broad investment opportunities eventually would be useful or assumed the entrepreneurs organizing and managing institutions would be of the same "school" as was traditional to the business. As one observer noted, the savings and loan business has always been conducted by "gentlemen."[11] In any event, many association managers were consumed by problems of survival and not thinking about what future problems the business might face.

Texas also has broad laws and liberal regulations. State-chartered institutions there have always been close to the political structure and historically quite entrepreneurial in instincts and actions. They, of course, welcomed a law that granted considerable freedom in operating their institutions.

Florida always had been dominated by federally chartered institutions. The state-chartered system was virtually nonexistent. State law was weak and supervision was under the state's Controller, instead of a special savings and loan department that states with a strong state-chartered system have. The present liberal law in Florida was enacted in several stages from 1980 to 1984. It developed at the initiative of the Florida League of Financial Institutions to provide an attractive state charter option for federal associations frustrated by the Home Loan Bank's policy on mergers and branch expansion.

The law, first enacted in 1980, followed faithfully the Model Savings and Loan Act developed by the U.S. League. It was made more liberal by legislative enactments in 1982, 1983 and particularly in 1984. The officers of the Florida League and state officials, anxious to make the law as attractive as possible, believed that management of the state's institutions would never abuse this wide-open authority. Little thought was given to the possibility that new owners and executives might exploit the liberal law or that supervisors could not prevent the kind of bad lending and abuses that did develop.

The new liberal laws for these state-chartered systems went far beyond what the Garn-St Germain Act provided for the federal system and what most people in the business thought was needed. In retrospect, the leadership of the state leagues and savings and loan

---

[11] This was hardly true of a number of savings and loan executives in California in the 1950s and 1960s as well as a few other states when capital stock charters were a road to riches for entrepreneurs.

executives in those states generally should have exercised greater oversight of their state legislatures. If they were following what was happening, they should have considered the consequences more carefully. Ultimately, these laws taxed the ability of the examination and supervisory systems and helped cause major losses at some institutions.

The following are highlights of broad investment powers provided for state-chartered institutions by statute or regulation in four of the most liberal states—Arizona, California, Florida and Texas.

ARIZONA

Real Estate Loans	No restriction on property type, purpose of loan, lien priority, or type of borrower.
Service Corporation Investment	Up to 6% of assets.
Commercial Loans	No limit.
Consumer Loans	No limit.
Leeway Investment	Investment in "any other investments not prohibited by regulation" authorized up to 10% of assets.
Loans to One Borrower	No limit.
Corporate Bonds	Limited to 20% of assets.
Common Stock	Limited to 20% of assets.

CALIFORNIA

Real Estate Loans	No limit on property type, type of borrower. Loans must be secured and are subject to varying limitations according to type. Variable rate loan limits of 40 years and 100% of value.
Real Estate Investment	No limit in real estate investments for income, inventory and sale or improvement, the erection of buildings for sale or rental.

Service Corporation Investment	Subject to regulations of the Commissioner; may invest, without limit, in stock or other obligations of service corporation, which may engage in any type of activity.
Commercial Loans	Limited to 10% of assets.
Consumer Loans	Limited to 10% of assets.
Leeway Investment	May invest not more than 5% of assets in securities deemed prudent by the association.
Loans to One Borrower	No one loan may exceed the lesser of association's net worth or 10% of deposits.
Investment in Corporate Bonds	Authorized with restrictions, but no maximum percentage of investment.
Investment in Common Stocks	Investment in securities authorized by Commissioner's regulation.

FLORIDA

Real Estate Loans	No restriction on property type or purpose of loan, providing 50% of assets invested in home or primarily residential loans for terms not more than 40 years.
Real Estate Investment	May invest up to the lesser of net worth or 10% of assets, for income, inventory and sale, improvement, including erection, sale or rental of buildings.
Service Corporation Investment	Up to 20% of assets.
Commercial Loans	No limit under "50-50" formula, i.e., 50% of assets must be invested in home or primarily residential real estate loans.
Consumer Loans	No limit under "50-50" formula.
Leeway Investments	Investments the Department of Banking and Finance may approve.

Loans to One Borrower	No limit.
Corporate Bonds	Limitation of 25% of assets.
Corporate Stock	Limitation of 20% of assets aggregated with service corporation investment.

TEXAS

The Texas law grants the commissioner complete discretion to issue rules governing authorized loans and investment, provided the rules are consistent with sound lending practices. In addition, investments must promote the purposes of the act. The following is a summary of provisions of the commissioner's rules adopted or amended through August 1986.

Residential Real Estate Loans	Loans or participations in loans authorized to 100% of appraised value of property secured by first lien, or if for purchase, the purchase price plus cost of improvements if less than appraised value. Loan period is not to exceed 40 years. Variable rate loans are authorized.
Commercial Real Estate Loans	No limit on percentage of assets to make or purchase participations in loans secured by first lien on commercial real estate to 100% of appraised value or, if for purchase, the purchase price, if less than appraised value. Loans must be repaid in 40 years. The loan may include amounts to pay interest and other fees provided that a detailed narrative underwriting the report is prepared explaining the loan. If the loan amount includes interest and fees, the association must have "recourse," and the loan must not exceed 90% of the appraised value. Recourse may be waived if the association determines that the security has generated "break-even" income.
Unimproved Real Estate Loans	No limit on the percentage of assets to make loans, or purchase participations in loans, secured by first lien on

	unimproved real estate up to 100% of the appraised value or purchase price if less than appraised value. Similar rules apply to the amount of interest and fees on commercial property loans.
Personal Property Loans	No limit on percentage of assets to make loans secured by personal property, in amount of 100% of appraised or market value or purchase price or, if for purchase, the purchase price if less than appraised value. Aggregate loans are limited to $100,000 for one borrower or 15% of the association's net worth, whichever is greater. Maturity is 120 months.
Oil and Gas Loans	No limit on percentage of assets to make loans secured by first lien on proven reserves of oil and gas and other minerals up to 100% of value. Aggregate loans to one borrower are limited to $100,000 or 10% of the association's net worth, whichever is greater. Loans must mature within 60 months.
Unsecured Loans	No limit on percentage of assets to make unsecured loans. Aggregate limits to one borrower cannot exceed $50,000, or 10% of an association's net worth, whichever is greater. Loan must be repaid in five years.
Real Estate Investment	Associations may purchase, sell, own, rent, lease, manage, subdivide, develop, improve, operate for income or otherwise deal in (improved or unimproved) real property. Aggregate investments may not exceed 100% of the association's net worth without written approval of the Commissioner.
Corporate Bonds and Corporate Stocks	Associations may invest in securities and obligations approved by the Commissioner.

Service Corporations   Up to 10% of an association's assets can be invested with the Commissioner's approval. Approval to exceed the 10% limit may be secured if the association is in compliance with FSLIC's net worth requirements.

While these four states probably have the most liberal laws overall, many others have similar features as the following examples show:

1. Illinois authorizes investment of 10% of assets in residential development. Associations may invest 5% of assets, plus an amount equal to 50% of regulatory net worth, in service corporations.

2. Louisiana authorizes investment of 10% of assets in service corporations and for other investments and loans including joint ventures for redevelopment. Aggregate direct investments in service organizations, real estate and equity securities are not subject to this limit and may be equal to or less than twice paid-in capital, surplus, reserves and undivided profits.

3. Michigan permits investment of 10% of assets for residential development and an additional investment in service corporations up to 5% of assets.

4. Mississippi permits investment in service corporations of 10% of assets which may be raised by the state supervisor to 15% of assets.

5. Missouri permits investment of 20% of assets in service corporations.

6. New York permits investment of 10% of assets in service corporations.

7. North Carolina has no statutory limitation for real estate investments. Institutions may invest 10% of assets in service corporations. No limit exists for any investment deemed appropriate by an association's directors, subject to state regulations.

8. In Ohio, an amount equal to net worth may be invested in real estate for business premises, and up to 10% of assets in "any other real estate." An additional 15% of assets may be invested in service corporations, and 10% of assets in any type of security.

9. Virginia permits investment of 10% of assets in service corporations.

10. Washington permits investment of 10% of assets in "corporations or other entities whether or not related to the association's business" including interests in service corporations and, presumably, equity securities of corporations.

For comparison, the following list describes loan and investment authorities for federally chartered savings and loan associations under Section 5 of the Home Owners' Loan Act, as amended, reflecting the provisions of the Garn-St Germain Act and regulations of the Board.

1. Loans or investments without percentage of asset limitations:
   a. Various liquid instruments, such as government and ' agency securities;
   b. Loans on security of residential property;
   c. Obligations of state and local governments (except that no more than 10% of an institution's net worth may be invested in obligations of any one issuer);
   d. Secured and unsecured loans for repair and improvement of residential property;
   e. Loans made for manufactured home financing;
   f. Investment or loans to state housing corporations secured by FHA loans;
   g. Shares in open-end management investment companies;
   h. Investments in financial instruments an association is permitted to make by law or regulation.

2. Loans or investments limited by percent of assets:
   a. Loans on security of nonresidential property are limited to 40%;
   b. Loans, secured and unsecured, for commercial, corporate or agricultural purposes are limited to 10%;
   c. Investments in tangible personal property (lease financing) are limited to 10%;
   d. Consumer loans are limited to 30%;
   e. Education loans are limited to 5%;
   f. Community development investments are limited to 5% of assets;
   g. Nonconforming loans (leeway authority for investments that do not comply with other limitations) are limited to 5% of assets;

h. Construction loans without security (line of credit construction lending) are limited to an institution's net worth or 5% of assets, whichever is greater;
i. Investments in service corporations are limited to 3%;
j. Small business investment companies are limited to 1%;
k. So-called AID guaranteed loans are limited to 1% of assets.

Clearly, many state rules for investment of assets rapidly became more liberal than those allowed traditional savings and loan associations. The liberalization came upon a business not equipped by background or experience to deal with it intelligently and at a rate which did not allow most savings association executives the time or opportunity to develop a real understanding of "market competition" and underwriting techniques in the new areas of authorized investments. Equally important in an atmosphere glorifying deregulation, "unwritten rules" of conduct were forgotten by many in a competitive atmosphere which was totally devoid of a sense of "right" in the conduct of financial institutions; self-interest and survival set the rules of the game for too many.

THE ROLE OF LIBERALIZATION

It is obvious from this review that the principal breakthrough with respect to broader loan and investment authority came with the liberalizing rules of the Board under Chairman Pratt (1981-1983) and under the Garn-St Germain Act. This reflects, of course, the spirit of deregulation that pervaded the Reagan Administration and the perceived need to permit the business to operate "in the marketplace" with respect to its asset authority.

It is also obvious that this was quite a lot of liberalization in a short time for a business that had been tightly regulated throughout its entire history.

The record of the business in using its new loan and investment powers is quite spotty. Only modest use has been made of the authority to make consumer loans, and the record, on the whole, has been quite good. A few institutions suffered heavy losses in credit card operations; but the relatively small volume of outstanding credits has not posed a serious problem or led to failures.

This is also true for non-real estate commercial loans similar to commercial bank loans or consumer loans. Some larger institutions have gradually entered commercial lending and, with few exceptions, the record has been quite good. Small and medium size associations generally have made little use of this authority.

For federals, limiting corporate bond investments to those in one of the four highest investment grades (rated by at least two national rating services) has acted to keep these investments out of the loss column.[12] A few state-chartered associations, however, have made major purchases of high-yield, non-rated bonds—the so-called junk bonds. About one-fourth of all such bonds have been purchased by savings and loan associations, according to one report. No significant defaults have occurred on these bonds. Because interest rates declined from mid-1984 to early April 1987, the market values of junk bonds performed quite well until the October 1987 stock market crash, when a flight to quality caused their prices to drop. Although these investments did not contribute to association failures studied in this work, they remain a potential hazard. Whether savings and loan officers buying these bonds exercised proper judgment in selecting issues remains to be seen.

Some state-chartered associations took advantage of the authority to invest in common stock. The extent of this investment has not been documented and, at this writing, how the stock market decline since October has affected this class of investment in savings and loan portfolios is unknown.

Loans and investments causing major losses at some institutions have been in real estate, the area of presumed expertise of the savings and loan executive. Problems have occurred in financing office buildings, industrial and retail properties in periods of much speculative construction and considerable overbuilding, and financing apartments and condominiums, particularly in the Sun Belt growth areas. Much of this speculative activity was fueled by income tax laws which allowed the creation of partnerships and syndicates with generous income sheltering opportunities. This made many uneconomic investments attractive to people in high tax brackets. Other opportunities were created for associations to form joint ventures with builders to acquire large vacant land holdings for later development and sale as large-scale housing projects. Problems were compounded by the ability of associations to lend in unfamiliar markets, especially distant states. Booming oil markets in Texas created anticipations of future growth which were not realized. Expected demand for housing in Florida fell short of estimates because the state's population did not increase according to projections. High levels of employment and personal income in California led to excessive supplies of very expensive housing, office buildings and industrial parks. Declining employment in the

---

[12] Federals have a small (1%) nonrated bonds category (12 CFR 545.75).

smokestack states and reduced demand for agricultural products were overlooked in the enthusiasm for capitalizing on generally favorable national real estate markets in the early 1980s.

Many lenders ignored the history of cyclical real estate markets in which excessive highs were invariably followed by new lows. The lure of immediate profits from loan points, fees, equity kickers and other immediate income blinded them to the potentials for real estate market downturns. This, coupled with financial ventures into unfamiliar types of lending and investing, set the stage for serious problems.

In fairness to associations, however, their focus in the early 1980s was on interest rate risk, not credit risk. After all, only a few had suffered losses on real estate loans since the 1930s.

DIRECT INVESTMENT, COMMERCIAL AND MULTIFAMILY PROPERTY LOANS

Much attention has focused on savings and loan losses in the broad category of "direct investments."

Either directly or through service corporations (which in some states permitted investments in almost anything), there were clear abuses, and some instances of fraud—as well as misguided judgments, or bad luck—with respect to financing land development and home building activities which in other hands, other times and other locations might have turned out satisfactorily.

Much publicity has surrounded the unorthodox ventures which some associations financed, or through their service corporations, invested in. These included such legal investments (in some states) as hotels, ski resorts, oil refineries, feed stores, water parks, large farms, plum and grape groves, gambling casinos, coal land, fast food franchises, a mushroom farm, a windmill farm, and an ethanol plant.

Some loans and investments in unusual nonresidential properties, of course, have been quite successful. Commercial banks and insurance companies for generations have made loans secured by a variety of types of real estate. The experience of savings and loan associations in this area, however, generally has not been successful. Perhaps this is because association executives are unfamiliar with nonresidential real estate financing. They also may not understand the objectives of institutions which make these loans, including the lure of extraordinary profits through the taking of extraordinary risks. All types of lenders, of course, have had many commercial real estate loans in Texas, Louisiana and other energy states fail.

A number of studies show the business' troubled experience with nonresidential financing. The Bank Board staff identified 37 institutions with direct investments exceeding 10% of assets in December 1983. By October 1986, 21 of these institutions had failed, become an FSLIC case, or were considered significant supervisory cases. The definition of "direct" investment that existed in 1986 excluded many acquisition, development and construction loans and essentially involved real estate.

The average net worth ratio of these 37 institutions in 1983 was 4.3% of liabilities. By June 1986, this ratio had declined to 0.23% and many had a negative net worth. For comparison, the business' net worth ratios were 4.03% in 1983 and 4.43% in June 1986. By the third quarter of 1986, more than half of the 37 institutions were losing money. They had an average annualized net income as a percent of assets of 0.47% in 1983. By June 1986, however, this had deteriorated to -3.63%. The business' average recovered to 0.27% in 1983. In the second quarter of 1986, 79% of all FSLIC-insured institutions were operating profitably and had a net return on assets of 1.03%.

The 37 institutions with direct investments exceeding 10% of assets in December 1983 held an average of only 37.73% of assets in one- to four-family mortgages and mortgage-backed securities compared with the business' average of 63.44%. In June 1986, 34 remaining institutions averaged 29.89% of assets on one- to four-family mortgages and mortgage-backed securities compared with the business' average of 54.02%.

Another statistical review of loan and investment performance resulting in association failures is provided by Dennis Jacobe, the U.S. League's director of research. He details the investment record of failed institutions seized by the Bank Board and placed in the Management Consignment Program (MCP).

Because MCP institutions have continued in operation but with new management and directors, they continue to report to the Board. Details of their balance sheets and operating statements are publicly available. There were 52 institutions with combined assets of $22.4 billion in this program at the end of November 1986. Jacobe wrote the following in a memorandum dated November 1986:

> "As the business struggled with the twin shocks of deregulation and record high interest rates in 1981 and 1982, management searched for ways to garner higher rates of return while reducing interest rate risk exposure. Most institutions chose to remain dedicated to residential

finance, while pursuing an effort to diversify and supplement earnings on the margin.

"The MCPs[13] took a different approach. They virtually deserted residential mortgage finance (Exhibit 1). Residential mortgages, which accounted for 66.9% of MCP assets in June 1982, fell sharply, to only 35.2% of assets by June 1986. This stands in sharp contrast to the bulk of the business, whose residential mortgages totaled 61.7% of total assets as of mid-1986.

"One avenue to higher rates of return for MCPs was commercial real estate lending (Exhibit 2). By June 1985, some 22% of MCP assets were in commercial real estate loans. This percentage declined to 18.7% on June 1986, as new management was installed and various losses were recognized. The non-MCPs now hold 9.3% of their assets in commercial real estate, up from 6.2% in June 1982.

"Another area of great interest to the MCPs was land acquisition and development loans and direct real estate investments (Exhibit 3). These investments increased from 4.6% of MCP assets in June 1982 to 14.1% in June 1984. They now represent 13.7% of assets. The rest of the business had only 3.3% of its assets in these types of investments in June 1986.

"The MCPs also devoted greater resources to service corporation activities (Exhibit 4). Service corporation investments increased from 1.4% of MCP assets in June 1982 to 7% of assets in June 1985. Currently they account for investments equal to 2% of assets in June 1986.

"Although financial institution executives will always debate the relative risks of various investments, it seems clear that the MCPs invested much more heavily in nontraditional assets than the overwhelming majority of the business (Exhibit 5). If nontraditional investments are defined to include commercial real estate loans, development and acquisition loans, direct real estate investments and service corporation investments, an incredible investment trend emerges for MCPs. These nontraditional assets comprised 17.7% of MCP assets in June 1982. By June 1985 they accounted for 42.3% of

---

[13] The Management Consignment Program (MCP) is discussed in Chapter 11. These institutions had failed and were turned over to a new board of directors and new management under a consignment program. The data referred to here reflect the operations of the failed institutions.

total MCP assets. Since then, they had declined to 38.7%. These nontraditional assets represented 14.6% for other savings institutions at mid-1986, up from 8.1% of assets in June 1982.

"The MCPs compounded the problems by adopting a rapid growth strategy (Exhibit 6). While the business grew 17.7% in 1983, the MCPs grew an incredible 84.8%. The MCPs grew 47.8% in 1984, still two-and-a-half times the growth rate of the rest of the business. The MCPs began to shrink in 1985 as the Bank Board took control, and have continued to do so. It should be noted that excessive growth has long been recognized as one of the best predictors of financial institution failures.

"The nontraditional investment and rapid growth strategy of the MCPs worked well in the short term (Exhibit 7). The MCPs had net after-tax income equal to −0.41% of assets in 1982. They watched their bottom line soar to +0.66% of assets in 1983. Thus, they were able to return to the good earnings days of the 1970s almost overnight. That year, the rest of the business had an after-tax ROA of only +0.23%.

"A detailed review of the comparative earnings situation shows that the MCPs were more profitable than the rest of the business in 1983 due to their much higher fee income and their very strong subsidiary income. This is not surprising, given their nontraditional investment and rapid growth strategy at that time.

"In 1984, the business saw after-tax earnings ease to +0.13% of assets before soaring to +0.49% in 1985 and an annualized +0.50% of assets in the first half of 1986. In sharp contrast, the ROA of the MCPs fell to -0.52% in 1984. By 1985, the MCPs showed phenomenal losses, with an ROA of -4.84%. During the first half of 1986, their ROA plummeted to -7.08%. Delayed adjustments show that actual MCP losses were even greater than what was reported in 1985 and early 1986.

"The losses of the MCPs can be traced to an explosion of problem assets (Exhibit 8). Repossessed assets represented 0.5% of total MCP assets in June 1982. By June 1986, however, they accounted for 6.0% of total MCP assets. The repossessed assets of the rest of the business have also increased. But as of June 1986, they represented less than 1.0% of total assets.

"Comparative net worth trends illustrate the problems the MCPs represent for the FSLIC (Exhibit 9). In June 1982, other savings institutions had a net worth to assets ratio of 3.8%. This ratio had increased steadily to 4.7% by June 1986. In sharp contrast, the MCPs had a net worth ratio of 3.3% of assets in June 1982. But by mid-1986, it plummeted to -6.7%. In fact, the June 1986 ratio would have been twice as bad if income capital certificates had been excluded from MCP net worth."

(Exhibits referred to above are included at the end of this chapter.)

Another study by Jacobe compared the investments of institutions that came into the management consignment program by September 30, 1986, with non-MCP institutions. The following table shows the distribution of assets of these institutions.

TABLE 18: COMPARATIVE INVESTMENTS OF MCP INSTITUTIONS & OTHERS (Data as of September 30, 1986)

	MCPs	Non-MCPs, Negative Net Worth	Non-MCPs, Positive Net Worth
Loans			
Single-family residential	20.9%	32.8%	41.5%
Multifamily	11.4	8.9	6.9
Commercial real estate	16.3	14.5	8.9
Acquisition and development	11.0	7.5	2.5
Commercial	2.8	2.7	1.5
Consumer	2.6	5.0	4.2
Other Assets			
Mortgage-backed securities	3.5	6.1	13.5
Foreclosed real estate	6.5	6.3	1.0
Real estate investments	4.4	2.3	0.5
Service Corporation investments	6.0	2.7	2.1
Cash investments and other assets	14.7	11.1	17.4
Total assets	100.0%	100.0%	100.0%

Source: FHLBs and U.S. League of Savings Institutions

Note that the more institutions departed from traditional lending, the more likely they were to get into trouble. Mortgage-backed securities should be added to residential loans to obtain a complete picture of single-family compared with other mortgage lending. Heavy investment in service corporations by institutions should also be noted.

The Bank Board also released statistics showing the marked difference in asset mix between solvent and insolvent institutions. (See Appendix C.)

In addition, institutions in Texas were studied by Ferguson & Company, a Texas-based public accounting firm. Its study divided Texas institutions into four categories:

Category A   All 281 Texas thrifts.

Category B   168 Texas thrifts with capital greater than 3% of liabilities as of 12/31/86.

Category C   72 Texas thrifts with capital between a positive 3% and a negative 5% of liabilities as of 12/31/86.

Category D   41 Texas thrifts with negative capital greater than 5% of liabilities as of 12/31/86.

Table 19 shows the data as of December 31, 1986, for these institutions.

The institutions with the worst record (Categories C and D) had the highest annual growth rate and the highest proportion of loans in the apartment, commercial and land category.

These kinds of loans are not in themselves bad loans nor necessary causes for lender failure. Therefore, problems associations had with these loans reflected management's underwriting inexperience, the attraction of high fees, points and equity kickers and a rather desperate need to rebuild seriously eroded net worth positions. Also, a small minority of institutions in collaboration with builders and joint venture partners perpetrated fraud with these kinds of loans.

ADC LOANS

The authority to make acquisition, development and construction loans was abused by a small number of associations. This led to a vast distortion of the income and net worth picture at some institutions.

In a typical ADC investment, a lender agreed to provide all funds to acquire, develop land and construct buildings (often condominiums). Frequently, a limited partnership providing tax shelters for investors was formed. At times, proceeds from loans were used to "pay back" cash or other equity contribution of the joint venture developer.

TABLE 19: COMPARATIVE INVESTMENTS OF TEXAS INSTITUTIONS
(December 31, 1986)

Category	A All 281 Texas Thrifts	B 168 Texas Thrifts	C 72 Texas Thrifts	D 41 Texas Thrifts
	(amounts in millions)			
Total assets	$ 97,244	$59,997	$ 24,292	$ 13,055
% of State total	100.00%	61.63%	24.96%	13.41%
Capital	$ 538	$ 3,376	$ 86	$ (2,923)
% to total assets	0.55%	5.63%	0.35%	(22.39%)
4th qtr. net operating income annualized	$ (2,100)	$ 7	$ (633)	$ (1,474)
% to average assets				
Gross operating income	7.81%	9.41%	7.38%	1.57%
Operating expenses	2.33%	2.17%	2.23%	3.20%
Cost of funds	7.63%	7.23%	7.76%	9.12%
Net operating income (loss)	(2.15%)	0.01%	(2.61%)	(10.75%)
Adjusted net income (loss)	(5.65%)	0.89%	(5.09%)	(35.00%)
Miscellaneous ratios:				
Annualized growth rate since December 1982	27.95%	26.12%	28.90%	36.13%
Apartment, commercial & land loans to total assets	37.23%	29.95%	49.10%	48.55%
Earning assets to interest bearing liabilities	87.37%	95.54%	86.11%	60.53%

Source: Ferguson and Company

In many instances, a borrower had title to the land but little or no equity in it. These transactions were often structured so that the lender participated in the expected residual profit on the property's ultimate sale or use. Expected residual profit was more than a reasonable amount of interest and fees earned by the lender. Lenders often funded the commitment or origination fees, or both. These were included in the loan and almost all interest and fees owed during the loan's initial years were added to the loan balance.

In many ADC projects, lenders had no recourse to the borrower's other assets. The borrower did not guarantee the debt. For the lender to recover the investment in the project, the property had to be sold to independent third parties, the borrower had to obtain refinancing from another source, or the property had to be placed in service and generate sufficient net cash flow to service the debt.

Foreclosure during the project's development and early years of operation as a result of delinquency was unlikely. The borrower was not required to make any payments on the principal until the project was completed, and interest payments for two to three years were funded in the original loan advance.

While most of these ADC loans were structured as a "loan," they were actually direct investments in land and construction projects.

The investment's quality, of course, could not be determined or judged until the project's completion. That depended on the project's quality and market for such a development when completed. Meanwhile, it appeared as a valid asset on the institution's books.

Empire Savings, Mesquite, Texas, was one of the first widely publicized failures of an insured savings and loan association. This institution was placed in receivership in March of 1984. A special inquiry by the Committee on Government Operations of the U.S. House of Representatives revealed that Empire Savings appeared to show continued growth of earnings and net worth by including interest and fees from such projects in its income. The House committee found that many "loans" were not loans but investments. The "borrower" took few risks while Empire Savings took the full risk of an equity owner. As a result, Empire should not have taken in the income from interest, points and fees from the transaction until the property was sold or otherwise disposed of.

IMPROPER ACCOUNTING

The House hearings also revealed that public accountants for Empire condoned treating transactions as loans rather than investments which inflated the association's income and net worth. The rules of the American Institute of Certified Public Accountants initially were ambivalent about treatment for ADC loans. Without guidance from either AICPA or the Financial Accounting Standards Board, accounting firms were free to compete for clients with rather lax accounting standards for ADC loans and the income from them. The result was to mislead the association directors, stockholders, the supervisory staff and the public.

Not until November 1983 did AICPA issue a "Notice to Practitioners" addressing the accounting for such investments. This notice specified certain characteristics that generally exist in real estate transactions that may be classified as loans in contrast to those that should be classified as investments or joint ventures. A second notice was issued by AICPA's Savings and Loan Committee in November 1984 dealing primarily with the "personal guarantee" issue present in some ADC arrangements.

It was not until April 1985 that the Bank Board adopted a statement of policy concerning regulatory accounting for certain real estate transactions. The Board indicated that this policy statement was issued in response to increased ADC activity by insured institutions in an environment that some perceived to lack authoritative accounting guidance. The Board thus adopted the first two "Notices to Practitioners" as its accounting policy, thereby putting into regulatory format the guidance developed by the accounting profession.

The accounting profession, through the AICPA, adopted a third rule in a February 10, 1986, "Notice to Practitioners" which superseded the two prior notices and reflected the public position taken by the chief accountant of the Securities and Exchange Commission. The Board then proposed on March 4, 1987, to amend its policy statement to reflect AICPA's revised views. This proposed rule is still listed as "pending."[14]

The Board notes in the proposed rule that for transactions to be properly considered a loan the following conditions must be met: (1) the lender must participate in less than a majority of the residual profit; (2) the borrower must have a substantial equity investment in the project not funded by the lender; (3) the lender would have recourse to other substantial salable assets of the borrower; (4) a take-out loan had been obtained from a creditworthy, independent third party; and (5) a noncancelable sales contract or lease commitment from creditworthy independent third parties must be in effect to assure net cash flow sufficient to service normal amortization. These rules essentially have been in effect since 1985, when the Board first dealt with this issue, and reflect AICPA standards.

Few ADC loans made by associations in 1983 and 1984 met these conditions. They were booked as loans, however, and fees and "interest income" from them inflated profits and net worth. Often the

---

[14]   The Board earlier had specified that ADC loans that were in fact direct investments would be treated as the latter for purposes of the direct investment regulations (see page 75).

"loan" or investment was predicated on inflated values supported by fraudulent appraisals and "land flips."[15] In these, the original owner of the land and presumed "borrower" booked all the transaction's profit at the beginning and had little interest in its successful completion.

The type of ADC loan that led to substantial losses, and was dealt with by the AICPA pronouncements and the Board developed around 1981. Accountants and examiners had little experience then in evaluating such lending. Rarely did they make on-site inspections of properties owned by associations as an investment for future development or used to secure ADC loans.

The issuance of the first bulletin in late 1983, and the fact that examiners and supervisors were becoming alert to the dangers of these loans and the misleading accounting accompanying many of them, did help eliminate losses from this type of lending or misleading accounting. The new AICPA rules, however, were not reflected in audits until 1984, and more likely for 1985. By then, much damage had been done. Board examiners were slow to audit based on the new rules. Examinations were not recycled to catch fringe operators, and the Board did not deal with this type of lending as a regulatory problem until April 1985. This gave some obstinate association executives plenty of reason to maintain that they were violating no rule or regulation.

Much work by examiners during 1984 and later involved looking beyond an institution's accounting of these loans and accountant certifications to determine their true nature. This required substantial discussions with management about details of transactions and whether the reported income and net worth were accurate, or improperly inflated. As noted, many of these transactions had a two- or three-year interest reserve built into the original "loan" disbursement in addition to the front-end fees. The loan was kept current through monthly interest and principal payments made by the borrower but, of course, financed by the association. This made it difficult for examiners to identify and separate problem loans from good loans when examining an association's record. Complicating their examination was the fact that management's record keeping was often inadequate, particularly at fast growing associations. This time-consuming problem came during a great shortage of examiners, especially in California and Texas.

---

[15]   For further discussions of "land flips" see page 135.

A major weakness in traditional auditing processes was a willingness to accept an apparently reliable "paper trail" even though in some instances records concealed fraudulent lending. For example, a professional looking, seemingly complete appraisal report with fully completed loan papers was sufficient evidence of a loan file's viability. Only rarely would accountants independently check the reliability and accuracy of appraisals or other papers.

While giving unqualified opinions according to generally accepted accounting principles, auditors rarely visited properties offered as collateral for loans or checked local markets to determine a proposed project's feasibility. In effect, they accepted crucial loan package instruments without sufficiently checking them independently. Paperwork that had to be checked was often complex and much of it was new to savings and loan auditors. As a result, they relied on information supplied by management.

Associations that grew rapidly and ended in failure were characterized as a "disarray of books and records," according to Bank Board officials. If these institutions had adequate mortgage department staff for record keeping, the fast pace of growth made keeping complete and accurate records almost impossible. Too much business was being done in too short a time. Managers of these institutions, of course, were concerned with putting loans on the books—not with providing perfect records for accountants and examiners. In fact, some managers may have purposely opted for incomplete records. Surprisingly, despite inadequate loan documents, public accountants gave unqualified opinions on quite a number of institutions that failed or became management consignment cases right up to the time of seizure by federal or state authorities.

The record of direct investments and loans on apartments and commercial real estate is not entirely negative. Many institutions have done well in land development and home building. Others have had good results (at least before the stock market crashed on October 19, 1987) in other investments, including common stocks. The apparent difference is in management's knowledge of markets and ability to conduct solid long-range planning to achieve profit goals. Disastrous mistakes were primarily made by greedy or inexperienced people.

Problems some associations have had with direct investments led the Bank Board in early 1985 to take the unprecedented step of regulating direct investment authority of state-chartered, FSLIC-insured associations. This has been the one regulatory step in recent years of narrowing, or limiting, association lending or investment authority.

In February 1984, the Bank Board's Office of Policy and Economic Research reported that direct investment in equity securities, real estate and service corporations accounted for only about 2% of total savings and loan assets nationwide. These investments, however, accounted for more than 10% at rapidly growing, state-chartered institutions in California and Texas by the end of 1984. During the first three-quarters of 1984, direct investments for the business increased at a 91% annual rate. At that rate, the level of direct investments would almost quadruple in two years and increase 15 times in four years. It was imperative the Bank Board get control of the direct investments problem by regulation!

The Board issued its final regulation January 31, 1985. A limit on direct investments was established at 10% of an association's assets or twice its regulatory net worth. This regulation was first proposed in May 1984 and reproposed in December. Therefore, it was discussed for almost eight months while many associations (primarily in Texas, California, Arizona and Florida) abused state laws and accumulated bad assets.

Like the Board's proposal for tightening net worth requirements, this regulation was also attacked. Opposition to net worth changes was widespread and typically from conservative executives. But opposition to proposed curbs in direct investments came primarily from those who had been reasonably successful investing in land development, nonrated bonds, common stock and other ventures. Many attacked the proposal as a threat to "states rights," suggesting that it would be a first step in federal control over state-chartered operations.

Threats of legal challenge, studies by economists and even congressional hearings by an oversight committee helped delay action on the proposed regulation. Unusually vocal opposition neutralized the U.S. League's stand on the subject for some time. Like the net worth proposals in early 1984, this should have been adopted promptly. Once again the Board was too patient in considering comments from the business. In addition, political pressure was placed on the Board.

DETERIORATION OF CREDIT QUALITY

Financing of residential subdivisions was another major reason some associations failed. The rush to make loans to increase earnings was pronounced in the early 1980s. The business' share of the residential mortgage market increased from 35% in 1982, to 41% in 1983 and

49% in 1984. Savings and loan share of construction loans rose from 30% in 1982, to 41% in 1983 and 48% in 1984. This type of lending was, of course, subject to greater risk than loans on existing homes. No doubt this significant increase in market share resulted from making many loans which associations would have declined in previous years. Not only did both large and small associations assume greater risk, but so did Fannie Mae, whose lending policies affected residential mortgage markets throughout the country. Fannie Mae and a number of association executives put their institutions in overdrive. One such institution was State Savings (later American Savings) of Stockton, Calif., an affiliate of Financial Corporation of America (FCA).[16]

While Fannie Mae was able to secure substantial funds through the sale of its obligations, State Savings and a few other associations developed a network of "money desks" throughout the country. They offered somewhat higher rates than those paid by institutions in each market and developed a substantial flow of cash. Some institutions offered fixed rate loans exclusively, often with low down payments. Others designed adjustable rate mortgage products with generous "buy downs" and negative amortization loans that attracted borrowers of all types. Fannie Mae was buying primarily through mortgage bankers, but also from savings and loan associations.

During this period, savings associations were creating offices in distant cities for mortgage banking affiliates. Loans were made on generous terms not only to owner-occupants, but also on vacation homes and to investors in residential units in resort areas on adjustable rate terms. Borrowers were qualified at ridiculously low "teaser" interest rates, the allowable ratio of mortgage payment to income was increased, and two borrower incomes were generously accepted. Marginal builders, with questionable abilities and records, were put into business by associations anxious to build a portfolio of high rate, variable rate loans and to improve current earnings with high up-front fees. There was a substantial deterioration of credit quality. This period was characterized by a significant increase in lenders and loan offices, producing keen competition and narrower spreads. Established lenders were tempted to allow credit quality to deteriorate to retain market share.

Many other types of lenders were writing fixed rate mortgages, usually for sale in the secondary market. Meanwhile, savings and loan associations were trying desperately to expand their holdings of

---

[16] State Savings merged in 1983 with American Savings of Beverly Hills, Calif. The new association was managed by the officers and staff of FCA.

adjustable rate mortgages. In many instances, creating a volume of ARM loans required offering very low first-year rates and inadequate spreads over the index to which the mortgage rate was tied.

Some lenders assumed that secondary mortgage markets and joint-venture lending through participations would provide a safe haven for loans which they did not wish to keep. Some miscalculated that the secondary market would accept the low quality loans offered. In other instances, however, savings and loan associations bought 90% participations in poor quality loans. Many lenders got burned by participating with State Savings of Utah, an early failure. A number of significant and "respected" institutions were among 75 institutions that purchased participations in loans originated by Vernon Savings, Dallas, Texas.[17] This reflected a serious management failure to know the kind of institution with which they were doing business and the quality of its loan portfolio.

Lending and credit excesses in this period contributed not only to failures then, but also to problems at the roughly one-fifth of all institutions with poor earnings and virtually no net worth today. Future FSLIC assistance may well be required to solve these problem cases.

To put this picture in perspective, all but a minority of institutions made intelligent use of their new powers. This minority, however, has seriously drained the FSLIC's resources. For most associations earnings improved, and the maturity of association assets shortened. It must be said, however, that some state legislatures acted irresponsibly. They had no price to pay for losses that might result from such wide open grants of authority, and little desire or ability to supervise the results of the authority they granted.

Losses from loans and investments certainly have not been confined to state-chartered associations. Of the 72 management consignment cases, 37 were federally chartered associations, and several federals are on the Board's "critical list" as a result of bad lending and investments.

As a result of deregulation on the asset side, it has been far easier for association management to make bad loans and investments. Losses might have resulted anyway because of depressed economies in energy and agricultural states. If lending and investment rules before 1981 still had been in effect, however, losses might have been far less.

---

[17] American Banker, Nov. 23, 1987.

EXHIBIT 1: THE MCPs DESERTED RESIDENTIAL FINANCE

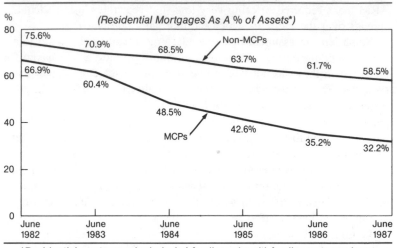

(Residential Mortgages As A % of Assets*)

*Residential mortgages include 1-4 family and multi-family mortgage loans and mortgage-backed securities.

EXHIBIT 2: THE MCPs INVESTED HEAVILY IN COMMERCIAL REAL ESTATE LOANS

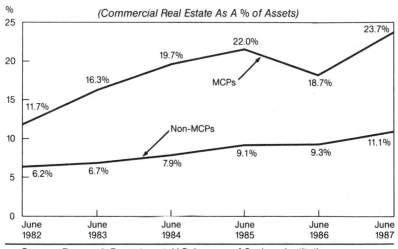

(Commercial Real Estate As A % of Assets)

Source: Research Department, U.S. League of Savings Institutions.

EXHIBIT 3: THE MCPs WERE BIG INVESTORS IN DEVELOPMENT AND ACQUISITION LOANS AND REAL ESTATE INVESTMENTS

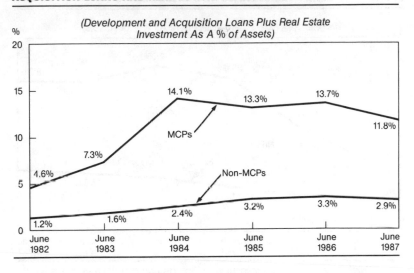

(Development and Acquisition Loans Plus Real Estate Investment As A % of Assets)

EXHIBIT 4: THE MCPs ALSO WERE BIG IN SERVICE CORPORATIONS

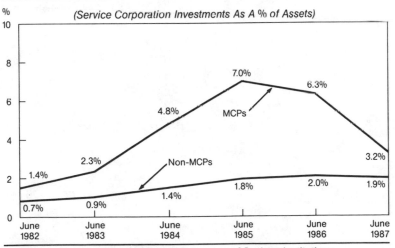

(Service Corporation Investments As A % of Assets)

Source: Research Department, U.S. League of Savings Institutions.

EXHIBIT 5: IN SUM THE MCPs REPLACED THEIR RESIDENTIAL MORTGAGE LOANS WITH HIGHER RISK REAL ESTATE INVESTMENTS

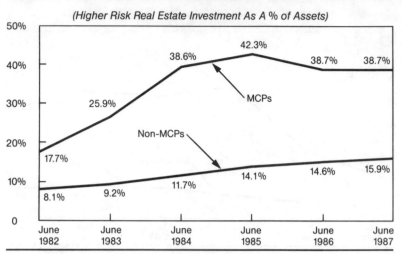

(Higher Risk Real Estate Investment As A % of Assets)

*Higher risk real estate investments include commercial real estate loans, development and acquisition loans, real estate investments and service corporation investments.

EXHIBIT 6: THE MCPs ALSO ADOPTED A RAPID GROWTH STRATEGY

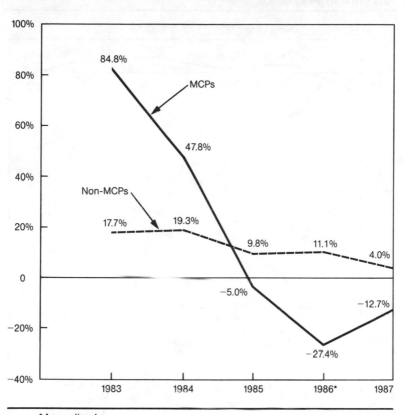

*Annualized.
Source: Research Department, U.S. League of Savings Institutions.

EXHIBIT 7: AS A RESULT, THE MCPs ENJOYED STRONG EARNINGS IN 1983 FOLLOWED BY BIG LOSSES

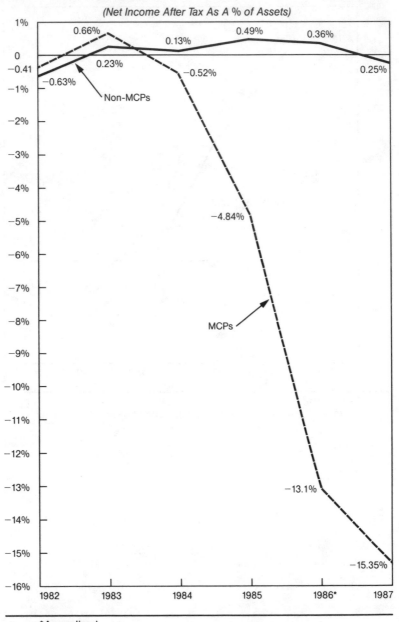

(Net Income After Tax As A % of Assets)

*Annualized.
Source: Research Department, U.S. League of Savings Institutions.

EXHIBIT 8: MCP REPOSSESSED ASSETS SOARED

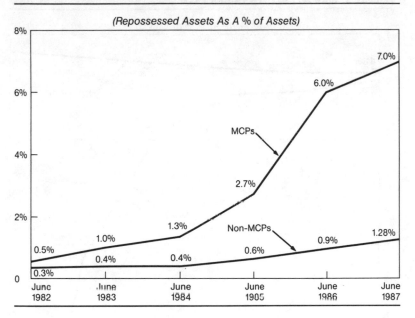

(Repossessed Assets As A % of Assets)

EXHIBIT 9: MCP NET WORTH PLUMMETED

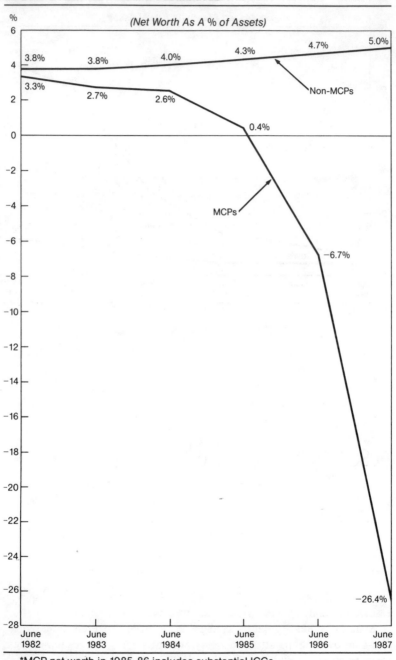

(Net Worth As A % of Assets)

*MCP net worth in 1985-86 includes substantial ICCs.

The New People 8

Of the 72 associations placed in the management consignment program from March 1985 until July 1987, about half were either managed or owned by interests new to the business since 1980. In California, 26 state-chartered institutions failed between March 1985 and March 1987 and were turned over to the FSLIC either as receiverships or under conservatorships. Of these, 21 were either new institutions or had been involved in change of control after the passage of the Nolan law referred to earlier.

The record of most new association executives and newly-chartered associations since 1984 has been quite good (see Savings Institutions, August 1987). But some who came during the early 1980s when net worth regulations permitted great leveraging of ownership capital to take advantage of liberal laws in Florida, California and Texas obviously wanted to make quick profits. They took chances and failed—while risking little of their own funds and a great deal of the FSLIC's.

PESSIMISM IN THE EARLY 1980s

In the early 1980s, there were few reasons to be optimistic about the business' future. Most conditions that had brought such a long period of prosperity to the business had changed. Existing management was happy just to hang on. What brought new people into the business was a somewhat different perception of the opportunities ahead. These were to stem not from the operation of the traditional savings and loan association, but from the ability to make money from a new charter granted primarily by state authorities, or from the purchase of an existing and typically small state-chartered association.

State laws and regulatory changes permitting brokered money and one-man ownerships attracted many entrepreneurs. One example may serve to show a trend that developed in California. New charters or acquisitions of small, existing, state-chartered institutions were actively promoted by a group of lawyers, or "consultants." These lawyers and consultants stressed that builders and developers could own an institution and continue operating a home building and land development business. They could use FSLIC-insured deposits to fund their ventures, rather than money obtained from commercial banks or other lenders at much higher cost. The old "conflict of interest" rules protecting associations from financing projects of insiders did not apply because the institution itself, not an individual or company owned by an "insider," was actually the builder-developer.

The result was the acquisition of many institutions by builders, land developers and other real estate entrepreneurs who had no intention of managing them in a traditional way.

To build or create an extensive state savings and loan system, some supervisory authorities began granting a significant number of charters. The state supervisor in California, who had come into office with the new Republican Administration of Governor Deukmejian, approved 172 charters from 1981 through 1984. When the next commissioner came into office (February 1985), 68 applications were pending. None was approved in 1985, only one was approved in 1986, and none was approved in 1987. From 1981 to 1984 the Texas commissioner granted 25 new charters, and supervisory authorities in Florida granted 24.

The Bank Board was expected—and under considerable political pressure—to insure deposits of these newly created institutions. Federal courts in the 1977 West Helena (Ark.) case ruled that the Board could not reject an application for FSLIC insurance on the ground that no economic need existed for an association's services. This complicated the Board's position in handling applications for deposit insurance. In Texas, Florida and California, moratoriums against new charter approvals imposed by the Bank Board brought angry exchanges between the state savings and loan commissioners and Chairman Gray. At this time, the examination and supervisory departments in these states were clearly inadequate. The Board on December 2, 1983, issued a regulation setting new and tighter requirements for federal charters and FSLIC insurance for newly chartered state associations.[18]

---

[18]   The following are conditions that govern operations of newly chartered or insured associations under the December 1983 regulation (Section 571.6):

1. Associations must have at least $3 million in initial capital stock or in the case of a mutual, $3 million pledged savings accounts, except that a $2 million minimum is acceptable for community-oriented associations located in communities with a population less than 50,000.

In addition to new, wide-open investment opportunity, three other conditions suggested the possibility of high profits: brokered money, easy acquisition of charters and minimum net worth requirements.

BROKERED MONEY

In March 1982, the FHLB Board, by action on deposit rate ceilings, repealed all restrictions on attracting deposits from brokers.[19] Some observers suggested that the repeal was the principal cause of failures in the business.

With the elimination of interest rate ceilings, associations could pay above market rates for insured deposits and advertise high rates in various publications, including special trade publications. The brokerage system permitted small institutions to raise funds easily and quickly from outside their operating areas. Thanks to the brokers, it was not necessary for an association to have great size or be in a large metropolitan area with many branch offices to grow rapidly.

The business once before had experience with brokerage money. From the early postwar years until June 1963, many associations, principally on the West Coast, attracted considerable deposits through small money brokers. Basically, these brokers ran ads in eastern

---

(Footnote 18 continued)

2. In the first full year, an institution must have a net worth of 7% of liabilities. The requirement is reduced to 6% thereafter.
3. The institution must operate according to a three-year business plan prepared as part of the application process. To deviate from the plan, management must receive prior approval from the institution's principal supervisory agent. Amendments are not considered unless the institution has been in compliance with its business plan during the previous two quarters.
4. Examinations are conducted quarterly during the first two years.
5. No more than 5% of deposits can be raised from brokered funds.
6. Interest paid on savings cannot exceed the average interest rate paid during the prior quarter in the institution's Federal Home Loan Bank district.
7. Investment in service corporations and real estate is limited to 10% of assets or the amount authorized by law, whichever is less.
8. A change in the managing officer of the institution must be preapproved by the principal supervisory agent.
9. A majority of the board of directors must be from the state in which the association is located and diversified and composed of individuals with varied business and professional interests.

[19] On September 30, 1980, under the chairmanship of Jay Janis, the Board repealed the limitation of 5% of deposits on funds for deposits, but left intact the maximum of a 2% sales commission and provided that such payment would be considered part of the interest payment subject to the Regulation Q ceilings applicable to such accounts, thus keeping an effective limit on the flow of brokerage funds to associations. The Depository Institutions Deregulation Committee in 1982 acted to exempt so-called finders fees or commissions from the limitations of Regulation Q.

newspapers and solicited business by mail from prospect lists, exploiting the fact that some associations paid a higher savings rate and that accounts were insured. At that time, the savings and loan account was very attractive because of its immediate liquidity and freedom from risk. Brokers generally charged 2% to 3% commission, and some were not above switching customer accounts from institution to institution to earn new commissions on the same funds.

The practice, while initially merely annoying to associations, became pernicious. It promoted paying higher rates than would otherwise have to be paid, led to excessively rapid growth at some institutions and caused many of those using brokers to develop 50% to 70% of their deposit balances with out-of-town—generally "hot"— money. The supervisory authorities, concerned about the health and future of institutions using excessive amounts of brokerage money, in June 1963 limited the amount of brokered funds associations could have to 5% of total deposits. Surprisingly, the Depository Institutions Deregulation Committee later opened the door to a rerun of these abuses. This move, however, was consistent with the deregulation philosophy of the Reagan Administration.

The end of Regulation Q ceilings and Board restrictions on brokerage money came just as associations were becoming competitive with money market mutual funds as a result of the Garn-St Germain Act's authorization of the money market account. Because associations could offer an account similar to money funds, the brokerage community began losing many new customers attracted from 1980 to 1982. In fact, some $100 billion flowed out of the money funds back into thrift institutions and commercial banks. Brokers saw a way to keep their customers and make money from them by directing their funds to deposits in institutions paying high rates.

With repeal of the old restrictions on brokered money, many associations took full advantage of the new freedom. They grew rapidly, bringing in money from all parts of the country. Often, however, they used these funds in unwise and ill-fated lending and investment programs. By June 1983, 485 institutions had a total of $15.6 billion in brokered funds, a fivefold increase in just one year.

More ominously, the number of institutions heavily dependent on brokered funds grew rapidly in the same period. In June 1981, only 32 savings institutions had more than 5% of total savings from brokered funds, and they accounted for only $2.5 billion in assets. By June 1983, 258 institutions, holding a total of $89 billion in assets, had brokered funds exceeding the former supervisory limit of 5% of savings.

The increase in brokered funds was even more dramatic after October 1, 1983, when the DIDC removed all remaining interest rate ceilings on retail deposits other than passbook and NOW accounts. By the end of October, brokered funds held by savings institutions totaled $26 billion in assets, a tremendous increase in only four months. The real problem, however, was that some rapidly growing institutions were relying almost entirely on funds obtained through brokers. Quite a few of these later headed the list of failing institutions. It was impossible to grow at the rate some of these institutions did and avoid serious problems.

Rapid growth at so many associations began to concern the Bank Board staff and Chairman Gray in late 1983. The Board's first move was to limit by regulation (or, in effect, prohibit) the acceptance of money from brokers by effectively denying FSLIC insurance to deposits from this source. The FDIC took parallel action.

The Bank Board's regulation was issued in final form in March 1984.[20] It had been in the works for several months as Chairman Gray sought similar action from the FDIC and also had to convince the other members of the Board of the need for such regulation. Meanwhile, of course, brokerage money continued to pour into institutions determined to grow rapidly and use the funds for apparently profitable loans and investments which later proved the source of major losses.

Although the brokerage regulation was supported by the U.S. League, opposition from institutions using brokered money and from the brokers producing it was intense. Opposition was reflected not only in appeals to Congress, but by action brought in the federal courts. This question was the subject of an inquiry by the Subcommittee on Commerce, Consumer and Monetary Affairs of the U.S. House of Representatives, chaired by Rep. Doug Barnard of Georgia.

The committee held hearings in March 1984. It learned from the Board and the FDIC that many institutions were growing rapidly and recklessly through the use of brokered money, but that brokers were not the only way institutions could and did raise large amounts of funds quickly.

FAIC Securities, Inc., and the Securities Industry Association sued in the federal district court to overturn the rules. On June 20, 1984, the court ruled that the FDIC and Bank Board had exceeded their

---

[20] Issued in proposed form January 23, 1984, and approved March 26, 1984, to be effective October 1 with an interim rule approved March 26, 1984, limiting accounts from brokers to 5% of assets by associations with less than 3% net worth.

statutory authority and enjoined them from implementing these rules. The agencies appealed the decision, but subsequently withdrew their rules and basically retreated to a system which relied on supervisory action to curb the most flagrant abuses. The Bank Board chose not to limit the most flagrant use of brokerage funds through use of cease-and-desist orders. Rather, it believed the best course was to curb the practice by a regulation equally applicable to all institutions.

ACQUISITION OF SAVINGS AND LOAN ASSOCIATIONS

A second condition making large profits possible quickly was the ease with which opportunists could acquire a savings and loan charter. Entrepreneurs could start an association with a relatively small investment, and it was possible to own an association with no, or only a few partners. A policy change made by the Bank Board when Richard Pratt was chairman reduced the minimum number of stockholders of an FSLIC-insured institution to one.

For years, a minimum of 400 stockholders was required. No one individual was allowed to own more than 25% of the stock. Directors also were required to come from communities institutions served. The end of these requirements meant that it was possible for single owners and directors to come from different cities and even different states. It put a vastly different complexion on the operation of newly chartered institutions and those acquired by new owners. This change was based on a philosophical conviction that savings associations should operate like other businesses—not as organizations designed primarily to serve local communities.

Not only were' new charters available, but entrepreneurs desirous of exploiting short-term profit opportunities could easily buy an existing institution for a relatively small investment. By 1982 and 1983, the net worth of many institutions had been seriously depleted. Many local managements and owners were discouraged and happy to sell their associations. With brokerage money available, it was not necessary to buy a large association and pay a lot of money for it to get into the business.

The Board also permitted individuals to contribute land or other real estate to an association in lieu of cash to meet nominal net worth requirements. This was particularly useful to land developers buying existing institutions, and was permitted as the institution grew and required additional net worth. Little is known about methods of valuing land contributed as net worth. The validity of some appraisals is suspect, however, considering the problems that later occurred with ADC loans made by institutions controlled by land developers.

MINIMUM NET WORTH REQUIREMENTS

A third condition making fast growth and large profits possible was the nature of the reserve or net worth regulation until January 1985 when the Board under Chairman Gray substantively rewrote it (after changes were first proposed on February 15, 1984) and later revised it in August 1986.

Until the 1985 revision, the net worth requirement was a maximum of only 3% of deposits based on regulatory accounting rules. These rules were easier in many instances than GAAP rules. More important for rapidly growing associations, the regulation permitted use of the five-year moving average arrangement in computing the necessary build-up in reserves to the 3% benchmark. For newly chartered or newly insured associations, the regulations permitted a 25-year period to reach the minimum benchmark, initially 5% and later only 3%. Combined with the moving average formula this meant that under the Board's new rules, newly chartered associations could grow rapidly with virtually no net worth.

Weak net worth rules made possible great leveraging of an investor's initial investment for an indefinite number of years based upon the FSLIC's credit—"playing on the house's money," as one person described it—whether operating a newly chartered association or purchasing a small existing one.

This condition attracted many who did not have the same instincts as traditional savings and loan executives, and who sought to build a different kind of business. Many newcomers were skilled in financial markets and knew financial opportunities when they saw them.

Two types of people, particularly, were attracted to the savings and loan business by this combination of circumstances: mortgage bankers and land developers/home builders anxious to use an association for their development and home building activities. Home builders have always struggled to obtain financing. Traditionally, they used their own funds supplemented by short-term borrowings from commercial banks. Many mortgage bankers faced problems of raising funds needed to finance their inventories of mortgages held for sale. In both cases, an association charter now provided them with a lower cost and more certain source of funds than commercial bank borrowings.

CHANGE IN CONTROL LAW

The possibility of risk-taking entrepreneurs coming into financial institutions and harming them has existed for a long time. In 1978 Congress passed the Change in Control law, applicable both to banks and savings and loan associations. It gave supervisory authorities an opportunity to review an applicant's biographical information to determine whether the applicant should be denied entry into the business. Supervisory authorities were given 60 days to declare that the new owner, or "controller," was unsuitable to control the institution.

The law was also designed to alert supervisory people about new ownership or management. They could then monitor the operation to make certain that problems did not develop. Unfortunately, the act failed both as a way of keeping the wrong people out and as an alert mechanism.

At some association failures, incoming management's record warranted the confidence of supervisory agencies. In the well-publicized case of Empire Savings, Mesquite, Texas, the chief executive officer had a good record with an institution in Austin, Texas. He had been elected president of the Texas Savings and Loan League and was serving as vice chairman of the Federal Home Loan Bank of Dallas before problems developed at Empire Savings.

At another institution which later became an MCP in California, the chief executive officer had been head accountant at the Bank Board in Washington, D.C., and on the staff of a Big Eight public accounting firm. A former governor of Illinois (1973 to 1977) bought a controlling interest in a small Illinois association later declared insolvent and taken over by the FSLIC. He later pleaded guilty to financial fraud in connection with the association. These are examples of people with good records or backgrounds that do not suggest imprudence. Deregulation and the ability to leverage profits, however, presented risky opportunities that led them into trouble.

The Board maintains that it is difficult to disapprove applications for control or ownership of institutions unless there is hard evidence of incompetence or a clear history of wrongdoing. In some instances when the Board was uncertain about an applicant for control of an association, but had no clear grounds for denying the application, it exercised a variety of delaying tactics. The Board also believed, however, that it should not limit the freedom or rights of association stockholders to sell their institutions. After all, who was to say that former home builders or mortgage bankers would not be appropriate savings and loan executives? Further, some incoming owners or executives had strong political allies, who could make it difficult for public officials to deny applications.

Significant changes in the control law were made by Congress in 1986 (as part of the Money Laundering Control Act of 1986) with identical changes in the Bank Control Act. Amendments strengthening the law:

1. Required the FSLIC to investigate the competency, experience and integrity of a person seeking to acquire control;

2. Provided supervisory agencies with authority to subpoena documents and records;

3. Mandated publication of the identity of a person filing notice under the Control Act; and

4. Permitted the FSLIC to seek injunctive or other relief under the Control Act or regulations issued under it.

These amendments came some years too late. It remains to be seen whether even they will do the trick. Clearly, however, inadequate use was made of the previous law.

9 Management Experience and Judgment

Newcomers weren't the only ones engaging in activities that led to association failures. Executives who had spent their careers in the business did, too.

A whole new group of salesmen and, at times, outright hustlers posing as consultants and specialists advised associations on how to take advantage of "opportunities" offered by deregulation. In most instances, management was unfamiliar with the new markets. Managers were not equipped to study, analyze and make proper judgments about markets suddenly opened to them. Thus, they needed outside assistance which often proved valuable, but which sometimes led to losses.

CHANGING MARKETS AND THE DRIVE FOR EARNINGS

The years 1981 and 1982 were traumatic for the business. Practically all associations saw their net worth seriously depleted. Many were concerned that violating the minimum net worth requirement would cause serious problems with regulatory supervisors and pressure to merge with another institution. For years the business had been conditioned to fear violations of regulations, particularly the net worth regulation. Although the minimum net worth requirement then was only 3% for most institutions, even that was above what many would show on their statements.

In late 1982 and in 1983, interest rates were still high, the economy was booming, oil prices were $30 to $35 a barrel and the tax law favored investment in real estate. Many institutions, survivors of the previous few years, thought they saw a way out of their low net worth and low earnings dilemma by using new lending and investment powers. They adopted aggressive expansion programs to improve earnings and balance their portfolios with adjustable rate mortgages, short-term construction loans and loans with 5-year or 10-year balloon payment maturities.

For some stock-owned institutions, the lure of high per share earnings and valuable stock options whetted their appetite for aggressive lending programs. Some institution executives reported that the supervisory establishment, taking its cue from Washington (when the Board was led by Richard Pratt), actively encouraged associations to make aggressive use of new lending and investment powers provided by Garn-St Germain as a way of improving earnings to build net worth.

One observer noted that the Pratt Board had a "sink or swim" approach to institutions in danger of exhausting their net worth. The Board was preoccupied with net earnings as the business' principal problem. There had, after all, been little Board experience with asset problems, and at the time the real estate economy looked rather solid. Of course, associations with little or no net worth should not have been encouraged to take risks beyond the range of management's experience. Greater risks should be taken by high net worth institutions, not those unable to absorb losses.

In addition to encouraging associations to use new powers to improve their earnings, regional Bank officials briefed association boards of directors on interest rate swaps and hedging, and reviewed broader investment powers provided by the Garn-St Germain Act. Instances occurred where associations took these suggestions without doing their homework. They rushed into commercial real estate lending without adequate knowledge of the risks involved. For example, some associations apparently took the advice to diversify geographically by acquiring loans in Texas.

The most logical targets for profitable lending were loans on condominiums and commercial structures such as office buildings, shopping centers and hotels. Construction loans on commercial properties appeared particularly attractive. Construction and permanent loans on non-single-family properties rose to 25% of total lending in 1984. For many associations the percentage was much higher. Also attractive were loans on condominium apartments. In many instances, an association not only financed a developer and construction of units, but also ultimate buyers, with investor-owned units financed on the same generous terms as owner-occupied units. Properties in resort areas proved particularly alluring to many savings and loan executives.

Land development ventures were potentially the most profitable. They were also the most risky, especially when the properties were in distant market areas. The Bank Board's Office of Policy and Economic Research noted that in early 1984 the savings and loan share of the nonresidential mortgage market increased from 11% in 1981 to 16% in 1982, 23% in 1983 and 29% in 1984. It also noted that in 1984 nonresidential construction loans accounted for 42% of all construction lending by the business.

Some $100 billion from the money market funds were deposited in associations as they became able to compete again for yield-conscious customers. Too much money at any one time frequently leads to lending excesses. This money was recycled by associations into loans on commercial real estate, much as the commercial banks recycled the Arab oil money in loans to developing countries in the 1970s. Other lenders also had a surplus of funds and wanted to make the more profitable commercial loans. If they could not find good loans, they were willing to make high risk loans as long as points and profit potentials were attractive. Developers, of course, will always build if generous financing is available.

Through 1983 and 1984, aggressive lending programs appeared quite successful. Earnings increased, and unless the deposit growth was too rapid, net worth ratios improved considerably. By 1985, however, overbuilt conditions began appearing in many markets from vacation condominiums to downtown and suburban office space. Nationally, office building vacancies rose from 5% in 1981 to more than 20% in 1986, and higher in the suburbs and some cities. In many cases, the developers' sales and rental projections proved overly optimistic. Projections were made to justify loans lenders wanted to make.

Inflation rates began to retreat in 1985, and by 1986 the cost of living index increased only 1.9%. Gross National Product rose 2.9% in 1986, a decline from 3.0% in 1985, and 6.4% in 1984. A considerable amount of steam began disappearing from the nation's economy. While the decline in interest rates helped interest rate spreads, improved profit margins were not enough for several hundred institutions to offset losses from an increasing proportion of nonperforming assets. In fact, the economic conditions that brought lower interest rates exacerbated the problem of poorly made loans on commercial property, land development projects and some single-family homes. Losses on single-family homes and condominium units would have been much greater if many loans had not been covered by private mortgage insurance.

APPRAISING

Appraisals made in the 1980s were based essentially on the standards and procedures set in the 1930s and 1940s when the basic textbooks on appraising were written. Beyond that, however, the market analysis supporting many appraisals was often inadequate and, even when appraisers did attempt to offer some warnings about future events through the use of "limiting conditions and assumptions" their concerns were often ignored by loan officers. Many appraisals were based on the overly optimistic assumption that property values would continue to rise.

The appraisal profession has suffered in prestige as a result of the wave of major losses in mortgage lending by all types of lenders. Standards of professional practice were inadequate, but loan officers and executives of failed institutions and government officials cannot pass the buck to appraisers. The appraisal is only one phase of loan underwriting. Appraisers have differing skills, experience and reputations. Executives have a responsibility to hire honest, competent appraisers. It appears that loan executives often hired appraisers expecting them to support a preconceived value estimate so that the desired loan could be made. In other cases, honest association executives unfamiliar with commercial and industrial property relied on appraisals that were too often superficial, or simply wrong. Executives perhaps accepted such estimates because they permitted the kind of loan with fees and interest rates an association wanted on its books. Analysis independent of an appraiser was considered unnecessary. The appraiser and the association executive were thus both naive and wrong. Appraisers, however, do not make loans. Loan officers and association executives do.

TEXAS AND THE SOUTHWEST

Chapter 7 referred to a statistical study of the Texas savings and loan system by Ferguson & Company, a public accounting firm. It noted that 41 Texas thrifts, with total assets of $13 billion, had negative net worth greater than 5% of liabilities as of December 31, 1986. This included eight institutions which at the end of 1986 were in the management consignment program. The Texas institutions, along with those in Louisiana, Arkansas and Oklahoma, were particularly hard hit by a substantial decline in real estate values which followed the collapse of oil prices beginning in late 1985 and early 1986. This price drop caused a major economic recession in much of the Southwest.

TABLE 20: REGULATORY NET WORTH/TOTAL ASSETS
(As of March 31, 1987)

State	Less than 0.0%		0 - 3.0%		3.0 - 5.0%		5.0%		Total
	% Firms	% Assets	% Firms	% Assets	% Firms	% Assets	% Firms	% Assets	Assets
California	12.1%	4.0%	5.6%	12.9%	26.2%	17.2%	56.1%	65.9%	100.0
Colorado	10.8	1.9	10.8	19.1	27.0	32.1	51.4	46.9	100.0
Florida	9.9	7.1	6.6	8.4	27.2	39.8	56.3	44.8	100.0
Georgia	3.0	0.6	10.4	12.2	26.9	35.4	59.7	51.8	100.0
Illinois	6.4	6.5	12.9	10.1	32.2	30.0	48.5	53.4	100.0
Michigan	7.8	3.6	3.9	1.1	43.1	51.9	45.1	43.4	100.0
Oklahoma	26.4	26.3	24.5	20.2	18.9	13.1	30.2	40.4	100.0
Texas	26.1	27.1	17.5	16.7	22.9	27.0	33.6	29.3	100.0
U.S. Total	8.6%	6.5%	9.3%	11.2%	25.5%	28.4%	56.6%	53.9%	100.0

Source: Untied States League of Savings Institutions.

Tables 20 and 21 give a recent assessment of the business' condition in Texas and Oklahoma (the states most affected by the oil price collapse) in comparison with some other states with large savings and loans.

TABLE 21: ANNUALIZED EARNINGS AS A PERCENT OF ASSETS
(First Quarter 1987)

State	Less than 0.0%		0 - 1.0%		More than 1.0%	
	% Firms	% Assets	% Firms	% Assets	% Firms	% Assets
California	22.9%	7.9%	40.7%	59.3%	36.4%	32.8%
Colorado	32.4	27.4	54.1	66.5	13.5	6.1
Florida	29.8	19.4	51.7	57.1	18.5	23.5
Georgia	3.0	0.6	47.8	77.9	49.3	21.5
Illinois	17.8	10.7	47.7	48.9	34.5	40.4
Michigan	11.8	4.1	62.7	55.5	25.5	40.3
Oklahoma	52.8	54.0	43.4	41.0	3.8	5.0
Texas	62.5	73.4	26.8	14.6	10.7	12.0
U.S. Total	21.3%	16.7%	46.2%	55.8%	32.5%	27.5%

Source: United States League of Savings Institutions.

Overall a 16% decline occurred in Texas real estate values from mid-1984 to the third quarter of 1985, with an 11% decline for single-family properties. Deflation was much greater in cities unusually dependent on the oil industry. The savings and loan business suffered not only from the fall in oil prices and subsequent decline in real estate values of all types, but from failed ventures launched during the heady days of an oil boom following the Arab oil embargo.

Some Texas savings association failures were clearly caused by high-risk, even reckless lending—some of which may prove criminal. Ultimate losses to the FSLIC because of these excesses could be extremely high. In most instances, however, institutions were hurt by a decline in energy prices and depression in real estate values.

In the early 1980s when oil prices went from $7.64 per barrel in 1975 to $34.50 per barrel in 1981, Texas' economy experienced an unprecedented boom, particularly in the real estate business. The Texas Savings and Loan League reported in 1987 that state building permits increased from $4.3 billion in 1976 to approximately $17 billion in 1983. Inflation in Texas real estate substantially exceeded the national rate as Table 22 shows.

TABLE 22: NATIONAL AND TEXAS REAL ESTATE INFLATION RATES

Year	National Inflation Rate	Texas Real Estate Inflation Rate
1976	5.8%	8.9%
1977	6.5	13.4
1978	7.7	14.9
1979	11.3	15.4
1980	13.5	15.1
1981	10.4	14.2
1982	6.1	11.2
1983	3.2	9.0
1984	4.3	6.0
1985	3.6	5.2
1986	1.9	(3.6)
1987	3.7	n.a.

Source: Bureau of Statistics, Texas Research League and Baylor University.

Given the euphoria created by the oil boom and depression-proof history of Texas, most Texas savings institutions pursued aggressive growth and investment practices that in earlier years would have been considered imprudent.

Institutions were established in Texas in the late '70s and early '80s, and many new owner and management groups came into the business. Of the Texas institutions put into receivership in 1986 and 1987, or considered substantially insolvent by mid-1987, some 50% were run by managers who entered the business after 1979.

Texas institutions willingly made loans on unusually high loan-to-value ratios. These ratios were based on values which clearly exceeded even current market values and could only be achieved by historically high economic growth rates.

Whether managed by new owners or more traditional ones, Texas institutions began to originate unprecedented amounts of commercial real estate loans and invest unprecedented amounts in land for development. Often, loan quality problems were compounded by associations becoming partners in unorthodox land and building ventures. Frequently partners were developers with questionable backgrounds.

As the report of the Texas League indicates, growth to generate income became a vicious cycle. Table 23 shows the pace of this frenzied growth.

TABLE 23: ASSETS OF TEXAS THRIFTS

Year	
1975	$14.1 billion
1976	20.0
1977	24.3
1978	28.2
1979	31.5
1980	35.3
1981	38.2
1982	43.5
1983	57.3
1984	78.4
1985	94.5
1986	97.3
1987	100.1

Source: Texas Savings and Loan League.

In three years (1981, 1984 and 1985), Texas institutions grew roughly three times the national average. They generally paid significantly higher rates for deposits than other institutions around the country. (See Table 24.)

TABLE 24: EFFECTIVE COST OF DEPOSIT FUNDS

Year	United States	Texas
1981	9.95%	10.32%
1982	10.40	10.55
1983	9.22	9.30
1984	9.51	9.70
1985	8.56	8.91
1986	7.42	8.00
1987 (through March 31)	6.54	7.20

Source: Texas Savings and Loan League.

Not only did rapid deposit increases fuel the state's real estate market, but associations in other states with more deposits than they could lend directed funds to Texas associations. As a result of higher money costs and competition to invest these funds in profitable real estate loans and investments, these institutions generally acquired poorer quality loans.

The Texas Savings and Loan League reported that real estate developers and real estate entrepreneurs began to acquire control of Texas institutions through actual purchase. According to a Dallas newspaper investigation, entrepreneurs with backgrounds in real estate development either own or owned 20 of the 24 most insolvent thrifts (the other four copied their tactics). Many of the newcomers, as well as some existing owners, also began to engage in illegal schemes to reap even larger profits from the business. The Texas League study further indicated that "the apparent increase in net worth of the acquired thrifts was, in many cases, illusory since it resulted from the contribution of real estate assets that lost substantial portions of their values in the subsequent real estate collapse and in many cases was artificially created through the use of 'push down' and purchase accounting." This illusory increase in net worth, however, was sufficient for RAP purposes, allowing thrifts to substantially increase their leverage. The result was a spiraling cycle of growth in liabilities and increases in commercial real estate loans and investments.

Institutions with the most rapid growth rates often worked with builders and developers of questionable ability and integrity. These arrangements included making loans which would have gone into default even without the substantial decline in oil prices.

When oil prices declined and real estate markets collapsed, associations were left with large portfolios of nonearning assets. A general downturn in Texas real estate markets caused price declines of 40% to 60% for better properties, and no sales at any price for more speculative projects.

During these years the Bank Board's examination and supervisory program at the Federal Home Loan Bank of Little Rock, Ark., was completely inadequate. Without a sufficient number of well-trained examiners, the supervisory program was unable to deal with these problem institutions. The situation became worse after the Bank moved to Dallas in 1983. Shortly thereafter, the Bank's president was replaced and the entire supervisory staff had to be rebuilt.

In 1985 and 1986, the Home Loan Bank of Dallas borrowed examiners from several Home Loan Bank districts just to learn what was happening at various Texas institutions. By 1985, however, it was too late: insolvencies had already occurred, or become inevitable.

It is also clear that from 1980 to 1984 the Home Loan Bank of Little Rock-Dallas' supervisory staff misjudged the motivations of many new people in the business and willingness of more traditional savings and loan executives to take risks in lending they had never taken before. Many institutions throughout the country, in effect, became "fee junkies." They were even more addicted in the Southwest.

Real estate problems spread to out-of-state associations that made loans and investments in Texas and bought loan participations from Texas associations. Substantial investments in Texas real estate and mortgage loans were made by some California associations already having problems with their own loans and investments.

DIRECTORS PARTIALLY TO BLAME

Traditionally, the role of savings and loan directors has been to leave an association's operations to management. Duties were almost perfunctory in well-run associations until deregulation brought significant changes. In the new environment, traditional directors were often in situations in which they had no experience, little business capacity, and almost no appreciation for the changes which were occurring. They were too willing to accept the advice and programs of young, new financial managers mesmerized by high levels of apparent financial success achieved by other entrepreneurs in the mortgage market and savings and loan business. Experienced directors, and some experienced assistant executives, were uneasy about the rapid growth rates of their institutions but were willing to tolerate what they perceived as new industry thinking. These directors also failed to heed the findings of their internal audit committees. At many associations, directors did not have an audit committee truly independent of management or owners to serve as their "eyes and ears" in reviewing managerial activities.

At some institutions, management did not tell board members about activities in which the institution was engaged, even large compensation plans for management. Board complacency made it possible for management to keep many key facts from directors. Directors should have been aggressive in hiring and firing executives, setting reasonable salaries, creating and enforcing lending policies, assuring the safety and soundness of an association's assets and exercising general oversight of management. Instead, lulled by apparently record high profits, they acted almost as spectators, content to accept management's assurances that new policies and programs were necessary because of changes in the lending and financing environment.

Directors are not expected to have experience in real estate finance or in investment areas opened by deregulation and new laws. They are, however, expected to have a modicum of good judgment with respect to banking activities. In some instances, the Bank Board asserts that directors were actively involved in the improper dissipation of the institution's assets. The Board has sought—and may win—judgments against directors of a number of failed institutions.

10 Supervision

Another reason—clearly one of the most important—for excessive and expensive savings and loan failures was inadequate supervision.

In the early years of the Reagan Administration and the brave new world of deregulation, it appeared that the objectives of savings and loan regulators were to give financial institutions more and more freedom to compete, take risks, find their own areas of service, do their own brand of credit underwriting, and maximize profits. The Board under Chairman Pratt certainly provided this freedom in full measure at a cost far above the FSLIC's resources and the business' ability to pay deposit insurance premiums.

While Pratt was forthright in dealing with those supervisory problems brought to his attention and delegated to Principal Supervisory Agents the power to initiate and issue supervisory agreements, the Board during his tenure failed to grasp that deregulation almost by definition meant the need for a dramatic strengthening of the examination and supervisory process. Its overriding interest in deregulation, developing drafts for what later became the Garn-St Germain Act and dealing with problems arising from the earnings squeeze caused the Board to neglect its examination-supervision side. The business did not get the tougher supervision needed until Edwin Gray's term as chairman.

EARLY SUPERVISORY OBJECTIVES

When the Bank Board was organized and for many years thereafter, supervision of savings and loan associations (and banks) was intended to:

1. Prevent failures, and particularly to avoid a repetition of the collapse of the banking system such as occurred from 1930 to 1933;

2. Assure that regulated institutions adhered to written laws and regulations;

3. Assure the honesty of operation and integrity of financial statements; and

4. Minimize conflicts of interest.

As noted earlier, most laws and regulations savings associations operated under in post-Depression years were designed to avoid failures. Preventing failures was always an important consideration in the Bank Board's evaluation of proposed laws to give the business greater flexibility.

A NEW EXPANSIVE ATTITUDE

Under the chairmanship of Preston Martin during President Richard Nixon's Administration, the Board encouraged the business to expand following a period of some failures and supervisory problems under the chairmanships of Joseph McMurray and John Horne. The Martin Board also moved to reform certain aspects of the business that had been increasingly criticized. These included management voting permanent proxies (solicited at the time of an account opening) at association annual meetings to perpetuate control of an institution; ownership by association "insiders" (management, directors or persons close to management) of insurance agencies that wrote an important percentage of the fire insurance policies on properties financed by the association; and ownership of escrow companies and appraisal companies. The Martin Board also moved to provide for disclosure of certain inside information, including salaries and personal information about officers and directors. A few years later, the Board under Chairman Tom Bomar developed an extensive set of regulations dealing with conflicts of interest.

CONSUMERISM

The Truth-in-Lending law passed in 1968. This marked the beginning of the consumer movement which blossomed during President Jimmy Carter's Administration and the Board chairmanship of Robert McKinney. Congress also passed the Community Reinvestment Act in 1977. Developing the regulatory framework for this and other consumer laws took much of the Board's time. Enforcement of these regulations required much of the examiners' time, too.

Even those at the highest federal levels in Washington or the Bank Board did not appear concerned about a worsening of a long familiar problem: rapid growth in 1978-79 of rate-sensitive short-term deposits (money market certificates) invested in long-term, fixed-rate mortgages. They were pleased that money market certificates helped avoid serious disintermediation, that mortgage money continued to flow and housing starts remained at high levels. The business later paid a high price for being used as an instrument to carry out federal housing policies, but had also greatly benefited by this same policy in previous years.

EXAMINATION VS. SUPERVISION

This work explained earlier why examination and supervision are separate: The U.S. League's leadership believed that during the Depression, examiners were given too much discretion and closed many banks that should have remained open.

Consequently, when the national savings and loan system was organized, examiners were to be purely fact finders, exercising little or no discretion. Discretion was the province of supervision, which in the field was headed by the presidents of the regional Federal Home Loan Banks with small supervisory staffs. In Washington, there were separate examination and supervision divisions. It remained that way until these two offices were merged into an Office of Examination and Supervision (OES) on January 1, 1964, when Joseph McMurray was the Board's chairman.

In the field, however, examiners continued to be separate from supervision. They were on the Board's payroll and reported to the staff officers in Washington, not to those responsible for dealing with the findings of the examiners.

This system worked satisfactorily, or so it appeared. The business was relatively simple, and given the highly regulated environment not many associations got into trouble quickly. The system proved completely inadequate, however, in the 1980s.

No system of supervision and examination would have prevented the failure and near failure of associations that have occurred as a result of the declining spread between investment and savings yield. But tougher regulations, a greater number of and more experienced examiners and supervisory staff, and different examination and supervisory procedures would have minimized the failures since 1984.

TIME LAGS IN SUPERVISORY ACTION

The supervisory establishment is often criticized for delays in effecting enforcement actions. This criticism has been common throughout the savings and loan business' history and, no doubt, in commercial banking.

It is instructive to review a number of papers as part of a study analyzing the savings and loan business, directed by professor Irwin Friend of the University of Pennsylvania. These papers were submitted to the Bank Board in 1969. One by H. Robert Bartell (former bank commissioner for the State of Illinois and former president of the Federal Home Loan Bank of Chicago) analyzed the Illinois savings and loan failures in the period 1963-68.

The study showed that supervisory officials were indecisive and the decision-making process—divided between the Federal Home Loan Bank of Chicago and the staff and members of the Bank Board in Washington, D.C.—was long and drawn out. Second and even third examinations were ordered before definite decisions were made to take enforcement action or close institutions. Appraisals were requested and then debated between management and supervisors. In some instances, as much as three years elapsed between the first suggestion of problems and final supervisory action, during which time asset deterioration continued and losses mounted. A clear lack of cooperation or coordination existed between federal and state supervisory authorities, who insisted on a preemptive right to supervise state-chartered institutions.

It was evident that supervisors were exceedingly cautious in taking definitive action. They had to have clear evidence of insolvency before closing an institution and were reluctant to deprive management of its institutional prerogatives, even though most institutions were mutual.

CAUSES OF ILLINOIS FAILURES OF THE 1960s

Bartell identified the following elements common to savings and loan failures in Illinois:

1. Rapid growth in savings, usually with money obtained from outside the association's normal trading area, and frequently obtained through brokers;

2. Heavy concentration of loans to a few large, multiple borrowers;

3. Heavy concentration of loans on income properties; and

4. High percentage of loans based on excessive appraisals.

These same elements characterized virtually all of the failures of insured savings and loan associations from 1984 to 1987. Dr. Bartell also noted that criminal intent played a significant part in some failures. Heavy borrowers on overappraised properties frequently had extensive personal business relationships with an association's officers and directors. In addition, at several institutions the same borrowers were involved, implying a conspiracy to defraud the associations. Apparently officers and directors benefited through kickbacks from large borrowers.

Surprisingly, by the 1980s the Board was too concerned with deregulation, freedom to compete and remaking the business to learn from Illinois' painful experience. The possibility of failures through bad lending, fraud and deflation in real estate and their cost apparently were not considered.

THE PENN SQUARE BANK

The Penn Square Bank, Oklahoma City, seized by the U.S. Comptroller on July 5, 1982, underscored many problems with the supervisory system.[21]

The Comptroller's supervisory staff knew for months that Penn Square was in trouble and its officers were negligent. However, the Comptroller would not, or could not, take action against the bank until it could be proven insolvent, if necessary, to a court.

In the last weeks of Penn Square's life, much supervisory time was spent trying to arrange a takeover by another bank. Many high level meetings occurred involving the Treasury, FDIC and Federal Reserve officials. They tried to explore ways to avoid closing the bank and to pay depositors only the amount covered by FDIC insurance.

A similar situation happened in many savings and loan failures. The general rule has been that FSLIC-insured institutions could not be closed and placed in receivership unless the institution was insolvent and the supervisory and legal staff was confident that, if necessary, insolvency could be proven in court.

There are legal risks in a declaration of insolvency and receivership, particularly in the case of proprietary or capital stock institutions. Supervisory staffs must make certain not to deprive

---

[21]   For a thorough discussion of the Penn Square disaster, see Belly Up by Phillip L. Zweig.

stockholders of actual or residual property rights. Although rarely successful, enough lawsuits have been brought by former owners of seized institutions to suggest that justifying supervisory actions in court is not just theoretical.[22]

Certain due process procedures have been built into supervisory law for both banks and savings associations. It is useful to review these protections for owners and managements and the history of supervisory law, basically written by Congress in 1966.

EARLY SUPERVISORY PROCEDURES

Not until the chairmanship of Walter W. McAllister Sr., during the administration of President Dwight Eisenhower did the Board contemplate that the examination and supervisory process would include making test appraisals and employment of review appraisers. Unlike commercial bank examination practice, examiners were not called upon to judge the value of an association's assets or given authority to require certain reserves against assets, although supervisory officials at the regional Banks have exercised such authority from the mid-1950s. Today examiners may recommend the establishment of reserves, but only the Bank President, acting as the Principal Supervisory Agent, or one to whom he delegates such authority can require the establishment of reserves.

Savings and loan executives have traditionally resisted the ability of examiners to judge the value of an institution's assets. This attitude remains today; the business was opposed to a classification-of-assets program the Board began in December 1985. Association executives generally are reluctant to see examiners have too much authority. Possibly this is because many believe that examiners do too much nit-picking, and were usually low-level (and low-paid) civil service employees.

In contrast, commercial bank examiners for a long time have had authority to require reserves against questionable loans, and to write down, or write off, certain loans. A great difference, however, exists between a loan against working capital, inventory or other short-term business loans and a long-term mortgage loan, or short-term loans to finance construction of residences or commercial structures. Many real estate loans are more complex than short-term business loans, and therefore more difficult to analyze.

---

[22] See for example, the case of Telegraph Savings and Loan Assn. v. William J. Schilling, Federal Home Loan Bank Board 807 F. 2d 590 (7th Cir. 1986).

For generations the savings and loan business has been wary of examiners and supervisors. The business has tried to keep examination costs and supervision to a minimum, possibly because its early leadership distrusted the whole supervisory process.

The commercial banking system has had a great deal of examination and supervision flexibility and operated with relatively few regulations governing banks. In contrast, savings and loan associations have always been, and preferred to be, guided by specific regulations. This preference still exists. Distrust of the supervisory process was exemplified by: the U.S. League's response to a request by the Gray Board to revise the basic supervisory law (discussed later), the reaction of the business to loan classification procedures, pressure on the Board in 1987 for a specific, written forbearance program, and forbearance provisions in the FSLIC recapitalization law for associations in depressed energy, agricultural and mineral states.

TAKEOVERS IN THE LATE 1950s

In the mid-1950s, the Bank Board became concerned about conflict-of-interest situations. It dealt forcefully with many financially sound institutions where evidence indicated that executives and others profited from the lending process. Using supervisory powers then available, the Board in effect dismissed managements at some half dozen associations basically for conflict of interest.

The Board took control of these associations by putting a "supervisory representative in charge." The business protested vehemently and defended the actions of executives at these associations. The Board was accused of enforcing unwritten laws; a demand was made that it express in writing, by regulation, the do's and don'ts. The business generally said it wanted a "government of law" and not a "government of men." The Board responded that it was impossible to codify safe, sound and proper practices.

In 1959, 1960 and 1961, a congressional oversight committee, under the chairmanship of Congressman John Moss, conducted extensive hearings and severely criticized the Board's examination and supervisory staff and chairman, Albert Robertson.

The result was a great many new regulations as the Board tried to follow the wishes of this congressional committee (and the business) and a substantial inhibiting of the examination and supervisory processes. This was evidenced in extreme caution and indecision in handling the Illinois institutions guilty of improper conduct in the 1960s.

The business subsequently became concerned about several well publicized failures in Illinois, as well as failures in a number of other states, notably California and Nevada. The business considered the examination/supervisory process largely to blame and became fed up with the proliferation of regulations.

THE SUPERVISORY LAW OF 1966

Time was ripe for a complete revision of the supervisory law, which had been discussed within the business, at the Board and in Congress for a number of years. The objective of the new supervisory law, passed in 1966, was to give the Board increased authority to deal with institutions case by case. Thus, the Board was given authority to issue cease-and-desist orders and, in certain instances, to remove an institution's officers and directors. This was described as the "rifle" approach in contrast to the "shotgun" method of having many regulations equally applicable to all institutions, whether weak or strong, or poorly or fraudulently managed.

Although little use was made of the cease-and-desist and removal authority, this law appeared to be quite satisfactory to the Board and the business until supervisory problems, stemming from bad assets, began mounting shortly after Edwin Gray became chairman in 1983.[23]

The Board's supervisory routines were frustrated by uncooperative managements of problem institutions. In many cases where supervisory agreements could not be obtained or directives were ignored, a cease-and-desist or removal order was the only alternative to an action for receivership which, in effect, required finding an association insolvent. Obtaining those orders was time consuming and pursued by the Board only reluctantly.

In many instances, it was difficult to determine the details of the association's financial condition because the books and records were in disarray. In at least one instance, association management frustrated supervisors by trading one piece of real estate owned for another, just as an appraisal of the first piece was in process. This delayed asset evaluation. Many transactions were complex and often involved faulty, if not fraudulent, appraisals. Endless arguments about the quality of loan appraisals occurred. Disputes erupted over accounting policies followed on loans the examiners believed should be classified as investments.

---

[23] No overtures were made either by the Board or the banking agencies to change the law until 1984.

Certain due process provisions built into the 1966 law were vexations. They permitted the Board to issue temporary cease-and-desist orders only to stop certain unsafe and unsound practices likely to cause insolvency, threaten a substantial dissipation of assets or earnings, or seriously weaken the institutions and prejudice the interest of depositors.

While such temporary cease-and-desist orders were immediately effective and enforceable by law, the act also gave those representing an association the right to apply to the federal district court for an injunction to limit, or set aside, the order pending an administrative proceeding. Right to an administrative hearing was also part of the "due process" procedure following issuance of a permanent cease-and-desist order. The 1966 law also gave the Board authority to remove officers and directors, but only for violation of a law, rule, regulation or order which had become final—or if the officer or director was participating in unsafe and unsound practices which constituted a breach of fiduciary duty. The Board could also remove managers if it found that an association had suffered substantial financial losses which could seriously damage or prejudice members. In addition, the Board could dismiss executives charged with a crime, dishonesty, or breach of trust punishable by imprisonment for a term exceeding one year.

In the discussions leading up to the 1966 act, the U.S. League and National Savings and Loan League vigorously worked for added due process provisions. State supervisors—both for banks and savings and loans—and many state-chartered banks and savings associations strongly opposed substantial revision of the law applicable to state-chartered associations. They alleged that it violated the concept of the dual system of charters by giving the federal supervisors (through the FDIC and FSLIC) too much authority over state-chartered institutions.

The act's final version, which also applied to commercial banks, was a compromise among the U.S. League, the state supervisory authorities and the Board, and the banks and the banking agencies. It gave the Board and the regulatory agencies considerable new authority over both federal and state-chartered institutions, but more barriers to quick supervisory action were built into the law than either the bank supervisors or Board officials felt wise.

As a result of protections for management and owners built into the law, the Board had to be able to prove that an association's actions were likely to cause insolvency. It also had to prove, if necessary, that such actions involved a substantial dissipation of assets, or serious weakening of the institutions. These provisions made the supervision of failing or recklessly managed institutions quite demanding and time consuming. Institutions served with a cease-and-desist or removal order could go to court and make the Board prove its case.

Also bothersome to supervisory authorities was the fact that inadequate records were not a reason for a cease-and-desist order, or other strong supervisory action. Inadequate record-keeping existed at many rapidly growing institutions and in most associations subsequently put into receivership, or otherwise taken over by the FSLIC. With records in a mess, it took examiners an extraordinarily long time to determine the institution's real condition. Supervisors often would see a deteriorating situation but, given a noncooperative or recalcitrant management, were unable to bring about corrective action. Supervisors found it difficult and time consuming to use stronger supervisory tools, such as a cease-and-desist or a removal order, until they had virtually an airtight case.

Proving insolvency, of course, can take a great deal of time. This permits further deterioration of assets, or continued dissipation of the assets for the personal benefit of management and owners. As the Penn Square Bank debacle shows, federal bank supervisors have faced the same problem.

REVISIONS IN SUPERVISORY LAW REQUESTED

Delays led the Board in early 1984 to draft and present for discussion proposed revisions in the basic supervisory law.

The Board proposed dropping the "substantial" and "seriously" modifiers from the basic authority to remove officers and directors, and equating "breach of financial duty" with "breach of fiduciary duty." Under the Board's proposal, an individual could be removed for any statutory or regulatory violation, or unsafe or unsound practices involving personal dishonesty or willful or continuing disregard for the institution's safety and soundness.

With respect to cease-and-desist orders, the Board also sought to eliminate "substantial" and "seriously" as modifiers of the power to issue orders where a violation of law, rule or regulation, or unsafe or unsound practice occurred which could cause insolvency or dissipation of assets and earnings, weaken the condition of the insured institution, or impair the interest of its insured members. At the same time, the Board sought to clarify its cease-and-desist authority with respect to service corporations, including second tier and partially owned service corporations.

The Board also sought to codify the term "unsafe or unsound practices." Such practices would encompass "any action or omission which is in the opinion of the FSLIC, contrary to generally accepted standards of prudent operation, whether relating to the association's internal management or to any external matter, the possible consequences of which, if continued, may pose abnormal risk of loss or damage to the insured institution, or any subsidiary thereof, to its stockholders, or account-holders, or to the FSLIC."

Finally, the Board sought authority to go into the U.S. District Court to obtain injunctions against officials for unsafe or unsound practices when it determined that its administrative enforcement provisions were insufficient to resolve problem situations.

The Board found it needed a "fast whistle," so to speak, in taking supervisory action and felt it needed these changes in the law to have a more effective supervisory operation.

The FDIC and the other bank supervisory agencies did not join the Board in this effort by seeking to improve their parallel law. Their inaction may have proved fatal to the Board's effort. Officers of the U.S. League had found that its members still distrusted the supervisory process. Management was apprehensive about reducing its rights to defend itself—its right to due process—not appreciating, perhaps, the ultimate costs to the business of a supervisory process whose effectiveness might be impeded by parts of the law the Board sought to change.

The League ultimately persuaded the Board to modify some of its proposals. Legislation was presented to the Congress in June of 1986, as H.R. 4998, incorporating a number of the League's suggestions. For example, a new standard, temporary cease-and-desist order could be issued without modifiers. The disarray of books and records was included as grounds for such an order, which would remain effective only for 90 days. After that, a temporary order would remain in effect only if the agency could demonstrate "substantial" dissipation of assets, or that the interest of the account holders was "seriously" prejudiced.

The Board's proposals, however, did not become law even with the League's modifications. One wonders how much less the losses from the institutions that subsequently failed might have been if the Board had been able to move more quickly under a law that did not give so much protection to managers and owners—the bad ones along with the good ones.

In any event, a paralysis gripped the Congress from 1983 through 1986 with respect to banking legislation. As a result, the Board's proposed strengthening of the supervisory law probably would have failed even if the business had supported it.

The connection between supervisory powers and losses from failures was not adequately made when the Board and business leaders discussed the question in 1984. By the time discussions between the U.S. League and the Board on the legislative draft had been concluded in 1986, most of the damage had been done. Supervisory law revisions will be useful only in preventing a new wave of failures.

11 Examination and Supervisory Routines

The traditional separation of the examination staff from supervisors contributed to delays which proved costly to the FSLIC. For example, until recently examiners were primarily fact finders and were not permitted to ask for corrections or to recommend loan write-downs. The supervisory process often had to wait for receipt of an examination report from FHLB regional staffs, separate from those responsible for the supervisory routines. It was said that the examination system was "calendar driven" and not flexible enough to schedule more frequent examinations or make special examinations of problem institutions and those with new management. In some instances, particularly after 1982, failure to conduct special examinations of problem institutions resulted from inadequate staffing.[24]

In the early 1980s, examiners were still looking for violations of regulations, with little concern for an association's overall financial health, and supervisors were still enforcing regulations. Increasingly, they are now first concerned with an association's financial viability (i.e., degree of maturity mismatch, quality of assets, managerial expertise, level of capital) and secondarily concerned with regulatory compliance.

Devoting too much time to noncritical aspects of an association's operation delayed reporting serious violations an examination would uncover. Problems were sometimes not reported or dealt with until an

---

[24] Instructions from the head of OES in Washington in 1974 were to schedule examinations on the basis of "need rather than fixed cycles." Associations with adverse ratings were to be examined more often than institutions considered to be relatively free of problems. To what extent this rule was followed other than in lengthening time between examinations for well-conducted institutions is not known. Problem institutions, or those that turned out to be problems, were not examined often enough or in adequate detail. Again, this might have been caused by a lack of examiners and misleading them with monthly reports and audits showing good earnings and high reserves.

entire examination was completed and a report finalized; computer use was at a minimum.

(As a result of losses and failures since 1983, a great many changes in the examination/supervisory process have been made in the last several years. The following describes the examination and supervisory process before 1984. Most subsequent changes took place in 1986.)

Examinations were conducted with an examiner in charge, generally supervised by a field manager. Field managers monitored groups of institutions and would be with examiners part of the time during examinations. Examiners in charge would collaborate with field managers in writing reports which went to district directors of examination for editing and review.

When examination reports with all of their schedules were finished, they went to deputy supervisory officials at district Home Loan Banks. Copies were sent to one of four regional supervisors at the Bank Board office in Washington.

For clean institutions roughly three weeks elapsed from the time examinations were completed to the time the supervisors received a final written report. For large, complex institutions, or institutions with problems, this process could take longer—at times much longer. (This procedure has been substantially improved in the last few years. Problem cases now go to supervisory officials much more quickly, often preceded by an informal, interim report.)

After receiving examination reports, supervisors in the district Banks sent a supervisory letter to an association's board of directors requesting they review it and respond within 30 days. Routine cases once took between 45 days to 60 days from a completed examination to receipt of a supervisory letter. This process took 90 days or longer—at times as long as six months—at problem institutions. (Again, this time schedule recently has been reversed between clean and problem institutions.)

Supervisory letters underscored deficiencies in an association's operations, violations of laws or regulations, and asked for corrective action. More serious cases usually meant longer delays before corrective action. In some instances, management and even entire boards of directors were called into a district Bank for conferences with supervisory officials.

Regional supervisors in Washington routinely received copies of every report, letter and conference report. Supervisory action often involved consultation by local supervisory officials with Washington.

As far back as October 1974, the director of the Bank Board's Office of Examination and Supervision instituted a supervisory reporting system. The implementing memorandum noted that if an association received a composite rating of either three or four, its supervisory agent should schedule a meeting promptly with the association's board of directors. In addition, a special reexamination should occur within 60 to 120 days of the date of such meeting with the board of directors. The extent these routines were followed as supervisory cases piled up after 1981 is unknown. In a number of publicized failures it is probable that examinations fell far behind and not enough examiners were available to conduct regular (or special) examinations with sufficient frequency. Reporting on the failure of one large institution in Arkansas in December 1986, The Washington Post noted that the association had not been examined between December 1982 and February 1985. (This article is reproduced in Addendum D.) This association was supervised by the FHLBank of Little Rock, which moved to Dallas in this period and lacked the necessary examiners and personnel.

Every effort was made to correct problems at the district Bank level. In most instances Bank officials succeeded. More serious cases required time-consuming policy discussions with Washington officials. Frequently, another examination would be ordered, together with property appraisals. Authority to request appraisals rests with the District Director of Examination in practice, or with the principal supervisory official or his designee.

The so-called supervisory agreement is a type of "consent decree" wherein management agrees not to do certain things it had done in the past, and to do other things that supervisors request. This is a step short of the cease-and-desist order and has usually been effective in correcting operating problems and what might generally be called management misconduct. Its use began in the 1970s and, while issued by the regional supervisor, was strictly a product of the Office of Examination and Supervision (OES), the Office of General Counsel (OGC) and its Office of Enforcement in Washington. While often recommended by the regional supervisory staff, the use of a consent decree and the terms involved had to be cleared through Washington, which took time. In 1982, preparation and issuance of supervisory agreements was delegated to supervisors in regional Banks and a Bank president as the principal supervisory agent. Widespread use of the supervisory agreements did not come until 1984 when 116 were issued after considerable insistence from Board Chairman Gray that regional supervisory agents crack down.

Cease-and-desist and removal proceedings can be issued only by Washington officials. These involved correspondence, memoranda and discussions between the Office of Examination and Supervision and the Office of the General Counsel (with its Office of Enforcement) with inevitable delay. The law requires that the full Board be officially involved in these actions.

Until a few years ago, Board action on cease-and-desist and removal orders was taken only at official Board meetings. Finding time with an often crowded Board calendar posed a problem. Now such matters are handled by "notational voting" on the basis of memoranda prepared for Board member study and action by the Office of Enforcement. Action on such orders has also been expedited by separation of the enforcement staff from the Office of the General Counsel. Requests for enforcement action now come to that office directly from the supervisory officials at the regional Home Loan Banks. The old system with the Office of the General Counsel and the Office of Examination and Supervision involved delay and at times passing the buck. Indecision in issuing cease-and-desist orders was often caused by fear of having a bad case (and losing) if the institution took the case to court on appeal.

The staff in Washington preferred that regional supervisory people obtain a supervisory agreement or persuade management to step aside whenever possible. This was the case with even flagrant abuses of "safe and soundness" standards. Cases involving criminal conduct are referred to the Department of Justice where delays in action can be almost endless.

The necessary "fast whistle" to prevent or minimize losses was simply not possible under the supervisory system that existed (and may still exist). In cases of honest differences of opinion, and particularly with noncooperative association executives or directors, the process took a great deal of time—the time of the examiners and staff, especially. If disputes occurred over loan quality, the value of properties underlying loans and real estate held for investment, or as a result of foreclosure, it took considerably more time. Appraisals had to be ordered, and there would be differences of opinion as to their validity. Meanwhile, unless there was substantial evidence of dissipation of assets, or insolvency was threatened, bad lending practices often continued despite admonitions of supervisory officials. It was possible for an association, through various legal devices, to delay the supervisory process for many months. At times association management would refuse to sign a supervisory agreement, or would argue over terms proposed by supervisors. Once signed, supervisory agreements would often be disregarded or deliberately violated. Even when issued, cease-and-desist order enforcement was sometimes delayed by court actions by association officers.

The reasons for ineffective supervisory action are debatable. Supervisory staff at regional FHLBs who encountered indecision and delays from Washington when requesting cease-and-desist and removal orders might have been affected as to the vigor of their work. The Bank president's personality and "taste" for or dislike of the job of principal supervisory agent also had an effect. A number of Bank presidents might clearly have preferred that Washington make the hard decisions and then blame Washington for whatever disagreeable action was needed. Indeed, Washington staff often preferred to make such decisions.

Based on memoranda from Chairman Gray to the principal supervisory agents, the Board in Washington felt regional supervisory authorities were particularly too lenient enforcing new net worth requirements in early 1985. Reports to the Board showed that excessively rapid growth was continuing in too many cases, especially in Texas. Gray issued memoranda on April 12, 1985 (with three memoranda of the same date from the acting director of OES); December 2, 1985; and an extensive memorandum dated February 12, 1986 dealing with interim examination reports. These memoranda pressed for more prompt and firm supervisory action. They clearly reflected increasing anxiety in Washington over the growing number of supervisory cases and mounting losses of failing institutions.

It is apparent that at least Gray felt the supervisory handling of improperly managed institutions had not been sufficiently resolute, and that the tools available to the Board under existing law and regulations had not been used adequately. With that, the great majority of savings and loan people would agree.

As noted, the examination and supervisory process has been accelerated. Computers are now used extensively. Examiners have computers on the job, and often write their report while still at an association. Interim reports are required in the case of problems suggesting prompt supervisory attention. Supervisory agreements are sought with more determination. When these are not forthcoming, supervisory orders are issued (under the authority of the net worth regulation, which usually has been violated by associations in trouble). Officers and directors understand that they may be liable for losses resulting from violating supervisory orders.

Delay and continued losses still result, however, if managements continue to misuse an association charter for personal gain and where regulations, such as those limiting loans to one borrower, are deliberately violated.

Since examiners were transferred to the Home Loan Banks, chief examiners have become officers of the Banks (along with chief supervisory officials) and some delay inherent in the separation of examination from supervision has been eliminated. Much better coordination and cooperation exists in dealing with problem cases. Also, examiners in the field have more authority to seek and obtain corrective action, although this has been a matter of considerable controversy. These changes, of course, all happened after damage had been done following deregulation and the great liberalization of investment authority by the Garn-St Germain Act and state legislatures.

ENFORCEMENT ACTIONS

The Bank Board has taken the following enforcement actions since 1975:

TABLE 25: ENFORCEMENT ACTIONS OF THE FEDERAL HOME LOAN BANK BOARD

Calendar Year	C&D Orders	No. of Individuals Removed and/or Prohibited	Supervisory Agreements	Consent Merger Resolutions	No. of Investigations Completed by Office of Enforcement	
					Formal	Informal
1975	13	—	10	N/A	41	N/A
1976	8	—	41	N/A	46	(combined)
1977	13	—	14	N/A	21	N/A
1978	9	—	9	N/A	37	(combined)
1979	7	4	7	N/A	20	(combined)
1980	3	1	1	0	6	10
1981	8	2	0	33	8	6
1982	13	6	5	49	10	10
1983	17	21	39	22	17	15
1984	13	22	116	38	24	20
1985	28	22	233	65	30	30
1986	58	48	214	130	30	25

The small number of cease-and-desist and removal orders may surprise and even outrage association executives who have seen great losses at improperly conducted institutions paid for by the FSLIC and ultimately by the business. Associations have expected examiners and supervisors to prevent violations of law and regulation and to make effective use of tools available to them. It might surprise them even more to learn that few of these cease-and-desist orders were the emergency or "temporary" type that supervisors were expected to use to stop wrongdoing promptly. The great majority of these orders were the regular type to be issued only after a hearing before an administrative law judge. Most of these orders were issued with the consent or voluntary approval of an association. They were obtained, of course, by supervisory authorities after discussion with an institution's management, which would agree to stop certain "unsafe and unsound" practices. This in turn would help prevent more drastic action by the supervisor. Violations of supervisory agreements sometimes lead to cease-and-desist orders, usually of the consent type. A copy of an actual cease-and-desist order issued to a supervisory case institution of the consent type is shown in Addendum E.

Cease-and-desist orders could have been used to prevent excessive deposit growth through brokerage money, yet there is no evidence of them being used in the program's early period—some say because of cautious lawyers at the Board. Gray began to publicly criticize brokerage practices as early as November 1983 and was quite outspoken about it in the early months of 1984. His program was to pass regulations limiting the attraction of brokerage funds, thus using the "shotgun" approach rather than the "rifle." As previously noted, this regulatory move was aborted by federal courts. Subsequently, supervisory agreements and cease-and-desist orders of the consent type did deal with the brokerage money question along with other major abuses in association operations. In retrospect, it appears the cease-and-desist routine could have been used earlier and effectively to prevent many of the problems that later developed from excessive growth.

It is interesting and useful to compare the number of cease-and-desist orders issued by the Federal Deposit Insurance Corporation and its use of other types of enforcement orders. The FDIC data follow.

TABLE 26: ENFORCEMENT ACTIONS BY THE FDIC

Year	Cease and Desist Orders	Orders to Remove Officers and Directors	Orders to Terminate Insurance of Accounts
1980	41	N.A.	8
1981	38	2	3
1982	69	8	18
1983	223	9	26
1984	138	13	32
1985	186	37	75
1986	135	14	59

Again, this is a small number of cease-and-desist orders considering that there are some 7,000 banks examined and supervised by the FDIC (state banks not members of the Federal Reserve System). A number of the FDIC orders related to violations of consumer laws, principally the Truth-in-Lending laws. As in the Bank Board case, practically all were of the regular or consent type versus the temporary type.

To obtain a regular cease-and-desist order (under Section 1730 (e)) the supervisor must have reasonable cause to believe that an association officer or director is about to engage in an unsafe or unsound practice, or is about to violate a law, rule or condition imposed in writing. The FSLIC issues and serves a notice of charges. The notice contains a statement of facts, substantiating alleged violations and fixing the time and place for a hearing to determine whether a cease-and-desist order should be issued.

A hearing is conducted before an administrative law judge, typically an attorney from another agency. If parties on which a notice is served fail to appear, their consent to the issuance of such order is automatic. Following a hearing, the FSLIC may issue a cease-and-desist order which is effective 30 days after service. It remains effective and enforceable except as modified or terminated by the FSLIC or a court.

A temporary cease-and-desist order (under Section 1730 (f)) may be issued whenever the FSLIC determines a violation (or threatened violation) of a regulation or stipulation, or unsafe and unsound practice has occurred and its continuation is likely to cause more serious problems such as insolvency. The FSLIC may issue a temporary order requiring an association (or directors and officers) to cease-and-desist from any such violations or practices. Such an order becomes effective upon service. Within 10 days after an institution has been served, it may apply to the United States District Court for an injunction to limit or suspend enforcement pending an administrative hearing required for issuance of a regular cease-and-desist order.

The small number of orders and the fact that most of them are of the regular type obtained with the institution's consent, and the fact that both the Bank Board and FDIC have used them sparingly, lend credence to the contention that the criteria for temporary orders are too demanding and that regular orders are difficult to obtain. Their use by the Board, and probably also by the FDIC, was also limited by the fact that a cease-and-desist order was not asked for unless both the Office of Examination and Supervision (OES) and the Office of the

General Counsel (OGC) were convinced that they had a good case. (OES is now the Office of Regulatory Policy, Oversight and Supervision.) They were concerned that losing cases in court would develop some bad case law, handicapping future supervisory efforts. This clearly brought a "degree of caution" (to use a Board attorney's phrase) in bringing cease-and-desist orders against an institution and explains the delay in the supervisory enforcement process. As previously noted, the Office of Enforcement has been separated from the Office of the General Counsel and now deals directly with the regional supervisory officials and the Board's members in bringing enforcement action. While not suggesting less caution in the use of enforcement orders, the decision process and paperwork has been shortened.

The limited use of cease-and-desist orders may be welcome to some in the business and a disappointment to others. Certainly to those involved in developing the supervisory law passed in 1966, it has not worked as expected or intended. The theory was that the Board (and FDIC, Comptroller and Federal Reserve) would use cease-and-desist and removal powers to supervise on a selective basis, taking action where needed against institutions and allowing those with capable, honest and careful management to proceed with a minimum of bureaucratic interference. Apparently too many safeguards against their use against good management (the due process provisions) have impeded their use against those for whom they were intended.

It may be, of course, that supervision has found it easier to regulate on a general rather than a selective basis, and that simple bureaucratic caution has worked against the use of this selective supervisory tool. It would not have been an appropriate tool to use against institutions having spread problems in 1980, 1981 and 1982. Certainly it has not prevented losses from improper lending and investing, excessive rates of growth, flagrant violations of rules against insider dealings and fraud. The business might consider improving cease-and-desist and other tools available to the supervisors.

The "due process" delays inherent in cease-and-desist and removal orders do not apply to discussions followed by supervisory agents obtaining "supervisory agreements." These sometimes "strong arm" procedures have caused much unhappiness in the business and have furthered the long-time antagonism between certain segments of the business and the supervisory establishment.

Over the years, the business has criticized the Bank Board for failing to close institutions which were insolvent and badly or dishonestly managed. In the case of state-chartered associations, the division of responsibility between state supervisors and federal supervisory operations has at times delayed supervisory process and deciding whether to put an institution in receivership or to force a change in management.

Before 1968, the Bank Board had difficulty in a few states having the FSLIC appointed as a receiver for a failed state-chartered, insured institution. Congress then gave clear direction that the FSLIC should act as receiver for state-chartered institutions. This authority was granted, incidentally, after protest by some state supervisors. The Garn-St Germain Act gave the FSLIC, on a temporary basis, extraordinary power to acquire failing insured institutions regardless of federal or state legal charter without necessarily having approval of state supervisory authorities. This authority expired October 13, 1986, with Congress' failure to enact any type of banking legislation, and was not restored until passage of the Competitive Equality Banking Act of 1987.

During this period, the declaration of insolvency and creation of a so-called pass-through receivership was held up for a number of state-chartered institutions whose state supervisors wanted to delay such final action and accompanying publicity. In other cases, takeover and the pass-through receivership delays have occurred because insolvency must be proved. The FSLIC will not take an institution into receivership, or otherwise deal with it as a failure, until (1) the FSLIC staff is satisfied that insolvency has been proved; (2) a "consent to merge" resolution has been obtained from the institution, or has at least been presented; and (3) the institution has been put up for sale in the state of domicile without any offer of FSLIC assistance and no buyers have been found. There would also have to be a recommendation from the principal supervisory agent, coming through the Office of Regulatory Policy, Oversight and Supervision, that the institution be put into receivership or otherwise dealt with as a case for FSLIC action either by an assisted merger, a liquidation or a pass-through receivership in the Management Consignment Program (MCP).

This MCP program was instituted in April 1985 to stem losses at some of the most severely troubled institutions and get the incompetent, or possibly dishonest, management out of the organization. Under the program, an institution's management and its board of directors are replaced with new management chosen by the FSLIC, generally from another well-managed and healthy association, under a management cost-plus contract; and a new board of directors is chosen by the FSLIC. Procedurally, the failed institution is declared insolvent, placed in receivership, and then all of its assets and liabilities are transferred immediately to a new federally chartered mutual association. The program has the advantage of delaying any cash outlay from the FSLIC and preserves the going concern value of the institution.

Some case resolutions have been delayed by a shortage of funds at the FSLIC. The pass-through receivership and use of the management consignment arrangement do not, of course, immediately involve any of the FSLIC's resources. Since this program was developed and first used in April 1985, 72 such actions in the space of a little more than 31 months have occurred, indicating considerable vigor dealing with failed institutions. Delay that does exist in the enforcement and receivership action at times comes from concern for an association's community image—and the need to avoid a "run." In addition, there's a willingness to let management find some way to bring in more capital or dispose of assets at a profit to return the institution to solvency. A shortage of FSLIC staff may also cause delays. As board members of management consignment institutions (one in California and one in Florida) the authors appreciate the amount of time FSLIC and regional Bank supervisory staff spend on these cases.

SUITS AGAINST OFFICERS AND DIRECTORS

To improve the moral tone of savings and loan operations and provide modest help in restoring the FSLIC fund, in 1983 the Bank Board began to sue officers and directors of failed institutions much more often, and forced them to restore funds to the institution or FSLIC. About 80 suits have been brought with about $150 million in judgments obtained. An unfortunate result has been the loss of fidelity and officer and director liability insurance protection for the business and a huge increase in premiums for insurance.

PERSONNEL WEAKNESS

While supervisory law provisions, the separation of examination and supervision and the procedures in place in the 1980s contributed to the inadequacies of the supervisory system and the subsequent FSLIC losses, the system also suffered far more seriously from personnel deficiencies—in number, ability and experience.

As problem cases piled up, not nearly enough examiners and supervisors were available. By 1984, many of the newly chartered institutions, or those acquired by new individuals, were growing at clearly excessive rates. Other institutions, managed by more traditional executives, were trying to grow out of their problems by entering new fields of finance and investing in ADC loans in distant markets. Reports flowing into the district Banks suggested that a great many institutions needed special examinations, supervisory attention and supervisory discipline, but the job simply overwhelmed the existing staff.

Importantly, the flow of data to the supervisory staff in the regional Banks was interrupted by a substantial revision in the nature and timing reports from all institutions to the supervisory staff. As part of the Reagan Administration's program to reduce reporting to government agencies, the Board eliminated (effective January 1, 1984) detailed monthly reports from associations to the regional Bank. It substituted a quarterly report and a bare-bones monthly report used essentially to permit the Board to continue its public reports of lending activities and savings flows.

New data were required for quarterly reports and many associations had trouble completing them. There were frequent errors. Some supervisory staff time had to be devoted to editing reports and sending them back for correction. Overall, this change to quarterly reports interrupted the flow of critical data to supervisors and to some extent destroyed continuous record keeping required for effective monitoring.

As access to brokerage money became available, associations could completely change in size and character between examinations. In addition, examinations often could not be conducted every year as they should be. Because data flows from monthly reports necessary for monitoring associations between examinations were interrupted, the checking between examinations was not as effective as it should have been. The Bank Board has now gone back to a rather detailed monthly report more useful to the supervisory process.

This situation permitted many new institutions and those with new managers or owners to proceed virtually undeterred with a rapid growth, high risk strategy. They, of course, filed the monthly and (later) quarterly reports and had the usual audits by professional accountants. Except for rapid growth, these typically showed no signs of trouble, given the misleading accounting for ADC loans which dominated their lending. In fact, national reporting services had many future failures heading their "most profitable" lists.

Not only was there a shortage of examiners, but many were simply not equipped, by background or experience, to understand and

TABLE 27: KEY CHARACTERISTICS OF SAVINGS INSTITUTIONS BY ANNUAL GROWTH RATES (Average of Institution Ratios)

Annual asset growth rate	Number of savings institutions	Assets of savings institutions	Annualized after-tax ROA	Net worth as a percentage of assets	Real estate development activities as a percentage of assets	Brokered deposits as a percentage of assets
First quarter 1984:						
5% or less	913	$227.4	−0.31%	4.16%	1.17%	2.21%
5% to 10%	504	125.2	+0.07	4.96	1.02	0.71
10% to 15%	466	114.1	+0.19	4.87	1.45	1.00
15% to 20%	314	91.4	+0.23	4.89	1.38	1.07
20% to 25%	205	72.4	+0.24	4.62	1.31	1.29
25% to 30%	124	33.9	+0.18	4.15	1.53	1.88
30% to 50%	264	81.6	+0.38	4.19	3.35	5.26
More than 50%	336	107.4	+0.62	5.08	6.42	12.27
Second quarter 1984:						
5% or less	1,020	$218.1	−0.02%	4.17%	1.31%	1.83%
5% to 10%	585	108.5	+0.40	5.13	1.13	0.46
10% to 15%	417	115.6	+0.46	4.68	1.20	0.84
15% to 20%	289	72.7	+0.40	4.44	1.78	1.39
20% to 25%	176	82.3	+0.58	4.27	1.88	2.40
25% to 30%	131	61.5	+0.55	4.31	3.54	2.79
30% to 50%	252	167.5	+0.71	4.37	3.91	5.85
More than 50%	275	114.5	+0.64	5.96	7.43	11.24

evaluate an association's operations. A review of investments in raw land required knowledge far beyond that of most examiners. ADC loans used very complex financing techniques, often involving land flips, fraudulent, though well documented, appraisals and participation sales to other savings and loan associations. Many associations began to finance commercial real estate ventures and condominium projects, often in distant cities, a field foreign to the experience of most of the examination and supervisory staff. Associations were also making commitments involving secondary markets and engaging in hedging techniques and other transactions in new financial instruments. In at least one district, examiners had to bring in a group of FDIC examiners to assist in their examination of a large institution's newly acquired portfolio of commercial bank type loans. In short savings and loan examination staffs had little or no experience in these areas. More serious, however, was examiner and supervisor naiveté with respect to transactions involving real estate.

There is literally no excuse for supervisors ignoring the fast growth at some institutions. They should have known even from their limited experience that fast growth—and particularly super growth—usually leads to serious problems.

For the savings and loan business, fast growth was closely correlated with the acquisition of high cost brokered deposits and heavy involvement in real estate development activities. Data published in the December 1984 issue of Savings Institutions underscored the problem. (See Tables 27 and 28.)

TABLE 28: GROWTH RATE IN FAST GROWING STATES
Growth of 50% or more annually (dollars in billions)

	Number of institutions		Assets of institutions	
	First quarter 1984	Second quarter 1984	First quarter 1984	Second quarter 1984
California	58	74	$ 43.9	$ 61.6
Florida	30	19	7.4	11.5
Texas	72	62	16.3	14.0
Three state total	158	155	$ 67.6	$ 87.1
Nationwide	336	275	$107.4	$114.5
Three states as a percentage of total	47%	56%	63%	76%

Source: Federal Home Loan Bank Board and U.S. League of Savings Institutions.

High-flying institutions that grew at annual rates of 50% or more during the first half of 1984 had the highest annualized after-tax return on average assets in the business, at 0.62%, and the highest net worth percentage, at 5.08%. Supervisors should have suspected that something was wrong; they should have instinctively known that such rapid growth and large profits could not have been sound. The same article in Savings Institutions noted that the super-growth savings institutions of the first half of 1984 were concentrated in the same three states that saw the worst disasters with real estate investment trusts (REITS) of an earlier period: California, Florida and Texas. These are the same three states with the most liberal laws for state-chartered associations. Forty-eight of the 72 associations placed in the management consignment program to October 6, 1987, were from these three states, as the following table notes:

TABLE 29: MANAGEMENT CONSIGNMENT CASES

California	25
Texas	16
Louisiana	8
Florida	7
Illinois	7

Dealing with the managements of these super-growth institutions, of course, may have been another matter, and there is no way of knowing without seeing their files what action supervisors might have taken. Supervisory officials say that these institutions were put on special examinations and efforts were made to monitor their activities, but this came at a time when examination staffs were stretched pretty thin. They did not take supervisory caution or suggestions seriously. Given the due process provision in the supervisory law and audited statements showing high earnings and strong net worth, it would have been impossible to issue cease-and-desist orders or supervisory directives and have the owners accept them. Fast and decisive supervisory intervention that might have prevented losses often was not possible even if supervisors had the foresight and toughness to take necessary action.

DISHONESTY

Congressional investigators, looking at association failures in California, concluded that fraud in many thrifts reached excessive proportions. In Texas, a task force of federal prosecutors and FBI agents is studying records of at least 290 developers, bank and savings and loan executives in what may be the largest white collar crime investigation in U.S. history. Those being investigated include public officials, developers and executives of financial institutions, both within Texas and in other states.

While many transactions, loans and investments that led to losses may or may not have been fraudulent, it is clear there were many cases of extensive and illegal insider dealings and apparent violations of rules dealing with loans to one borrower. Some transactions between associations involved moving loans around to inflate profit figures. Called "daisy chaining," loan trades were used to hide or disguise illegal transactions and to increase earnings. This practice of land-flips, "Texas style," was described in an article in the Dallas Times Herald which is reproduced in Addendum F. Land-flips first came to the attention of the Board staff in 1982. It was a difficult practice for examiners to deal with, almost requiring a special task force to trace complex transactions, understand them and develop a case for supervisory action.

Unfortunately, the practice began to spread in Texas as the 9th District Bank was moving from Little Rock to Dallas with accompanying supervisory personnel weaknesses throughout the district. Threats to the solvency of institutions from this practice really did not become known to the business until the publicity about Empire Savings of Mesquite (from Congressional hearings on that case in 1984). Illegally inflated earnings were at times used as the basis for high dividends to owners of institutions.

One of the egregious transactions involved State Savings and Loan Association of Salt Lake City, which was purchased by J. William Oldenburg of San Francisco in 1983 for $10.5 million. As reported in the San Francisco Herald-Examiner issue of April 29, 1984, Oldenburg on March 20, 1984, caused State Savings to buy for $55 million a 363-acre property he owned in Richmond, California, known as Glen Park Estates. Newspapers reported that he bought this parcel of land in 1977 for $874,000, paying $80,000 down. In 1979, the land was appraised at $8.5 million. Two years later, an appraiser hired by Oldenburg appraised the land at $32.5 million although nothing had been built on it. The Herald-Examiner reported that in 1982 the same appraiser reappraised the land at $83.5 million ($229,000 per acre). After securing a second appraisal for the same amount, the land was sold to State Savings for $55 million. The transaction was more than seven times the legal limit of State Savings for a single real estate investment.

Illegally inflated earnings were at times used as the basis for high dividends to owners of institutions. Insider stock deals apparently were also involved in at least one association in Arkansas with insiders withholding information about the institution's deteriorating status while selling a portion of their own stock. (See Addendum D.) Bad loans were often hidden by selling them to insiders who, in turn, borrowed from the institution, allowing the institution to take such loans off its books while replacing them with loans that would be current for at least a short time.

Supervisory officials report that it is extremely difficult to detect cases of some types of lending that violate rules against insider transactions and loans to one borrower. It takes a determined examiner to go through all the transactions that may be involved, often through multilevel corporations with disguised ownerships.

Ways perpetrators of illegal transactions can cover up their activities include multilevel corporations, unrecorded loan transactions and dishonest internal audit practices. Reports made to directors, examiners and outside auditors may deliberately be inaccurate and misleading. Cooperation between examiners and management is completely absent. Examiners can spend hundreds of hours trying to determine the nature and extent of fraudulent transactions. This often helped delay the supervisory process.

Because of publicity emphasizing the more sensational aspects of association mismanagement, there may be an overemphasis on the extent to which dishonesty was responsible for savings and loan failures in recent years. Many flagrant instances of dishonesty and indictable offenses undoubtedly occurred. Material provided in November 1987 to the House Subcommittee on Commerce, Consumer and Monetary Affairs by the Board's Office of Enforcement indicated that, in the past three years, criminal misconduct and insider abuse were the principal factors or "significant contributing factors" in 20% of the institutions closed, merged or placed in the management consignment program. In the previous three years, the indicated percentage was 23%.[25]

---

[25] The following is an excerpt from material presented to the Committee on November 19, 1987, with respect to losses from January 1, 1985, to June 30, 1987, by the FSLIC from "misconduct" by insiders and affiliated outsiders: "A.1. The Board does not have sufficient data to enable it to attribute a specific dollar amount of the losses suffered by the Federal Savings and Loan Insurance Corporation ('FSLIC') insurance fund to insider misconduct. However, the staff has given its best estimates of the ultimate losses FSLIC will suffer in failed institutions where insider misconduct contributed significantly to failures. Of course, these figures are greater, and may be significantly greater, than the losses attributable to misconduct alone. Given (various estimating) limitations,

The House study supports our basic finding that causes far more fundamental than dishonesty led to most association failures during the 1980s, including management failure to adhere to high standards of prudence. In most instances, conservatism gave way to unusual risk taking because of pressures of the marketplace, including pressures to rebuild net worth and, as noted, suggestions from supervisors to take advantage of opportunities provided by new laws and liberalized regulations.

The question is sometimes raised, why didn't savings and loan managers "blow the whistle" on institutions whose reckless operations and lending practices must have been known to their peers. This question was put to several savings and loan executives, who made the following generalized comments.

Competing managers did not have access to the operating data going monthly, and then quarterly, to the Home Loan Banks. The only data they had were reports, certified by the public accountants, made public annually. In many instances, as noted, these were misleading. As for lending and investment practices, the high flyers frequently made their most risky loans in distant markets, or purchased participations from other high flyers. No executive would have a factual basis for criticism of these loans or lending practices.

Managers would often express to Home Loan Bank officials concern about high growth institutions. They knew instinctively that excessive growth in a short time often leads to bad lending. Observations made to supervisors, however, would usually be returned with essentially "no comment." Supervisors are proscribed from discussing supervisory cases outside the supervisory establishment, particularly with competitors of the criticized institutions.

Association executives generally assumed that supervisors were doing their job. Those serving on boards of regional Home Loan Banks were given no supervisory information and carefully kept out of the supervisory process. Also, at times high flyers received good press and showed up on the national listings of the most profitable and

---

(Footnote 25 continued)

the estimated potential loss to FSLIC from all causes where misconduct is a significant contributing factor was $88.92 million in 1984, $53.4 million in 1985, $1.77 billion in 1986, and $1.87 billion for the first half of calendar year 1987. This represents estimated losses from 43 institutions, or 20% of the 210 institutions closed, merged, or placed in conservatorship or the MCP program. By comparison, the Board's estimate given to this Subcommittee in 1984 was that in 23% of the 30 thrifts placed in involuntary receivership between January 1980 and June 1983, criminal misconduct was a major contributing factor."

best reserved institutions. Criticism of them to the supervisors often had the ring of sour grapes or competitive jealousy. This is not to suggest that savings and loan executives did not often raise questions with supervisory authorities. Whether they told supervisors anything not already known is, of course, not reported. As noted frequently in this book, supervisors needed reasonably hard evidence of wrongdoing or insolvency before taking strong enforcement action.

FAILURE TO EXPAND EXAMINATION STAFF

There was no move during the latter years of the 1970s to beef up the examination and supervisory staff. No progress was made in this direction under Board Chairman Pratt, although the vital legislative underpinning of reform was secured with Garn-St Germain. Table 30 shows the size of the district or field examination staff from 1976 through 1985.

The totals for years before 1976 were approximately as follows:

1936	155
1946	262
1956	510
1966	755

It is easy to note that the number of people in the field with respect to the examination process, as distinct from supervision, clearly did not grow in proportion to the growth of the business, and certainly not in proportion to the complexity of the business. It is particularly disturbing that the number of examiners in the field actually declined each year from 1981 through 1984.

The Board in its budget submitted to the congressional Appropriations Committees in 1984 actually requested 38 fewer positions in the Bank Board's field examination staff resulting in a "saving" of $300,000. Testimony in behalf of the budget to the Senate Appropriations Committee on May 5, 1983, was presented by Chairman Gray, who assumed that position only five days previously. Gray has indicated that the budget materials he presented were developed and prepared by the staff under the previous chairman, Richard Pratt. The material submitted to the Appropriations Committee in support of the requested budget suggested that the reasons for the staff reduction were:

1. Reduction in the number of institutions being examined;

2. The expectancy of a healthier business in fiscal year 1984;

TABLE 30: OFFICE OF EXAMINATION AND SUPERVISION; DISTRICT OFFICE POSITIONS

	1976	1977	1978	1979	1980	1981	1982	1983	1984	1985 Est.*
District Directors	12	12	12	12	12	12	12	12	12	12
Asst. District Directors	45	43	45	45	45	45	45	44	42	42
Civil Rights Specialists	—	—	—	12	12	12	11	8	7	7
Real Estate Appraisers	16	16	14	13	13	13	13	12	9	14
Field Managers	98	98	88	90	90	90	90	89	94	94
Examiners	534	535	651	638	638	652	631	613	596	613
Clerical	110	109	109	109	109	113	115	113	115	115
TOTAL	815	813	919	919	919	937	917	891	875	897

Source: Federal Home Loan Bank Board

*Budget authorization. District examiners transferred to Federal Home Loan Banks effective July 7, 1985.

3. Expected savings as a result of management efforts to reform the examination process through greater reliance on computer-based analysis and monitoring in the examination office.

By early 1983, of course, the bad asset problems had not begun to surface and, in fairness to the Board under Chairman Pratt, it had not taken an extraordinary number of examiners or "super examiners" to assess the spread problems that had dominated the Board's supervisory concerns in the Pratt years. It was obvious when institutions were close to zero net worth. At the same time, the Reagan Administration was engaged in economy moves and efforts to reduce the federal work force. These efforts were directed at the Bank Board as well as taxpayer-supported government departments.

Chairman Pratt left office just as new entrepreneurs were entering the business, new laws were being fully utilized by an increasing number of institutions, and ADC loans with their questionable accounting were rapidly emerging.

It was not until Chairman Gray had been in office for about a year that the need for reform in this phase of the Board's operation began to receive the chairman's attention and became a priority project.

The examination and supervisory staff that was adequate during the 1960s and 1970s should have been built up along with the moves toward deregulation and the broadening of the scope of savings and loan operations. During the Carter Administration, there were few problems in the business and examiner attention turned to the enforcement of the consumer law and thrust of the Community Redevelopment Act, with its anti-redlining concerns. Little thought apparently was given in the early 1980s to the examination and supervision side of the Board's operation by Chairman Pratt, his senior staff and the Board members. Supervision, both at the regional Banks and in Washington, was then concerned with the severe earnings squeeze and dealing with the problems of shrinking net worth, and closing, merging, or putting into "Phoenixes" those institutions whose net worth had disappeared.

Instead of concentrating on the examination and supervisory process, the Pratt Board primarily was interested in remaking the business. The Board wanted fewer associations and to move the business away from its tradition of community, mutual organizations devoting almost all their resources to home loans to a business that theoretically would be able to survive the full force of market competition in attracting funds. Thus the Board took off the asset regulatory limits, drafted Garn-St Germain's liberalizing investment powers and welcomed similar action for state-chartered associations.

The Reagan Administration's concept of deregulation was fully tried on the savings and loan business. The Board devoted its creative thinking to that direction, not realizing the future perils of lower inflation rates, overbuilding in many real estate markets, and the inevitability of new entrants into the business.

The Board's ability to maintain a competent examination and supervisory staff—indeed an adequate staff throughout its entire operation—has always been limited because expenses are subject to the congressional appropriations process. From the standpoint of the Board chairmen, meeting staff needs was limited by how much the Office of Management and Budget was willing to allow the Board to request of Congress. OMB's pressure on the Board to limit its authorized staff, including the examining staff, goes back at least to the Carter Administration. Board chairmen had little choice but to generally go along. The Board could not ask congressional committees for a greater authorization than the OMB would permit.

In the Reagan Administration, OMB zealously promoted deregulation, reductions in government personnel and reports required of the business. OMB was determined to control the Board's operations and displayed an intransigent attitude toward the Board's budget and staff size. The OMB rigidly opposed transfer of examiner forces to regional Banks.

As noted earlier, the Board requested fewer examiners for fiscal year 1984. This was done in part from an honest belief that examinations could be done with fewer people and also a desire to accommodate the OMB. Examination forces also suffered from excessive turnover and lack of experience, both of which can be attributed to generally low salaries.

Table 31 shows entry level and average salary of Bank Board examiners in comparison with salaries of the Office of the Comptroller of the Currency, the FDIC and Federal Reserve Board.

TABLE 31: SALARY COMPARISONS OF BANK REGULATORY AGENCIES 1984

	FHLBB	OCC	FDIC	FRB
Entry Level	$14,390	$ 17,000	$ 17,750	$ 17,690
Diff. from FHLBB		$ +2,610	$ +3,360	$ +3,300
Average Salary	$24,775	$ 30,764	$ 32,505	$ 37,900
Diff. from FHLBB		$ +5,989	$ +7,730	$ +13,125

Source: Federal Home Loan Bank Board .

TABLE 32: TURNOVER RATE AMONG EXAMINERS (by grade)

Grade	1980			1981			1982			1983			1984		
	A	B	C	A	B	C	A	B	C	A	B	C	A	B	C
GS-05	7	39	18%	9	68	13%	12	41	29%	13	41	32%	12	70	17%
GS-07	11	54	20	11	58	19	12	68	18	13	41	32	5	71	7
GS-09	7	113	6	13	84	16	12	78	15	5	87	6	9	79	11
GS-11	22	123	18	11	148	7	18	143	12	14	143	10	24	129	19
GS-12	30	231	13	18	231	8	20	245	8	36	231	16	28	199	14
GS-13	9	138	6	10	140	7	14	132	11	11	126	8	16	147	11
TOTAL	86	698	12%	72	729	10%	88	707	12%	92	669	14%	94	695	14%

Source: Federal Home Loan Bank Board

Column A: Separations.
Column B: Number in grade.
Column C: Turnover Rate (%) = Column A ÷ Column B

Table 32 shows the number of examiners in each grade and the turnover rate, i.e., the number of separations in the year as a percentage of the total in the grade from 1980 to 1984.

The turnover rate in fiscal year 1984 for each district is shown in Table 33.

TABLE 33: TURNOVER FOR FHLBB EXAMINING STAFF
(Fiscal Year 1984)

District No.	Percent
1	8.8%
2	12.8
3	9.8
4	28.3
5	9.6
6	21.9
7	13.3
8	14.5
9	23.5
10	22.5
11	10.8
12	23.7
Total District	16.1
Government-wide	11.4 (FY 1983 data)

Source: Federal Home Loan Bank Board

The following are cited as reasons for the resignations:

28% resigned to enter private industry;
12% transferred to other federal agencies;
13% resigned for personal reasons;
2% terminated for unsatisfactory performance;
The remaining group gave no reasons for leaving.

It is interesting to note the percentage of trainee examiners, i.e., those with experience of two years or less in several of the districts, compared with the total number of examiners. (See Table 34.)

TABLE 34: PERCENTAGES OF TRAINEE EXAMINERS (GS-5/7) IN SELECTED DISTRICTS (Fiscal Year 1984)

District 4, Atlanta	27%
District 7, Chicago	22%
District 9, Dallas	43%
District 10, Topeka	19%
All Districts	22%

Salaries for examiners and all Board personnel, except those appointed by the President and in certain exempt positions (department heads, for example), are subject to the Personnel Classification Act of 1949 and under the Office of Personnel Management's control. This agency administers the compensation system for the entire federal government. It provides for the Board pay scales and compensation system to be identical to those of the rest of the federal government, except for a few agencies exempt from the Personnel Classification Act. The agencies exempt from this act include the FDIC, Federal Reserve and the Office of the Comptroller of Currency. This explains generally low starting salaries and average pay for examiners compared with those for banking agencies.

Chairman Pratt had problems with OMB in the area of FSLIC authorizations. OMB wanted to control not only the overall total of the Corporation's expenditures, but also the amounts that could be disbursed in the variety of ways FSLIC insurance cases could be settled. Specific amounts were allocated to various programs, and Chairman Pratt was severely criticized by OMB for essentially transferring funds allocated for one type of insurance settlement to another. The problems of Chairman Gray with OMB finally resulted first in the transfer to the Federal Home Loan Banks of the examiner force out from under control of the appropriations process and OMB, and later the transfer of the Office of Examination and Supervision to the Home Loan Banks in the Office of Regulatory Policy Oversight and Supervision. This is further discussed in the next section.

Chairman Gray was hindered in not being able to go over the head of the OMB deputy director responsible for the operations of the Board and some 15 other federal agencies. He was never able to communicate directly with the head of the OMB and did not receive responses to his requests to the OMB director for added staff and higher grade personnel. It can safely be said that the OMB is partially to blame for a breakdown of the examination and supervisory processes and losses that resulted.

Other government departments and agencies over the years have had similar problems with OMB. Some believe such problems became worse with the Reagan Administration and its determination to reduce the size of the government. These problems were the same regardless of whether the agency was financed with taxpayer funds or funds of the business being regulated, such as the Bank Board.

OMB and Office of Personnel Management (OPM) control of the Board's personnel (both its number and compensation, including the Civil Service classification rules for hiring, advancement and firing) contrasted with the greater budget and personnel freedom long enjoyed by the FDIC, Federal Reserve, and to a lesser degree by the Office of the Comptroller of the Currency. The reason for subjecting the Board to the congressional budget process is shrouded in history, but the business was never enthusiastic about changing the situation. In fact, historically, the business took certain comfort from the fact that the Board had to go to the Congress to get authority to "spend our money." It provided an oversight operation over the Board and helped keep the bureaucracy and number of examiners to a minimum, which the business welcomed. The business always complained about examination costs and alleged examiner and supervisory "nit-picking."

Occasionally, the Board made an effort to get out from under the budget process. It rarely had much chance with or without the business' support. The business failed to realize that the Board's ability to do an effective examination and supervisory job was key to preventing additional FSLIC assessments and using the Home Loan Banks' net worth to bring needed funds into the FSLIC. However, since 1983 the U.S. League has supported moves to get the Bank Board out from under OMB control.

The FSLIC's resources had always been adequate. The business, after all, under its narrow laws and Regulation Q protection, undertook few risks and the large institutions were responsibly managed. The business assumed that the pipeline to the Treasury was usable, and that the full faith and credit of the government—not surviving institutions—stood behind the FSLIC as Congress by resolution had affirmed.

EXAMINER TRANSFER TO FHL BANKS

To the credit of the business, it did support the Bank Board's program to move examiners from the Board and Civil Service system to Federal Home Loan Banks. This initiative came after the Office of Management and Budget repeatedly failed to respond to the Board's pleas for a larger, better paid examination force, and after Congress once again failed to remove the Board from under OMB and the budget process.

Examiners moved to regional Home Loan Banks on July 6, 1985. Since then, the examination force has increased from 747 to 1,424 as of October 31, 1987. Data by Bank districts are shown in Table 35 on the following page.

TABLE 35: NUMBER OF FHLB EXAMINERS

FHLBank of	7/06/85	12/31/85	12/31/86	10/31/87
Boston	34	40	58	50
New York	60	81	120	103
Pittsburgh	42	50	69	52
Atlanta	95	123	203	199
Cincinnati	72	94	138	131
Indianapolis	33	49	74	59
Chicago	80	102	147	141
Des Moines	57	67	99	107
Dallas	116	160	251	210
Topeka	33	50	79	81
San Francisco	90	138	223	232
Seattle	35	49	63	59
Totals-Examiners	747	1,003	1,524	1,424

Source: Federal Home Loan Bank Board

Average salaries of experienced senior examiners increased about $7,000 to $10,000 from 1985 to mid-1987. The top salaries are today some $10,000 higher than in 1984. Entry level salaries are now $20,000 compared with $14,390 in 1984.

Also significant has been the examination system's new ability to have flexibility to acquire experienced, senior level staff and pay them well above entry-level salaries. For example, they can now hire CPAs, computer scientists and various financial analysts. This was not possible before examiners moved to the regional Banks.

A great increase in examiner training has also occurred. At least in some districts, training costs average about $15,000 per examiner over a two-year period. The program involves 45 training days in addition to on-the-job experience. Today enough examiners are available to do the job and a system is in place to improve examiner ability and experience.

At the same time, supervisory staff at regional Banks has roughly doubled, and substantially higher salaries are paid to Bank supervisory officers. The Board's Office of Examination and Supervision has been transferred from the Board to the Federal Home Loan Bank System and reestablished as the Office of Regulatory Policy Oversight and Supervision. It is now funded by assessments levied on the Federal Home Loan Banks, thus coming from under the Board's OMB-Congressional budget process. This helped improve the size and salaries of Washington's supervisory staff and permitted hiring professionals with greater experience.

All of this reorganization and upgrading, however, came several years too late. By July 1985, when improvements began, losses the business must pay for today were already inevitable. These steps should have taken place along with, or even before, deregulation—not four years later.

An increasing part of the supervisory routine and decision-making authority has been delegated to the Home Loan Bank staffs, thereby accelerating the process and helping prevent delay and indecision. Supervisory operations in regional Banks evidently have responded to directives to supervisory agents issued by Chairman Gray in 1984 and 1985 with more effective and resolute action. A greater willingness to make prompt use of the supervisory tools available to the Board has also occurred. Delay in placing failed institutions into receivership or the management consignment program throughout most of 1987 was caused by the FSLIC's lack of funds and some disarray at the Board in Washington, not the examination and supervisory process.

The supervisory staff has been learning from experience. It realizes that the business is no longer conducted by "gentlemen," as one former Board official noted, and that institutions can get into trouble in far more ways than they could before deregulation.

EXAMINATION AND SUPERVISORY SYSTEM IN RETROSPECT

Reviewing the history of the Board's examination and supervisory operation in the early 1980s, including its failure to expand and strengthen the examination and supervisory staffs until 1985, it is apparent that the Board's leadership overestimated the ability of savings institution managers to respond to deregulation and handle new powers given them by liberalizing or repealing of regulations and the passage of Garn-St Germain. The Pratt Board clearly did not foresee the extent to which some state laws would be liberalized and abused by unscrupulous entrepreneurs.

Throughout the history of the Board, the examination process dealt with little beyond regulatory compliance. Perhaps this is because of the presumption that examiners were to be purely fact finders and that the "do's and don'ts" were expressed in regulations and written rulings. The Examination Operations and Procedures Manual also had a lot of material irrelevant to the financial soundness of an institution, such as checking for compliance with the Community Reinvestment Act and the complex Truth-in-Lending regulations. Examiners were instructed to check for regulatory compliance, but were not trained or experienced in financial analysis.

In the latter months of the Pratt administration, a program was started to train examiners in financial analysis and to help them understand the new world in which the business was operating. The Director of Examination and Supervision suspended arbitrary adherence to the examination manual. The goal was to encourage examiners to concentrate on financial ratios and other measures of the quality of an institution's loan and investment portfolio.

By mid-1983, new powers were on the books and being used, but the wrong kind of people were coming into the business. The examination staff was not equipped by experience or ability to become financial analysts instead of fact finders. For years, they had been trained to check for regulatory compliance; it would take years before they could be counted upon to do much more than that. In contrast, commercial bank examiners had always been prepared to look for more than regulatory compliance. There were, however, few regulations applicable to commercial bank operations. Bank examiners had always looked at the financial side of a bank's operation and were trained to evaluate a bank's loan portfolio. In this connection, we've reproduced an article in Addendum G which outlines the examination and supervisory procedures of the FDIC. Readers should note the heavy emphasis on loan quality, capital adequacy and the steps used to secure compliance with examiner findings and recommendations.

In March 1983, just as institutions started to use powers given by the Garn-St Germain law, Richard Pratt resigned the chairmanship of the Board. With him went the Board's general counsel, the director of the Office of Examination and Supervision, the director of the FSLIC and the chief economist. Not only did the department heads leave, but so did many of their deputies.

Edwin Gray became chairman April 29, 1983. Along with Gray came two new members, Donald Hovde and Mary Grigsby. All had excellent backgrounds but were unfamiliar with the rising challenges facing the Board. The Board and its new office directors had to learn the nuances of their positions. Some important staff positions remained vacant for months. Throughout the personnel change in mid-1983, it is fair to say that the Board was unable to see the emerging problems for five or six months—a critical period in the development of problems that surfaced later.

It should also be noted that in the first months of 1983, the business had reason to be quite optimistic. Interest rates had peaked,

Garn-St Germain was on the books with its promise of a new life for institutions, savings were flowing back with the new money market deposit accounts, a building boom was underway and institutions were writing a significant number of ARM loans. Those institutions still around congratulated themselves on surviving a few years of deeply red income statements. At this point, the business really had no way of knowing that a number of institutions were being operated in a reckless and fraudulent manner. Without some lead from the Board or Bank presidents, there was no reason for the business to worry about the adequacy of the Board's supervisory and examination personnel, or to question the Board's ability to deal promptly with its problem cases.

This same optimism must have been felt by the Board as it prepared its budget for fiscal year 1984 and made future plans. Chairman Gray's initial speeches did not express any need for caution or spread any alarm. After some six months in office, however, he realized that new charters were being granted and given FSLIC insurance much too freely. As a result, the Board put in a regulation tightening the requirements for FSLIC insurance of de novo institutions. He began to express concern about what was happening in the business. In a speech to the U.S. League's convention in November 1983, he pointed out the problem of brokerage money. His public remarks in early 1984 dealt extensively with the potential problems to the FSLIC from rapid growth at institutions using brokerage funds. With the FDIC, the Board then began its effort to curb the use of brokerage funds through regulations (which later were aborted by the Federal Court). In February 1984, the Board proposed a substantial revision of the reserve regulations in an attempt to slow down rapid deposit growth not supported by adequate capital.

Beginning in late spring of 1984, Chairman Gray began to raise the specter of losses stemming from bad assets, a theme he emphasized regularly thereafter, and in May the Board proposed its so-called direct investment regulation. It also began to draft a substantial revision of the supervisory law, as discussed earlier.

Empire Savings of Mesquite, Texas, was closed in March 1984, and the details of its operations became public with the July 31 report of the House Committee on Government Operations. State Savings of Salt Lake City failed in early summer of 1984 after extensive publicity in the San Francisco press about the transactions of its owner, J. William Oldenburg. A major front page article about State Savings appeared on June 8, 1984, in *The Wall Street Journal.* Then came the overpublicized failures in Ohio and Maryland of associations insured or guaranteed by state funds (instead of the FSLIC) and subsequent runs on other non-FSLIC-insured associations in these states.[26]

From late May 1984 until at least early fall, the Board and its senior staff had to spend an inordinate amount of time on problems surrounding Financial Corporation of America and its affiliate, American Savings, then the largest association in the world.[27]

It was not until November that the Board reassessed developments in the business generally and reproposed the net worth regulation in substantially modified and improved form. By then, opposition by the business to a regulation designed to slow down the growth rate of the many institutions obviously growing too fast had lessened. The Board was convinced it had to go ahead with this regulation and the direct investment regulation, which was reproposed in December. Unfortunately, the final promulgation of these regulations was delayed in part by early opposition from a large segment of the business, the preoccupation of the Board with the FCA, various congressional inquiries and dealing with the problems in Ohio and Maryland. It permitted the "high flyers" another year of unfettered growth and the acquisition of billions of assets that must now be dealt with by the FSLIC and by institutions in the management consignment program.

For a period afterwards, the net worth regulation was apparently not enforced in a way to curb excessive growth in some districts, and

---

[26] Actually, the number of failed institutions was far less than the publicity led most to believe. Of the 72 state fund guaranteed associations in Ohio, only two were outright failures. The failure of Home State Savings in Cincinnati and an affiliate association in Dayton led the governor to close the remaining 70. Twenty became FDIC banks or were merged into commercial banks, 32 obtained FSLIC insurance and resumed normal operations and 18 were merged into FSLIC-insured associations. In Maryland, four associations were placed in receivership, four were taken over by commercial banks with financial assistance from the state, one association is being resolved, two have continued to operate but with restrictions on withdrawals, two more remain closed with an uncertain future; a total of 13 state guaranteed associations which might be considered failures.

[27] The mid-1984 controversy with FCA developed with an announcement on May 20 by the corporation that it would issue $225 million in subordinated debt and use the proceeds to purchase approximately one-quarter of its outstanding common stock. This announcement was made without the prior approval or knowledge of the Bank Board, which then stated that this transaction could not proceed until FCA made application for and had received Board approval. This statement caused some increase in withdrawals, which accelerated after the Board, on June 20, announced that it disapproved the transaction. Then, in August, the Securities and Exchange Commission announced that it was ordering FCA to reverse some transactions involving mortgage-backed bonds which would result in FCA having a loss instead of a substantial gain in income. This caused a substantial "run" on the institution and the subsequent removal by the Bank Board of the chairman and chief executive officer and installation of a new management selected by the Bank Board.

there were delays in the supervisory process in many districts. In spite of warning signals raised by the failure in Mesquite, Texas, and Salt Lake City, the extensive publicity given to the abuse by their owner-managements and a few other early failures, the business perceived these as examples of supervisory negligence, or failure "to do its duty," as isolated breakdowns of supervision rather than basic weaknesses of the system. In his speeches, Chairman Gray made clear his concern. The business, however, began to grow weary of hearing Chairman Gray speak out about such problems. The extent of potential future losses and the need for examination, supervisory and regulatory reform was not really understood by the business until later.

NEW REGULATIONS THAT SHOULD HELP

Along with substantially improved examination and supervisory staff, a number of new Bank Board regulations (some still in proposed form) and provisions of the Competitive Equality Banking Act of 1987 should be helpful in reducing the probability of failures in the future. These are:

1. The new net worth regulation, first issued in January 1985 and substantially revised in August 1986. By action effective May 5, 1987, the Board acted to tighten the definition of regulatory capital. Effective July 27, 1987, the Board amended its net worth (regulatory capital) regulation to require incremental capital of up to 10% for all equity risk investments in addition to the direct investments, including land loans and nonresidential construction loans with loan-to-value ratios greater than 80%. This supports the direct investments regulation noted below. As of September 20, 1987, the Board has "on notice" a proposal to change the method of computing the annual calculation of the business' profits to determine compliance with the net worth regulation. The current net worth requirements should eliminate the possibility of excessive leveraging which contributed so much to the fast growth and careless lending in 1982, 1983 and 1984. This regulation has also slowed growth. Supervisory agents report that since the new net worth requirements have been in effect and strictly enforced, new supervisory problems seem to have abated.

2. The Competitive Equality Banking Act of 1987. This gave the Board clear authority to establish case-by-case capital

requirements for individual institutions (in contrast to the Board's historical practice of a general regulation applicable to all institutions). It will be required to conform, over time, its minimal benchmark requirements to those of the other federal banking regulators. The Board is also given the same authority that federal banking regulators have had to issue capital directives to institutions and to decide which directive may be enforced in court as a final agency order. This procedure completely short-circuits normal due process protections. Regulations implementing this authority were finalized in late December 1987.

3. The Board's so-called direct investments regulation. For the first time this put the Board in control of at least some investment and lending activities of state-chartered institutions. It has curbed speculative excesses and reduced the potential for exposing the business to greater risks generally inherent in nonresidential financing. The first direct investment regulation was effective March 1985 and substantially revised and tightened effective April 16, 1987.

   Effective July 27, 1987, the Board expanded its direct investments regulation to include land loans and nonresidential construction loans with loan-to-value ratios greater than 80%. At the same time, the Board amended the diversification requirements in single real estate projects applicable under the direct investment rule. It provides that no institution may invest without prior supervisory approval in any one real estate project an amount greater than its applicable aggregate loans to one borrower limits.

4. The Board has proposed a regulation to strengthen the loan to one borrower limitations, basically to prevent loans to one borrower in excess of 25% of net worth, or $500,000. Issued on September 20, this proposal is still out for comment by December 1987. A number of institutions suffering major losses made loans to one borrower beyond prudent limits. The new proposed limits, together with more vigorous enforcement of the rules, should reduce major losses.

5. A regulation issued November 4, 1983, tightened the requirements for new federal charters and for insurance of newly chartered state institutions. The Board did not,

however, deal with the question of minimum number of stockholders.

6. In connection with the examination process, the Board in December 1985 adopted a classification of assets program similar to one used for commercial bank supervision. This regulation was intended to speed up and improve the review of institutions with a great number of troubled loans and investments, and to deal with those institutions with inadequate net worth. This routine became highly controversial. Reflecting its long history on the question of examiner-supervisory discretion, the business opposed the authority. It also feared that associations could be declared insolvent more easily as problems developed in the energy and agricultural sectors and loan delinquencies mounted in even conservative loan portfolios. On May 5, 1987, and again on October 2, the Board published a proposal modifying this classification of assets program. The latest revision was required by the Competitive Equality Banking Act of 1987 which requires the Board to publish a classification of assets system consistent with that of the federal banking regulators. This act vests principal supervisory agents with authority to require institutions to establish additional general loss reserves based on asset evaluation and to make classification determinations with regard to restructured assets. This regulation was finalized in late December 1987.

7. To deal with the problem of inadequate and often fraudulent appraisals, the Board in September 1986 revised its Series of "R" memoranda dealing with appraisal policies and practices. A new Memorandum R-41-(c) replaced Memorandum R-41-(b), issued in March 1982, which continued a series of memoranda dealing with appraisals initially issued in June 1977. The R-41-(c) Memorandum proved faulty; on May 5, 1987, the Board proposed a substantial revision in the form of a regulation dealing with appraisal practices. This proposed regulation was withdrawn on October 2. It was re-proposed in accordance with the Competitive Equality Banking Act of 1987 which directs the Board to adopt an appraisal standard consistent with that of the federal banking regulators. In addition, the

agency is directed to use GAAP in reevaluating security property obtained in foreclosure (or in lieu of foreclosure). This regulation was finalized in late December 1987.

8. In May 1987, the Board adopted a regulation requiring federally insured institutions to switch to GAAP beginning January 2, 1989. The change affects primarily mutual institutions, as federal securities laws already require stock chartered associations registered under the 1934 Securities Act to report using GAAP. This action reverses some policies of the previous (Pratt) Board which permitted a number of "loose" accounting practices to help associations maintain reserves at the regulatory minimums. By its May 1987 move, the Board indicated that the number of institutions with negative net worth would increase from 252 to 461. The accounting for the business was put on a uniform basis and liberal accounting methods, as a way to maintain net worth, were eliminated. Again, in accordance with the Competitive Equality Banking Act of 1987, the Board rewrote this rule. The law provides that institutions may continue to use subordinated debt, goodwill, loan loss deferral and amortization in meeting reserve and other regulatory requirements. In addition, GAAP is not required where to do so would result in a savings institution and its holding company being treated differently than a bank and its holding company (considered on a consolidated basis), or where a transaction is not currently consistent with GAAP but was when completed. Institutions which demonstrate to the Bank Board's satisfaction that it is not feasible for them to achieve compliance with GAAP requirements by January 1989 may be permitted to comply by a later date, but not later than December 31, 1993.

9. Changes made by the American Institute of Certified Public Accountants and the Bank Board in 1984 and 1985 with respect to the accounting for acquisition, development and construction (ADC) loans have gone a long way in properly classifying these assets as between loans and direct investments, thus bringing them into greater supervisory control. The Board on March 4, 1987, proposed to tighten its statement of accounting policy relating to acquisition, development and construction (ADC) loans. By the end of December 1987, this proposal had not been finalized.

10. The 99th Congress rewrote the Change in Control law for banks and savings and loan associations effective October 27, 1986. If used properly and forcefully, it should give the Board much greater protection from reckless entrepreneurs. At the same time, the Board's supervisory staff must be more forthright in using the law's provisions and prevent individuals from taking control of FSLIC-insured institutions. Where questions arise about a person's, or group's, fitness to own or manage an association, an institution should certainly be put on a watch list. Supervisory agreements should then be put in place as a condition for approval of the change in control and carefully enforced.

11. It also should be noted that the two most recent budgets for the Bank Board and FSLIC, approved by the Congress, authorize a substantial increase in FSLIC and other Board department staffs. The Office of Management and Budget must finally have realized that its program of trying to hold down the Board's staff size was counterproductive. Losses to the FSLIC cost billions of dollars in federal funds and are included in the federal government's budget totals, although the tab for the outlay is picked up by the savings and loan business.

    Whether this improved examination and supervisory procedure, together with new regulations and an added staff of examiners and supervisory personnel will result in minimizing failures remains to be seen. In the U.S. financial system, failures cannot be prevented, nor should there be a system that would entirely eliminate failures. There has, however, been too much exercise of the "right to fail," at least in the savings and loan system. The costs of failures to the FSLIC and, in turn, to the institutions that have avoided failures have been too great.

OTHER CHANGES THAT MAY BE NEEDED

Still more regulatory changes probably will be needed by the Bank Board and in the Bank System. Regulations, guidelines or broad examiner and supervisor discretion will be needed to monitor association transactions in money and secondary mortgage markets, in financial instruments (such as financial futures, options and interest rate swaps) and practices such as risk-controlled arbitrage.

The business, through payments for FSLIC insurance, has too much at risk to permit irresponsible state legislatures to control investment of their funds, particularly in light of the relatively weak enforcement provisions in many of the state laws and the inadequacy of most state examination and supervisory staffs. A limit must be placed on the price the business pays for a dual system in an era of modern communications and financial systems.

Also needed would be passage of the Board's proposed revisions of the supervisory law incorporated in H.R. 4998, presented to the 99th Congress with the modifications suggested by the U.S. League. There have been instances, possibly many, where associations violated provisions of supervisory agreements, directives and cease-and-desist orders. The law should provide means for rapid enforcement of these agreements or orders. The Board cannot control the high flyers and deal effectively with those whose operations can cost the FSLIC billions in losses with a law and system that permits these institutions to thwart supervisors. This, however, means giving the Board greater supervisory discretion over all the institutions—not just those identified as high flyers by more conservative associations.

The Bank Board has changed its supervisory system to become more like the commercial banking supervisory system. This involves giving examiners and supervisory agents more discretion, and not limiting them essentially to enforcing written regulations and rules. The commercial bank system, however, has not prevented failures and losses for the FDIC; the FDIC's record compared with the FSLIC's is not clear, given that the FDIC has not set up contingency reserves to reflect probable losses, as has the FSLIC.

Another lesson from the recent past is the importance of capital in operating financial institutions and the hazards of excessive leveraging. Measuring capital adequacy has always been, and will be, an inexact science. But efforts in that direction should not be abandoned as they were by the Board in 1980, just when the assets-based net worth requirement, operating in tandem with the traditional percent-of-savings test, should have been perfected instead of eliminated. At that time, however, the business was beginning to experience the effect of spread problems. A type of net worth "forbearance" for the business was generally the top priority. The Board's present thinking with respect to net worth in establishing net worth minimums or benchmarks to permit certain types of investment or lending activities is clearly appropriate. Institutions should be able to afford risks before taking them.

Hopefully, the business will support changes needed to prevent expensive mistakes, such as those made following deregulation—mistakes which exposed the business and the supervisory establishment's inability to deal with problems and risks inherent in a deregulated environment. The business can no longer afford to support all proposals for liberalizing laws and regulations and resist all new restrictive regulations as it has often done.

It is also to be hoped that the regulators will use any new authority in an intelligent and timely manner. The Board must be aware that the competitors of savings and loan associations are not subject to detailed regulations, and must be careful not to overregulate good institutions and those with competent management.

12 Deposit Insurance in a Deregulated Environment

Until at least the late 1970s, as this work shows, the purpose of supervision in the savings and loan field was essentially to prevent failure. Strict laws governing association operations and relatively inflexible supervision was the price (although grudgingly paid in many instances) for deposit insurance and the obvious benefits it brought—public confidence in a system which allowed institutions to obtain money at relatively low cost.

The government's response to the financial trauma of the late 1970s and early 1980s was to loosen this supervision and broaden the laws governing the business. This was done without ever confronting and thinking carefully about the basic conflict between a system of deposit insurance and deregulation of depository institutions.

American banking history is replete with examples of high failure rates accompanying an unregulated or underregulated banking system. There is some evidence to suggest that the government's financial policymakers were willing to accept a high failure rate as the price of deregulation.

Two key concerns were missing from this line of thinking. First, there seems to have been no worry about the adequacy of the FSLIC fund, based as it was on a premium level of 1/12 of 1%. Second, there certainly was no concern about who was going to supply the resources to meet massive failures caused by such extraordinary economic events as the rise and fall of serious inflation, variations in international currency exchange rates or the rise and collapse of energy prices.

First, consider the FSLIC premium of 1/12 of 1%. Some economists have argued that the current wave of failures and consequent drain on the FSLIC should be financed by the surviving FSLIC-insured institutions because they were benefiting in the past from a premium which was too low. This ignores the fact that the premium was quite adequate for the years before deregulation and that the premium rate was set on the assumption that the federal government was responsible for preventing failure and keeping the FSLIC solvent. Should the government fail in this responsibility, it would pay the price. That was the meaning of the "pipeline" to the Treasury and the promise by congressional resolution that the full "faith and credit" of the federal government stood behind the FSLIC.

In the past seven years, however, the government has indeed failed in its responsibility to prevent massive failures, thus necessitating the extra deposit insurance premiums. This governmental failure was manifested in many ways, all seemingly part of the Reagan Administration's deregulation philosophy, the liberal laws it sponsored and the Pratt Board's reformist approach. Contributing to the government's failure were the unwillingness to let the Bank Board build an adequate examination and supervisory staff; the lack of administration support for a strengthened supervisory law; the failure to make timely use of cease-and-desist orders; and the failure to adopt needed regulations promptly, with or without business support.

These governmental lapses presumably would have increased the number of savings institution failures in any event. Coupled with the unprecedented economic conditions generated by inflation, soaring interest rates, currency exchange variability, and energy and agricultural sector collapse, however, they all but guaranteed disaster for the business and the deposit insurance fund covering it.

Apparently no one considered the historical acceptance of limited risk-taking as the basis for a workable deposit insurance system. The limitations were removed, but no compensating adjustment or strengthening of the supervisory system was instituted.

In the 1930s, when deposit insurance was debated in banking and savings and loan circles, the choice was between free banking with minimum government interference with financial institutions on the one hand and public confidence gained by deposit insurance and federal supervision on the other.[28]

---

[28] Because of the way deposit insurance came to commercial banking immediately after the March 1933 bank holiday, commercial banks had no choice but to accept controls associated with it. Savings and loan and savings bankers, however, did exercise a choice. Thus, the co-operative banks and savings banks in Massachusetts did not come into the federal deposit insurance system until 1985 after the failure of state savings and loan insurance funds in Ohio and Maryland. This was true of some savings and loan associations and co-operative banks in other New England states as well. Most of the large, nonfederal savings and loan associations in the District of Columbia did not join the FSLIC until World War II. Many small associations in Ohio, Pennsylvania and Maryland stayed out of the federal deposit insurance system until 1985. A few other associations throughout the country, notably in Illinois, joined the system some years after it was first available in 1934, and then only reluctantly after federally chartered institutions aggressively promoted their insured deposits.

Deposit insurance proved to be worth a considerable loss of freedom for managers of financial institutions, and it certainly has been of immeasurable benefit to the American public. Since 1981, however, the goal has been to have both deposit insurance and more freedom for financial institutions. This has not worked well.

Both commercial banks and savings institutions have failed in numbers unheard of since the early 1930s. Whether the unhappy experience of the FSLIC provided enough warning to the FDIC to save it from a similar debacle is uncertain.

What is clear is that policymakers have not recognized the basic incompatibility of making insured deposits available for unregulated lending and investment. Commercial banks take international deposits amounting to billions of dollars, much of it then loaned to foreign borrowers, yet do not pay an insurance premium against these deposits. Large banks clamor to get into investment banking. The FDIC is caught with a "too big to fail" policy if things go awry.

A number of savings institutions have seized the opportunity of the past seven years to pursue reckless growth and unregulated investment, and the well-managed survivors are asked to pick up the cost of the resulting failures. Yet, these same survivors do not want to be fettered themselves in pursuing their own fund-gathering and investment policies.

The result is that the business today faces a decision somewhat like that made in the 1930s. This is not a decision whether or not to have federal deposit insurance or even to radically revise the present system. The public will not accept such ideas as reducing the insurance limit to $40,000 or $50,000, or requiring coinsurance whereby a depositor suffers the first 10% or 20% of loss. Variable premiums may evolve or higher net worth requirements may be keyed to levels of higher investment risk; but deposit insurance is here to stay.

The choice today, therefore, concerns the type of regulatory and supervisory system that should be developed to protect the deposit insurance funds. In the case of savings institutions, the choice relates to how the Bank Board should be empowered through a revision of the supervisory law enacted in 1966.

The options are (1) a system which relies on supervision enforcing written rules with examiners essentially checking for regulatory compliance, as in the past; or (2) more reliance on examiner and supervisor judgment (as in commercial bank supervision) and enforcement procedures with less due process protection to management and owners.

If the business prefers limited authority for supervisory officials to take over an institution, remove its officers and directors, and issue cease-and-desist orders (as under present law), then it must live with a regulatory system that spells out a great many of the 'do's' and 'don'ts.' Such a system must limit the business' ability to engage in activities beyond one- to four-family home loans. In effect, the business must be reregulated.

To have maximum freedom under the Garn-St Germain Act and even greater asset and liability freedom, and to leave untouched the authority of state legislatures to determine their own systems under which state-chartered institutions will operate, will require an examination and supervisory system that gives examiners and field supervisors considerable discretion. This includes the valuation of assets and the supervisory tools necessary promptly to enforce their orders.

The cost of deposit insurance for savings institutions must become comparable with that for commercial banks. If this is to occur, the business must avoid the kinds of massive failures and losses that have caused special FSLIC assessments and the great cost of the FSLIC recapitalization program to both the Federal Home Loan Banks and their member institutions.

The business must decide—and live with the decision—how to revise the regulatory and supervisory system to avoid yet another massive wave of failures.

Addenda

ADDENDUM A: Federal Savings and Loan Associations Act (Section 5 of the Home Owners' Loan Act of 1933) from the Conference Report No. 210 of the House of Representatives, June 8, 1933

Sec. 5. (a) In order to provide local mutual thrift institutions in which people may invest their funds and in order to provide for the financing of homes, the Board is authorized, under such rules and regulations as it may prescribe, to provide for the organization, incorporation, examination, operation, and regulation of associations to be known as "Federal Savings and Loan Associations", and to issue charters therefor, giving primary consideration to the best practices of local mutual thrift and home-financing institutions in the United States.

(b) Such associations shall raise their capital only in the form of payments on such shares as are authorized in their charter, which shares may be retired as is therein provided. No deposits shall be accepted and no certificates of indebtedness shall be issued except for such borrowed money as may be authorized by regulations of the Board.

(c) Such associations shall lend their funds only on the security of their shares or on the security of first liens upon homes or combination of homes and business property within fifty miles of their home office: Provided, That not more than $20,000 shall be loaned on the security of a first lien upon any one such property; except that not exceeding 15 per centum of the assets of such association may be loaned on other improved real estate without regard to said $20,000 limitation, and without regard to said fifty-mile limit, but secured by first lien thereon: And provided further, That any portion of the assets of such associations may be invested in obligations of the United States or the stock or bonds of a Federal Home Loan Bank.

(d) The Board shall have full power to provide in the rules and regulations herein authorized for the reorganization, consolidation, merger, or liquidation of such associations, including the power to appoint a conservator or a receiver to take charge of the affairs of any such association, and to require an equitable readjustment of the capital structure of the same; and to release any such association from such control and permit its further operation.

(e) No charter shall be granted except to persons of good character and responsibility, nor unless in the judgment of the Board a necessity exists for such an institution in the community to be served, nor unless there is a reasonable probability of its usefulness and success, nor unless the same can be established without undue injury to properly conducted existing local thrift and home-financing institutions.

(f) Each such association, upon its incorporation, shall become automatically a member of the Federal Home Loan Bank of the district in which it is located, or if convenience shall require and the Board approve, shall become a member of a Federal Home Loan Bank of an adjoining district. Such associations shall qualify for such membership in the manner provided in the Federal Home Loan Bank Act with respect to other members.

(g) The Secretary of the Treasury is authorized on behalf of the United States to subscribe for preferred shares in such associations which shall

be preferred as to the assets of the association and which shall be entitled to a dividend, if earned, after payment of expenses and provision for reasonable reserves, to the same extent as other shareholders. It shall be the duty of the Secretary of the Treasury to subscribe for such preferred shares upon the request of the Board; but the subscription by him to the shares of any one association shall not exceed $100,000, and no such subscription shall be called for unless in the judgment of the Board the funds are necessary for the encouragement of local home financing in the community to be served and for the reasonable financing of homes in such community. Payment on such shares may be called from time to time by the association, subject to the approval of the Board and the Secretary of the Treasury; but the amount paid in by the Secretary of the Treasury shall at no time exceed the amount paid in by all other shareholders, and the aggregate amount of shares held by the Secretary of the Treasury shall not exceed at any time the aggregate amount of shares held by all other shareholders. To enable the Secretary of the Treasury to make such subscriptions when called there is hereby authorized to be appropriated, out of any money in the Treasury not otherwise appropriated, the sum of $100,000,000, to be immediately available and to remain available until expended. Each such association shall issue receipts for such payments by the Secretary of the Treasury in such form as may be approved by the Board, and such receipts shall be evidence of the interest of the United States in such preferred shares to the extent of the amount so paid. Each such association shall make provision for the retirement of its preferred shares held by the Secretary of the Treasury, and beginning at the expiration of five years from the time of the investment in such shares, the association shall set aside one third of the receipts from its investing and borrowing shareholders to be used for the purpose of such retirement. In case of the liquidation of any such association the shares held by the Secretary of the Treasury shall be retired at par before any payments are made to other shareholders.

(h) Such associations, including their franchises, capital, reserves, and surplus, and their loans and income, shall be exempt from all taxation now or hereafter imposed by the United States, and all shares of such associations shall be exempt both as to their value and the income therefrom from all taxation (except surtaxes, estate, inheritance, and gift taxes) now or hereafter imposed by the United States; and no State, Territorial, county, municipal, or local taxing authority shall impose any tax on such associations or their franchise, capital, reserves, surplus, loans, or income greater than that imposed by such authority on other similar local mutual or cooperative thrift and home financing institutions.

(i) Any member of a Federal Home Loan Bank may convert itself into a Federal Savings and Loan Association under this Act upon a vote of its stockholders as provided by the law under which it operates; but such conversion shall be subject to such rules and regulations as the Board may prescribe, and thereafter the converted association shall be entitled to all the benefits of this section and shall be subject to examination and regulation to the same extent as other associations incorporated pursuant to this Act.

ADDENDUM B: Asset Composition and Net Worth Index

Asset Category	Minimum Net Worth Percentage

First Mortgage Loans and Contracts:
Insured or guaranteed mortgage loans 2

Mortgage loans, participations, and mortgage-backed certificates insured or guaranteed by an agency or instrumentality of the United States (except excluded assets) 2

Conventional mortgage loans
Single-family dwellings 3
Homes – 2-4 dwelling units 5
Multifamily – more than 4 dwelling units 6
Other improved real estate — commercial and industrial 7
Developed building lots and sites 6
Acquisition and development of land 8
Undeveloped land 8

Nonconforming mortgage loans and contracts to facilitate sale of real estate owned 8

Other loans:
Property improvement, alteration or repair
  Insured or guaranteed loans 3
  Other than insured or guaranteed loans 5
Educational loans
  Insured or guaranteed loans 2
  Other than insured or guaranteed loans 6
Mobile home chattel paper
  Insured or guaranteed 3
  Other than insured or guaranteed 6
Equipping and consumer loans 6
Unsecured consumer loans 15

Real Estate:
Foreclosed and in judgment 10
Held for development or investment 7
Office premises –
  Land and buildings 3
  Leasehold and leasehold improvements 3

Investment securities — Non-liquid:
    Securities other than those that qualify as liquid assets
    under Par. 523.10(g) or would so qualify except for maturity
    (except excluded assets) 3

Other assets:
    Furniture, fixture and equipment 10
    Investment in service corporations and other subsidiaries 5
    All other (except excluded assets) 3

(a) The following are "excluded assets" and shall not be included in any asset category under such Index:

    (1) Cash on hand and demand deposits in banks;

    (2) Loans on the security of savings accounts;

    (3) Prepaid FSLIC insurance premiums and secondary reserve prepayments;

    (4) Securities that qualify as liquid assets under Paragraph 523.10(g) of this chapter or would so qualify except for maturity;

    (5) Other securities fully guaranteed as to principal and interest by the United States, including any securities guaranteed by the Government National Mortgage Association;

    (6) Any obligations of, or participations or other instruments fully guaranteed as to principal and interest by the Federal Home Loan Mortgage Corporation;

    (7) Time deposits and bankers' acceptances that qualify as liquid assets under Paragraph 523.10(g) of this chapter;

    (8) Stock of a Federal Home Loan Bank or the Federal National Mortgage Association; and

    (9) Prepaid expenses.

(b) Deferred income (in any form) may not be deducted from any asset item.

(c) Accrued interest with respect to any asset shall be included in the same asset category as such asset.

NOTE: In computing the minimum net worth required under this formula, the five-year averaging arrangement (used in computing the alternative minimum) was not included.

ADDENDUM C:

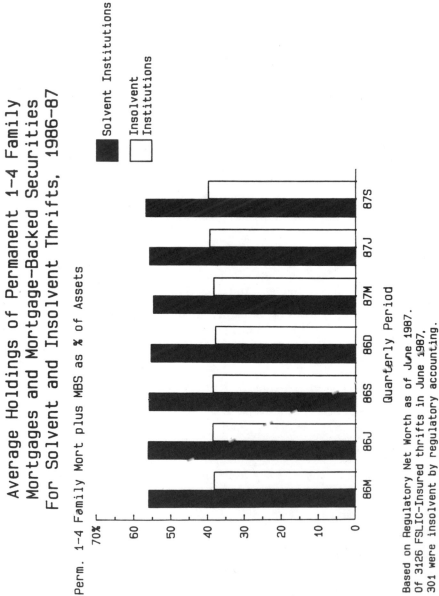

Average Holdings of Permanent 1-4 Family
Mortgages and Mortgage-Backed Securities
For Solvent and Insolvent Thrifts, 1986-87

Perm. 1-4 Family Mort plus MBS as % of Assets

Quarterly Period

- Solvent Institutions
- Insolvent Institutions

Based on Regulatory Net Worth as of June 1987.
Of 3126 FSLIC-Insured thrifts in June 1987,
301 were insolvent by regulatory accounting.

ADDENDUM D: Reprinted with permission from the August 30, 1987 *Washington Post*

Boom to Bust In Arkansas

Only Lawsuits Remain for FirstSouth S&L

By John M. Berry
Washington Post Staff Writer

LITTLE ROCK, Ark.—By the fall of 1983, Howard J. Wiechern Jr. had put it all together. With the help and encouragement of federal regulators, Wiechern had turned a small, stodgy savings and loan association in Pine Bluff, Ark., into the state's largest thrift institution. Southern Building and Loan had grown into FirstSouth FSB and its stock was snapped up by investors eager to share in its future.

Four years later, First South is gone. Last December federal authorities closed it down because it

was running out of cash. At the end, First South was still holding loans and other assets supposedly worth $1.7 billion. But it was so short of cash that it had sold its furniture and many of its branches and was leasing them back. The once-sought stock was worthless.

Officials involved in sorting out what is left of FirstSouth say it probably will take seven to 10 years to sell off its assets and pay whatever money is left to a multitude of creditors, many of whom may get only a few cents on the dollar. Depositors have been protected by the Federal Savings and Loan Insurance Corp., but the FSLIC now has to salvage what it can from FirstSouth's bad loans and bankrupt investments.

The loan losses at FirstSouth are so large that its failure is likely to be the most costly savings and loan collapse in history, costing FSLIC several hundred million dollars, said an official at the Federal Home Loan Bank Board, the federal agency that regulates savings and loan associations.

When the bank board ordered FirstSouth closed, more than $500 million worth of loans were in default and others have gone bad since. More than $600 million in loans to stockholders was discovered, though not all of them were in default or illegal.

Ultimately, American taxpayers may have to cover a share of the losses at FirstSouth, as well as at scores of other insolvent but still operating thrifts around the country. The FSLIC insurance fund has just been given a $10.8 billion bailout by Congress and may need billions more. FirstSouth is a prime example of why.

FirstSouth failed not just because of the plunge in oil prices that depressed the Sun Belt real estate markets in which it made many loans, but also because of stunningly sloppy business practices, reckless real estate speculation and massive insider loans, many of them illegal.

The Federal Bureau of Investigation is looking into allegations of fraud and FSLIC has sued Wiechern and other former FirstSouth officials for $150 million.

Summing up charges against FirstSouth executives, the FSLIC lawsuit said the defendants "recklessly and negligently allowed First-South to become a source of funds for favored real estate speculators and developers who gambled First-

South's resources away at little risk to themselves and at great cost to FirstSouth."

Though federal officials are now aggressively cleaning up after FirstSouth's fall, they not only consented to, but encouraged its rise and failed to monitor its explosive growth.

Despite danger signals flashed by earlier audits, FirstSouth was not examined by federal regulators between December 1982, and February 1985, Home Loan Bank Board officials admit. During that time, FirstSouth absorbed about a dozen smaller thrifts that regulators thought were or were about to be in financial trouble, and would be better off under the wing of FirstSouth.

Instead, the affiliation with FirstSouth pulled them into a whirlpool. During the critical 26 months when examiners weren't watching, FirstSouth grew from a $500 million institution to one with assets of $1.3 billion. Eventually it had more than $1.8 billion in assets on its books, though their true value was hundreds of millions less than that.

Howard Wiechern's strategy for growth was to deemphasize long-term home mortgages—the safe, stodgy mission for which federally insured savings and loans were created. The Wiechern method—as it came to be called in Arkansas—did not demand waiting to earn interest over the life of a 20-year loan, it paid off immediately. FirstSouth concentrated on generating big up-front fees by making so-called acquisition, development and construction loans. Though enabling FirstSouth to pocket the equivalent of points on a home mortgage, development lending proved to be a disaster.

Since it was paying high interest rates to its depositors to attract funds from around the country, FirstSouth also charged its borrowers high rates—which meant it attracted borrowers who had been turned down by lenders charging lower rates.

Among those eager to borrow at First-South's high rates were several of the S&L's major shareholders, who borrowed millions to finance real estate speculation, much of it in the Dallas area.

Some of the insider loans were so large they violated the legal limits on loans to a single or related group of borrowers, the bank board charged. Hundreds of millions of dollars worth of insider loans were in default when the institution failed. FirstSouth's biggest stockholders became its biggest debtors.

Meanwhile, FirstSouth's approach to making loans to those who didn't have inside connections was just as loose. In one instance FirstSouth agreed to give a $20 million mortgage on a Palm Springs, Calif., condominium called Sundance, owned by Clint Murchison, the well-known Texas oil man and then owner of the Dallas Cowboys. It was the largest single loan the institution had made up to that time and Murchison personally guaranteed it.

Murchison's name was apparently all FirstSouth needed to know. Before making the loan, no one at FirstSouth checked with Seafirst Bank of Seattle, which held a smaller existing mortgage on the property. If FirstSouth loan officers had asked, they would have discovered the original loan was already in default and the bank was pressing to have it paid off immediately.

No one at FirstSouth asked why none of the 60 condo units had been sold during the 10 months since several Dallas Cowboys and cheerleaders presided over the grand opening. Nor did anyone inquire into the unaudited financial statements provided by Murchison, or question the strength of Murchison's personal guarantee. Before he sold his beloved football team and went bankrupt, Murchison had given hundreds of millions of dollars worth of such guarantees, which proved worthless when Sundance failed.

And while no one at FirstSouth was looking too deeply into the loans being made, no one at the Federal Home Loan Bank Board was paying much attention to FirstSouth.

A closer look by federal authorities might have turned up not only insider loans, but insider stock trading. The bank board later said some of FirstSouth's biggest stockholders violated regulations prohibiting changes in control of an S&L without board approval. According to board officials, some of the investments in FirstSouth stock have been tied to the insider loans and were made to prop up the price of the stock.

A stockholder suit has charged that Wiechern and other FirstSouth officials withheld key financial information about its deteriorating status while some were selling portions of their own stock. The stock is now worthless, and the investors blame the FSLIC for not warning them that the S&L was heading for failure.

According to court records, depositions of FirstSouth officials, statements by federal regulators and other information that has come to light since the institution was closed, Wiechern and other top FirstSouth managers arranged a complicated series of transactions beginning at the end of 1983 to hide the fact that the institution was in serious trouble.

In one set of transactions, $25 million worth of bad loans was hidden for more than two years by selling them directly or indirectly to corporations controlled by E. Harley Cox, a former Arkansas Bar Association president who was the S&L's counsel. Cox's corporations bought the bad loans with money borrowed from FirstSouth, allowing the institution to take the overdue loan off its books and replace it with a new loan backed by a prominent borrower. But the loans still didn't get paid and eventually FirstSouth had to take them back and report them as losses.

Hiding bad loans was critical to maintaining FirstSouth's appearance of good financial health when it was selling stock to the public. At the end of 1983, the S&L had assets of $885 million—almost triple its size four years earlier—but it had a net worth of only $20 million.

FirstSouth reported profits of $4.6 million for the year, but if it had acknowledged the bad loans and added money to its loan loss reserves to cover likely losses, it could have wiped out 1983 earnings and eaten into its already paltry capital base. Investors never would have bought its stock.

FSLIC, as receiver for FirstSouth, recently filed a suit in federal district court here seeking $150 million in damages from Wiechern, FirstSouth Chairman Del L. Brannon and several outside directors. A similar claim was filed earlier in a bankruptcy proceeding involving Roderick D. Reed, president of FirstSouth and Wiechern's right hand man.

The suit charged that the FirstSouth officials "made staggering sums of money available to certain favored borrowers on terms and conditions in flagrant disregard of prudent lending practices and with serious adverse effects on FirstSouth's financial condition." It also charged that:

■ "A substantial amount of FirstSouth's resources [were] devoted to speculation in high-risk real estate transactions in which loans were made without proper underwriting procedures;

■ "Favored borrowers were not required to put any equity into the properties or projects on which they received loans;

■ "Loan payments were taken from the loan proceeds themselves or from refinancings;

■ "The security pledged for the loans was frequently insufficient to cover potential losses upon default.

Wiechern, Brannon and the six outside directors named in the suit all filed responses denying any wrongdoing in managing FirstSouth's affairs. Reed has also denied any wrongdoing. Wiechern, Reed and Cox all declined comment on FirstSouth or failed to return phone calls.

Howard Wiechern's Baby

Whatever happened at FirstSouth during the early 1980s, people familiar with its operations agree it was Howard Wiechern's baby.

Wiechern, 49, was from Ft. Worth but attended the University of Arkansas. His wife, whom he met in college, is from Pine Bluff, an Arkansas River town about 30 miles downstream from here. The Wiecherns moved to Pine Bluff more than 25 years ago and he went to work in a clothing store. In 1963 he joined the small Pine Bluff savings and loan association that was to grow into FirstSouth.

By 1976 Wiechern had moved up to executive vice president and in 1980 he became president and chief executive officer, setting the stage for the institution's dramatic rise and fall.

FIRST SOUTH

As CEO, Wiechern succeeded Del Brannon, described by some who know him as a genial, well-meaning man with far less drive than Wiechern and far less ambition for the institution.

At the time Wiechern took control, FirstSouth, like its counterparts across the nation, was being squeezed between a portfolio of single-family home mortgages yielding low, fixed returns and tight money markets in which interest rates were soaring to the highest levels since the Civil War. In Arkansas the squeeze was particularly severe because a provision in the state constitution strictly limited the interest rate that could be charged on any kind of loan.

Partly in response to this squeeze, federal legislation was passed in 1980 to begin eliminating virtually all restrictions on the interest rates financial institutions could pay on deposits other than regular checking accounts. The same legislation and another law passed in 1982 also opened up new lines of businesses to S&Ls and broadened the variety of loans they could make.

With deregulation of the industry under way, Wiechern moved aggressively to change FirstSouth's way of doing business. According to FirstSouth's descriptions of its business activities, it began in 1981 to concentrate on making land acquisition, development and construction loans from Florida to California.

These so-called ADC loans were "short-term, with adjustable, market-sensitive interest rates and included origination fees in excess of those which could be obtained on single-family loans," explained a FirstSouth press release. "The origination of these commercial real estate loans produced sufficiently high fee income and interest income to return the association to profitability" after 1981.

The prospectus offering to sell FirstSouth shares to the public in November 1983 described the new loans this way: "The ADC loans are typically made in amounts covering full cost of construction or development of the project, including the full cost of acquiring the underlying property, if applicable, and loan fees, interest and other carrying costs during the construction term."

In other words, the developers did not necessarily have to put up any money at all—no down payment, no fees, nothing. The so-called "interest reserve" meant that no payments would be required for many months. Instead, FirstSouth agreed to take the interest out of the loan itself and to collect its upfront fees from the money it loaned the borrower.

This meant the borrower could speculate with FirstSouth's money—money the S&L had gotten from depositors by paying high rates insured by the federal government. It meant FirstSouth could record the up-front fees as profit, even though it was simply taking back money it has just loaned. With no payments due soon, any danger of default on a bad loan was delayed. And when loans did come due, it turned out, FirstSouth often was happy to refinance the loan, collect new fees up front and postpone again the inevitable failures.

In addition to the up-front fees, the prospectus explained to investors, FirstSouth was also entitled to receive a "profit participation" in any gain when the property was sold.

FirstSouth not only kept a piece of the action for itself, it sold pieces of the loans to other financial institutions, so they too could share in the profits of the Wiechern method. FirstSouth received fees for collecting payments and keeping an eye on the deals and was supposed to keep at least 10 percent of each loan, so that it had its own money at stake.

In one case, FirstSouth officials discovered belatedly that they had sold more than 100 percent of a loan to other institutions. They had to hastily repurchase some of the participations and even so ending up with less than 1 percent of the loan, according to an attorney familiar with FirstSouth affairs. One of the other problems with the Wiechern method, it turned out, was that FirstSouth loan officials were not experts on the real estate markets of places as diverse as Palm Springs, Basalt, Colo., Destin, Fla., and Plano, Tex.

Why take the risk of making loans in far away places? Gerry E. Powell, a FirstSouth board member who is president of Ben Pearson Manufacturing Co. Inc., of Pine Bluff, a well-known maker of archery products, provided one answer in a deposition taken in a suit filed by a number of financial institutions that had bought participations in the Sundance loan in Palm Springs.

Branching out from Arkansas mortgages to Dallas development loans was "more or less as a directive from the chief of the Federal Home Loan Bank. If we couldn't make a profit, we would not exist if we hadn't gone into that business. And I think you are going to find some of the participants [the suing institutions] in the same situation."

"Was FirstSouth in a loss situation in 1980-81," asked Allan Gates, the Little Rock attorney questioning Powell.

"We sure weren't making any money consequence," said Powell. "We had loan the books of 7 or 8 percent, you know, and we were paying 12 and 14 percent for the money, or more. So, there was a dead-end there."

Dallas Federal Home Loan Bank President Roy Green offered a variant of this view in testimony this spring before a House Banking subcommittee, "In a sense," he said, "we had a problem with an industry that was locked into single-family home portfolios" that did not pay enough interest to cover an institution's cost of funds, much less other operating expenses.

Noting the laws that began deregulating savings and loans, Green continued, "Both the 1980 and 1982 legislation were necessary landmark initiatives which have provided us with both benefits and challenges.

"The legislation deregulating portfolios in order to combat interest-rate-spread problems also placed new responsibilities on the thrift industry and the regulators. We believe the industry and the regulators have in large measure responded promptly and appropriately.

"However, the new deregulated environment was vulnerable to abuse by some individuals," Green declared. "The excessive growth that these so-called entrepreneurs directed FSLIC-insured institutions to pursue for quick profits has resulted in asset portfolios that fall far short of industry standards for long-term value and sound underwriting."

Or as he also put it, more simply: "Some individuals reached too far."

The End of the Rope

Howard Wiechern reached the end of his rope in April 1986. Citing poor health, he unexpectedly resigned as FirstSouth CEO and Rod Reed took over, but only briefly. Federal regulators, by then, were taking an increasing interest in the institution's problems. In August they forced Reed out and the FirstSouth board accepted a "supervisory agreement" with the Federal

Home Loan Bank Board that gave the bank board a major say in the S&L's management.

Soon after, the FirstSouth board hired the Washington law firm Wilmer, Cutler & Pickering to investigate just what had been going on.

In a report delivered to the board last November barely a month before FirstSouth failed, the law firm said there were indications of possible criminal actions by the former management and grounds for civil

FirstSouth officials "made staggering sums of money available to certain favored borrowers on terms and conditions in flagrant disregard of prudent lending practices and with serious adverse effects on FirstSouth's financial condition."

—FSLIC suit

suits against a number of parties, including former FirstSouth officials, several major stockholders and some mortgage brokers. Concerned about confidentiality, the law firm named no names. Now that FirstSouth is broke, the firm is no longer working on the case.

The cautiously worded Wilmer, Cutler report raised questions about other lawyers who represented FirstSouth. The report said the Washington firm was "investigating situations where the lawyers apparently participated in transactions that hid bad loans and affected the stock price and earnings of FirstSouth by allowing FirstSouth to recognize income or fail to recognize loss [typically just at the end of an annual or quarterly reporting period], without adequate regard for the substance and circumstances of the transactions.

"In addition," the law firm's report said, "there appear to be a number of transactions in which the lawyers, acting as principals in transactions, participated in the parking of non-performing loans outside FirstSouth and funneled FirstSouth funds to other borrowers in order to provide those other borrowers with the means to make payments on their loans, which otherwise would be nonperforming."

FirstSouth's principal attorney was E. Harley Cox, a member of the firm of Ramsay, Cox, Lile, Bridgeforth, Gilbert, Harrels(Starling of Pine Bluff. Both Cox and the firm's managing partner, Louis Ramsay, are former presidents of the Arkansas Bar Association.

One set of transactions of the sort questioned by Wilmer, Cutler and Pickering involved the 38-unit Sandpiper condominium project on the Colorado River in Parker, Ariz. Over three years, FirstSouth lent more than $5.2 million to Sandpiper before declaring the loans in default.

Trying later to recover some of its losses, FirstSouth sued two Arizona appraisers, blaming their work for the loan losses. Defending the appraisers, Phoenix attorney Thomas K. Irvine discovered records showing FirstSouth had not lost money on the failed condos, but had sold the loans in 1983 for full value.

Irvine said the Sandpiper loans were sold by FirstSouth to a Dallas firm, Wagner & Nelson, in September 1983. A short time later Wagner & Nelson sold them to Sunbelt Service Corp., a subsidiary of a Dallas S&L. Sunbelt in turn sold the loans to Multistate Real Estate Management Co. and other corporations owned by FirstSouth's attorney, Harley Cox.

Irvine argued that his clients didn't owe FirstSouth anything, since FirstSouth hadn't lost any money.

Cox responded that though the loan had been sold several times, the S&L had always been at risk. His corporations had bought the loans at face value, he agreed, but the "cash" mentioned in the records was actually two new loans from FirstSouth to his companies.

Moreover, Cox added, it was understood at the time the loans were purchased that his firms were supposed to recover as much as possible on the various projects and that FirstSouth was supposed to insure that neither Cox nor his companies would suffer a loss.

The Sandpiper loans were among $25 million worth of properties that moved directly or indirectly from FirstSouth to Cox's companies late in 1983.

During most of the two years that those bad loans were off the books, FirstSouth reported steadily rising earnings and set aside only relatively small loan loss reserves. FirstSouth's 1984 annual report listed only $8 million worth of "slow loans" that were 60 to 90 days past due and another $3.4 million in foreclosures.

About 18 months later, however, the Cox loans were transferred back to FirstSouth according to documents in the Arizona suit. Twelve days after that Wiechern announced a $17 million addition to its loan loss reserves—the first public statement by the S&L that it had financial problems.

Wiechern also said FirstSouth was going to return to concentrating on single-family home mortgages instead of the more risky acquisition, development and construction loans. The Wiechern method was dead.

The announcement claimed FirstSouth still had a net worth of $47 million after the $17 million writeoff. But the $17 million turned out to be only the beginning of the bad debts.

The Big Loser

FirstSouth's largest losses are likely to be on a series of loans to the Watson & Taylor Realty Co. of Dallas, according to knowledgeable sources. That one company had $148 million worth of loans at FirstSouth, far more than Federal Home Loan Bank Board regulations allow to go to any one borrower from an institution of FirstSouth's size and net worth.

Watson & Taylor is a development company owned by George S. Watson and A. Starke Taylor III, son of Dallas Mayor A. Starke Taylor Jr.

When FirstSouth failed, Watson, young Taylor and two associates owned or controlled more than one-fourth of the S&L's common stock, according to Bank Board documents. Under such circumstances, Bank Board regulations limit loans to no more than $100,000.

The Bank Board didn't audit FirstSouth during the time when most of the loans were made and didn't know Watson & Taylor had purchased so much stock.

The controling stock in FirstSouth has been purchased without Bank Board approval, and early last year the two men agreed to sell their interests. However, as the bad news about FirstSouth's condition began to become public, they reportedly were asked by federal officials to hold off, since putting such a large block of shares on the market might have led to such a loss of confidence that FirstSouth would have failed immediately.

Beginning in 1985, federal authorities began to put pressure on FirstSouth to reduce its lending to Watson & Taylor, but that never happened. According to the FSLIC suit against Wiechern and the other officials, the institution went to elaborate and costly lengths to give the appearance of complying with the federal mandate without actually doing so.

Watson and Taylor have told reporters they never sought to control FirstSouth and did not get special treatment. However, the FSLIC suit details some remarkable deals made with Watson & Taylor, as well as some other major stockholders.

FirstSouth began lending to Watson & Taylor in March 1982. By 1983 they had borrowed $73 million, more than the S&L's entire net worth. The following year, when the two men began buying stock, their loan total hit $126 million, more than double FirstSouth's reported net worth.

The FSLIC suit detailed a number of Watson & Taylor loans, including those on some unimproved real estate in an area known as Frisco, north of Dallas. Without investing any of its own money, Watson & Taylor borrowed more than $50 million in mid-1983 to acquire the land, the suit said. As was the case with many such deals, the loans covered the purchase price, fees, interest, taxes and closing costs.

The following year, when the loans were about to fall due, FirstSouth refinanced them, raising the total to more than $59 million. Again, Watson & Taylor put up no money and no added security, and all the upfront fees were paid out of the loan proceeds. "At maturity in 1985, the loans were extended to September 1986," the lawsuit said, and along with the extension, the two stockholders got another loan for $5.6 million on the property. FSLIC has foreclosed on the loan.

Also borrowing heavily from FirstSouth were board members John P. Wagner and William C. Nelson Jr., owners of Wagner & Nelson Inc., another Dallas real estate firm, and of Wagner & Nelson Mortgage Ltd., a mortgage brokerage involved with a substantial number of FirstSouth transactions.

Wagner and Nelson collected brokerage fees on loans made to themselves or joint ventures in which they participated, according to the FSLIC lawsuit. By August 1985, loans to Wagner and Nelson and their ventures exceeded FirstSouth's net worth, the suit said.

Another series of loans in excess of $70 million went to Jerry L. Grigsby of Malvern, Ark., who owned more than 10 percent of FirstSouth stock, the suit continued:

"Grigsby invested none or virtually none of his own funds in projects financed by the Grigsby loans. Proceeds of each loan funded reserves to pay interest on the loan as it accrued. In addition, the Grigsby loans regularly were renewed or refinanced with no reduction in principal. Grigsby thereby had the free use of FirstSouth's money."

Grigsby, Wagner, Nelson, Watson & Taylor all would not discuss the loans, which are now involved in court cases.

Sorting Out the Pieces

Today, FSLIC receivers are trying to sort out the pieces of the FirstSouth wreckage. About $200 million worth of assets have been sold. Many others have been foreclosed including the Watson & Taylor loans.

Each day the legal fees and other costs mount, eating away at the value of the FirstSouth remains and increasing the losses to the FSLIC insurance fund and other creditors.

But if the losses are mounting for the federal government, the bank board and FSLIC can only blame themselves—because above all else, FirstSouth is a monument to regulatory failure.

Roy Green, of the Dallas Home Loan Bank—the region's regulator of S&L's—acknowledged as much in that congressional hearing this year.

The Dallas district, like most others around the country, he said, did not have enough bank examiners and those they did have generally were poorly paid and not very good.

"Because of salaries and regulations, we were not able to attract staff and expertise," Green said. That changed in 1985 when the examiners became employes of the 12 district banks, which technically are private institutions not subject to Civil Service regulations and pay scales.

One particular problem with the Southwestern regional home loan bank was that in the summer of 1983—under political pressure from Texas—it was moved to Dallas from Little Rock. About 40 percent of its employes refused to follow their jobs to Texas. A significant number of them went to work for FirstSouth.

"It was an advantageous time for FirstSouth," recalled Rebecca Vail, director of communications for the Dallas bank. "It was growing and they painted an advantageous picture for employes whose jobs were ending and wanted to stay in Arkansas."

The Little Rock financial community is small and there were many ties between FirstSouth and the regulatory bank. One-time CEO Reed was a bank board alumnus. And Bank Board Chairman Green once headed one of the little S&Ls taken over by FirstSouth.

Some Little Rock attorneys and others involved with the aftermath of the FirstSouth failure are convinced that ties between the former regulators on its payroll and those regulating them was a significant factor in causing the authorities to turn a blind eye to the institution for so long.

After the long-delayed examination of FirstSouth in early 1985, the regulators began to press for changes, but not very successfully. Many transactions that form the basis of the FSLIC suit took place after that increased scrutiny began.

Even when Wiechern unexpectedly resigned—everyone agrees he was not forced out—he stayed on the payroll. The board gave him a job with a subsidiary with no cut in his $440,000 salary.

Only after the board found out he had made about $1 million in loans and never told them about it, was Wiechern fired. According to the directors, the offense was not the loans, which he had the authority to make, but the failure to report them.

Finally, last August, the Dallas Home Loan Bank imposed its management agreement and ousted Reed as the death throes began.

Like so many of the savings and loan associations around the nation that decided to grow fast, FirstSouth had relied on the twin attractions of high interest rates and federal insurance up to $100,000 per account to attract deposits. A major share of the deposits were in $100,000 jumbo certificates of deposit.

As the FirstSouth news got worse and worse, depositors began pulling out their money when their CDs matured.

Last November, virtually none of the CDs were renewed, recalled a bank board spokesman. If that happened again in December, as appeared likely, FirstSouth would run out of cash and have no way to borrow any. Thus the Bank Board decided the only course was to close it.

The necessary papers were filed in federal court here on Friday morning, Dec. 4.

The Feds moved in at a key moment. A state court judge that morning was planning to sign an order directing FirstSouth to pay six other institutions more than $12 million in a lawsuit claiming they were defrauded by FirstSouth on loan participations in Clint Murchison's Sundance project.

The judge had concluded that FirstSouth management had committed "constructive fraud" in the transactions.

Before the fraud victims could collect, however, the FSLIC took over. The institutions are now FirstSouth creditors. The Sundance condos, being operated as a hotel, are up for sale.

Only a few FirstSouth depositors lost any money in the failure—those with more than $100,000 in their accounts. Only $14.4 million turned out to be uninsured, most of that interest on Jumbo CDs, Bank Board officials said.

The loss to depositors was so small in part because FirstSouth employes—at the urging of Bank Board officials—had been advising depositors to organize their accounts so that as little money as possible remained uninsured.

The Monday following the closing, a new institution, Riverside Federal Savings Association, opened for business in place of FirstSouth.

It took over all of FirstSouth's accounts that had had less than $100,000 in them, a small portfolio of good single-family mortgages and a whopping promissory note from FSLIC to cover its liabilities.

Nobody Is Talking

None of the principals in the FirstSouth rise and fall will talk about it.

Howard Wiechern still goes to an office he rents in the FirstSouth building here, reportedly working as a financial consultant.

Harley Cox has not been sued by FSLIC, though efforts are under way to collect from an insurance company that provided a bond for him.

Rod Reed filed for bankruptcy early this year. He has come up with a plan—if the bankruptcy court approves—to pay his creditors part of what they are owed.

There will be nothing much left to satisfy the $150 million claim FSLIC filed against him for mismanaging FirstSouth, or the added $1 million in punitive damages FSLIC has demanded.

The FSLIC also wants $150 million and damages from Wiechern, Brannon and the outside directors, but collecting that is doubtful as well.

Watson & Taylor are suing and countersuing FirstSouth, in another of the pack of legal disputes that will live on after FirstSouth.

The FSLIC attorneys, trustee and S&L salvage specialists have set up shop in Little Rock to continue the clean up.

They don't know how long it will take. FSLIC has never closed the books on an S&L liquidation.

ADDENDUM E: Text of a "Stipulation and Consent to Entry of Order to Cease and Desist" and of the accompanying "Order to Cease and Desist"

UNITED STATES OF AMERICA
Before the
FEDERAL SAVINGS AND LOAN
INSURANCE CORPORATION

In the Matter of:

AND LOAN ASSOCIATION

Federal Home Loan Bank Board
Resolution No.

Dated:

STIPULATION AND CONSENT TO ENTRY OF ORDER
TO CEASE AND DESIST

The Federal Savings and Loan Insurance Corporation ("FSLIC") and _____ Savings and Loan Association, _____ (hereafter _____ or "the Association"), hereby agree as follows:

1. *Consideration*. Whereas the FSLIC, being of the opinion that the necessary grounds exist to initiate an administrative proceeding pursuant to Section 407(e)(1) of the National Housing Act, as amended ("NHA"), 12 U.S.C. § 1730(e)(1) (1982, against _____ _____ Savings and whereas _____ Savings wishes to cooperate with FSLIC and avoid the initiation of administrative litigation, _____ Savings hereby stipulates and agrees to the following terms in consideration of the FSLIC's forebearance from initiating such administrative litigation on the subjects covered by the attached Order to Cease and Desist ("Order").

2. *Jurisdiction*. _____ Savings acknowledges that _____ Savings is a savings and loan association chartered by the _____ that maintains its principal place of business in _____. The savings accounts of _____ Savings are insured by the FSLIC, which makes it an "insured institution" as that term is used in

the NHA and the Rules and Regulations for Insurance of Accounts ("Insurance Regulations") and therefore subject in all respects to the NHA and the Insurance Regulations.

3. *Consent.* _____ Savings, without admitting or denying violating any laws, regulations or rules or engaging in any unsafe or unsound practices, hereby consents and agrees to the issuance by the FSLIC of the attached Order, and further consents and agrees to comply with the provisions thereof upon its issuance. The terms of this Stipulation shall be incorporated by reference into said Order.

4. *Finality.* _____ Savings stipulates and agrees that the attached Order upon its issuance shall become effective and enforceable as a "cease-and-desist order which has become final" as defined in Section 407(r)(1) of the NHA, 12 U.S.C. § 1730(r)(1) (1982), and that the Order complies with all requirements of law.

5. *Enforceability.* _____ Savings stipulates and agrees that the FSLIC has the power to enforce the terms of the Order under the provisions of Section 407(k)(2) of the NHA, 12 U.S.C. § 1730(k)(2) (1982).

6. *Waiver of the Notice of Charges and Hearing.* _____ _____ Savings hereby waives its rights to any notice of charges and any administrative hearing provided by Section 407(e)(1) of the NHA, 12 U.S.C. § 1730(e)(1), and further waives any right to seek judicial review of the Order that is otherwise provided by Section 407(j)(2) of the NHA, 12 U.S.C. § 1730(j)(2) (1982).

7. *Effectiveness.* _____ Savings stipulates and agrees that the Order shall be effective on the date of the resolution of the Federal Home Loan Bank Board, as operating head of the FSLIC, authorizing the Secretary (or Acting or Assistant Secretary) thereof to execute this stipulation and attached Order.

WHEREFORE, in consideration of the foregoing, the FSLIC and _____ Savings, by its directors, hereby execute this agreement.

FEDERAL SAVINGS
AND LOAN   _____ SAVINGS
INSURANCE CORPORATION   AND LOAN ASSOCIATION
By: by its directors
                                                            on behalf of the

Jeff Sconyers   _____
Secretary

UNITED STATES OF AMERICA
Before the
FEDERAL SAVINGS AND LOAN INSURANCE CORPORATION

In the Matter of:

_____

AND LOAN ASSOCIATION

Federal Home Loan Bank Board
Resolution No.

Dated:

ORDER TO CEASE AND DESIST

Whereas, _____ Savings and Loan Association (_____ or the "Association"), by execution of the attached Stipulation and Consent Agreement, the terms of which are incorporated herein by reference, has stipulated and agreed to the issuance of this Order to Cease and Desist ("Order"), which is issued by the Federal Savings and Loan Insurance Corporation ("FSLIC") pursuant to Section 407(e)(1) of the National Housing Act (12 U.S.C. § 1730(e)(1) (1982));

NOW THEREFORE, IT IS ORDERED that _____ _____, its directors and the Association's officers, employees, and agents shall cease and desist from any violations, or the aiding and abetting of any violations, of:

1. Section 563.4 of the Rules and Regulations for the Federal Savings and Loan Insurance Corporation ("Insurance Regulations") (50 Fed. Reg. 5232, 5234 (February 7, 1985) (to be codified at 12 C.F.R. § 563.4)); and

2. Section 562.9-8 of the Insurance Regulations (50 Fed. Reg. 6312 (February 19, 1985) (to be codified at 12 C.F.R. § 563.9-8)); and

3. Section 563.17 of the Insurance Regulations (12 C.F.R. § 563.17 (1985)); and

4. Section 563.17-1(c) of the Insurance Regulations (12 C.F.R. § 563.17-1(c) (1985)); and

5. Section 563.17-4 of the Insurance Regulations (12 C.F.R. § 563.17-4 (1985)); and

6. Section 563.17-5 of the Insurance Regulations (12 C.F.R. § 563.17-5 (1985)); and

7. Section 563.23-1 of the Insurance Regulations (12 C.F.R. § 563.23-1 (1985)).

IT IS HEREBY FURTHER ORDERED that:

1. Unless legally obligated in writing to do so as of the date of this Order, _____ shall not make or commit to make, purchase or commit to purchase, refinance or commit to refinance, disburse or commit to disburse, all or any part of any loan secured by real estate or any personal, business or commercial loan, except:

   (a) loans secured by one-to-four residential units not to exceed $250,000 to any one borrower or on the security of any one project; and

   (b) consumer loans not to exceed $10,000, in the aggregate, to any one borrower; and

   (c) loans approved by the California Savings and Loan Commissioner under the terms of the Cease and Desist Orders issued by the California Department of Savings and Loan (the "Department") on February 1, 1985 and May 7, 1985, as modified or amended by the Department as of the date of the issuance of this Order.

2. _____ shall not disburse funds on existing loans in process, except to the extent indicated below, until the Association has obtained:

   (a) all applicable information required by Section 563.17-1(c) of the Insurance Regulations;

   (b) an appraisal of the security property complying with the requirements of Section 563.17-1(c)(1)(iii) of the Insurance Regulations and meeting the guidelines contained in Federal Home Loan Bank Board ("FHLBB") Memorandum R-41b;

   (c) sufficient documentation to determine that _____ _____ Savings is legally obligated to disburse the funds; and

   (d) a certification from _____ Board of Directors or a senior officer that the request for disbursement has been reviewed, that the requirements of Section 563.17-1(c)(1)(vi) have been complied with, and that adequate documentation justifying the disbursement (*i.e.* inspection reports, vouchers and architect's certifications) has been received by the Association.

With regard to appraisals of the security property referred to in subparagraph (b) above,

(a) in those instances in which the Association has no appraisal of the security property in its possession, the following must occur prior to the disbursal of any additional funds:
(i) an opinion of value from a qualified, board approved appraiser must be obtained, and
(ii) an appraisal of the property, complying with all aspects of the above-stated regulations and guidelines, must be commissioned through a qualified, board approved appraiser, and
(iii) the Association must obtain a commitment from said appraiser for delivery of the completed appraisal within 90 days;

(b) in those instances in which the Association has an appraisal of the security property in its possession which has not been reviewed and certified to be in compliance with the above-stated regulations and guidelines, an opinion of value from a qualified, board approved appraiser must be obtained prior to the disbursal of any additional funds, and the Board of Directors must:
(i) designate an employee to review the appraisal within 30 days of the disbursal of funds and determine whether the appraisal is in compliance with the above-stated regulations and guidelines, and
(ii) if it is not, an appraisal complying with all aspects of the above-stated regulations and guidelines must be commissioned through a qualified, board approved appraiser, with a commitment from said appraiser for delivery of the completed appraisal within 90 days.

3. _____ shall not purchase or commit to purchase, directly or indirectly, any additional direct investments as defined in Section 563.9-8 of the Insurance Regulations, including but not limited to real property for investment or development. Further, the Association will not invest or commit to invest additional funds in existing real estate development projects held for investment until it has obtained a certification from its Board of Directors or a senior officer

that the information set forth in FHLBB Memorandum R-38 has been obtained, reviewed, and determined to be adequate. In those situations in which the Association is unable to make the above-required certification because of incomplete or non-existent documentation set forth, as applicable, in sections (5), (9), (10) or (11) of FHLBB Memorandum R-38, _____ Savings may invest additional funds, with the prior approval of the Supervisory Agent, providing a certification is obtained from the Board of Directors or a senior officer that:

(a) the missing information required by sections (5), (9), (10), or (11) has been commissioned through qualified, board approved individuals; and

(b) the individuals commissioned to provide the missing documentation will do so within 90 days; and

(c) all other applicable information set forth in FHLBB Memorandum R-38 has been obtained, reviewed, and determined to be adequate.

The Supervisory Agent's approval should not be construed as a determination of the economic merits or viability of the subject real estate project.

4. _____ Savings shall not increase or commit to increase the dollar amount of funds placed at the Association by deposit brokers ("brokered deposits") above the level of such deposits at the Association on the date of service of this Order. The Association shall, within 7 days of the date of this Order, submit to the Supervisory Agent a list of all brokered deposits at the Association as of the date of this Order. In addition, _____ Savings shall, within 15 days of this Order, develop and submit a plan to be approved by the Supervisory Agent to reduce brokered deposits in an orderly fashion and within a reasonable time. The Association shall implement this plan immediately following approval by the Supervisory Agent.

5. _____ Savings shall not take a position in any additional futures contracts, forward commitments, or financial options. Within 30 days of the date of this Order, _____ Savings shall submit to the Supervisory Agent an interest-rate-risk management policy for the Association as required by Section 563.17-6 of the Insurance Regulations. Further, _____ Savings shall dispose of its outstanding positions in futures contracts, forward commitments, and financial options at little

or no loss to the Association. This disposition of the Association's outstanding positions shall continue until the Supervisory Agent determines that _____ Savings is in full compliance with the requirements of Sections 563.17-3, 563.17-4, and 563.17-5 of the Insurance Regulations and that retention of those positions is part of its policies and guidelines to reduce interest-rate risk. Further, _____ Savings shall develop and maintain:

(a) a register of all its outstanding futures contracts, forward commitments and financial options, in accordance with Sections 563.17-3, 563.17-4, and 563.17-5 of the Insurance Regulations and prepared in a manner sufficient to enable the Supervisory Agent to determine the Association's total outstanding positions and the unrealized profit or loss therefrom; and

(b) a record of specific futures contracts, forward commitments and financial options, the purpose of each such investment made, the present or anticipated positions(s) or cash market transaction(s) against which they are matched, and, in the case of the futures contract entered into in connection with anticipated reinvestment of mortgage repayments, a statement of facts that adequately justifies entering into the futures transaction.

6. Within 30 days of the date of this Order, _____ Savings shall adopt and submit for the Supervisory Agent's review and approval, written proposals designed to:

(a) reduce the aggregate amount of direct investments, as defined in Section 563.9-8 of the Insurance Regulations, to an amount equal to or less than the level permitted by that regulation; and

(b) reduce the outstanding aggregate amount of delinquent loans and real estate in foreclosure.

These plans shall be implemented immediately upon notification of approval by the Supervisory Agent.

7. _____ Savings shall immediately develop and maintain such accounting systems, records, and controls, as required to provide a complete record of all business transactions involving the Association and accurately present its past and current financial condition. Specifically, _____ Savings shall:

(a) capitalize interest on its investment in real estate development projects in accordance with FHLBB Memorandum T 59-3a.

(b) recognize its construction loan fee income and profits on sales of real estate owned in accordance with Section 563.23-1 of the Insurance Regulations.

(c) account for earned but uncollectible interest income on loans in accordance with Section 563c.11 of the Insurance Regulations.

(d) prepare its financial statements and other reports to the FSLIC in accordance with the FHLBB regulations, policies, and directives, and with generally accepted accounting principles where there are no specific FHLBB guidelines, as required by Section 563.23-3 of the Insurance Regulations.

8. _____ Savings shall accurately reflect the level of its scheduled items and delinquent loans in its own records and in reports to the FSLIC and the Supervisory Agent. Loans in default shall not be treated as or deemed to be current unless funds covering all payments in arrears are actually received. On or before the 20th of each month, _____ Savings shall file with the Supervisory Agent a schedule containing the following information as of the last day of the preceding month:

(a) Balance of scheduled items;

(b) A description of each parcel of REO acquired during the preceding month;

(c) Balance of real estate held for development or investment;

(d) Loans modified or extended while delinquent; and

(e) Balance of loans in foreclosure.

9. _____ Savings shall not (a) modify the terms of any delinquent loan; (b) except where it obtains value, in cash, as hereafter defined, sell any real estate owned ("REO"); (c) make any loans to facilitate the sale of REO; (d) release any borrower or guarantor from liability under any loan except where full payment of the loan, in cash, is obtained; or (e) otherwise effect a "workout" arrangement for any transaction, or series of transactions, with a value exceeding $500,000 without providing 10 days prior written notice to the Supervisory Agent. For the purpose of this paragraph, "value" shall be defined

as the higher amount of the current appraised value or the Associations book value. The Supervisory Agent shall have 10 days within which to direct the Association not to effect the proposed action, and _____ Savings shall comply with such directive.

10. _____ Savings shall promptly establish all specific reserves for losses as directed in writing by the Supervisory Agent, as required under Section 563.17-2(c) of the Insurance Regulations.

11. _____ Savings shall not accept deposits from the general public that are not insured by the FSLIC.

12. The Board of Directors of _____ Savings shall appoint a qualified independent person as full-time chief executive officer of the Association within 45 days of the date of this Order. This appointment shall be subject to approval by the Supervisory Agent. The new chief executive officer shall be hired on a salaried basis and charged with full administrative and managerial responsibilities of the Association under policies established by its Board of Directors. In the event of this officer's removal, incapacity or resignation during the three year period following the date of this Order, the continuation or succession of competent management will also be subject to the Supervisory Agent's approval. An "independent person" is a person not related to the Association, its subsidiaries or its affiliated persons and who is otherwise free of any relationship that would interfere with the exercise of independent judgment. For purposes of this paragraph, a person is "related" to another person if he is an affiliate or associate of that person within the meaning of Section 563b.2(a) (1) and (4) of the Insurance Regulations.

13. The Board of Directors of _____ Savings shall submit a management plan to the Supervisory Agent, for approval, within 4 days of the date of this Order. The management plan shall include, at a minimum, the following information:

(a) the association's loan underwriting policies and procedures; and

(b) a three-year operating plan with pro forma financial statements, prepared in accordance with the forms and guidelines previously provided the Association by the Supervisory Agent.

Further, the management plan shall describe the duties, responsibilities, qualifications, and financial institution experience of each officer of the Association. It also shall identify the present holders of such positions or plans to fill such positions.

14. The Directors of _____ Savings shall take whatever steps are necessary to ensure full compliance by _____ _____ Savings with the requirements of this Order.

15. All technical words or terms used in the Order, for which meanings are not specified or otherwise provided by the provisions of this Order, shall, insofar as applicable, have meaning as defined in the _____ (Revised Edition) of the Federal Home Loan Bank Board, and any such technical words or terms used in this Order and undefined in said _____ shall have meanings that accord with the best custom and usage in the thrift industry.

By The Federal Savings and
Loan Insurance Corporation

ADDENDUM F: Reprinted with permission from the August 16, 1987 *Dallas Times Herald*

S & L FRAUD PROBE

Boom to bust: FSLIC flips over Texas land-sale chase

By Ross Ramsey

OF THE TIMES HERALD STAFF

Dallas real estate investor Louis G. Reese III bought land in south Fort Worth at the peak of the real estate boom.

And he bought it, and bought it and bought it — first for the development firm that bears his name, then in a partnership, next in the name of his children and finally in the name of a corporation of which he was president and treasurer.

In the course of those transactions and two others over a period of 26 months, loans against the land ballooned from $17.25 million to $64.737 million. The amount loaned per acre on the last sale was five times what had been loaned on the first.

All of the outstanding loans are now in default; the current owner of the property is tangled in bankruptcy proceedings; the four savings and loan institutions that financed the land purchases technically have gone broke, accumulating $1.1 billion in debt largely from real estate loan losses; and almost every person who had anything to do with any of the deals is under investigation by the FBI.

Of all the real estate loans made in Texas when the high-fliers were at their greatest altitudes, regulators chose these to show Congress the kinds of loans that had virtually bankrupted the Federal Savings and Loan Insurance Corp., the agency that must pay up to $100,000 per account when a savings institution runs out of money.

Though he didn't use names in his congressional testimony in March, Roy Green, the president of the Dallas Federal Home Loan Bank, cited loans that funded these transactions as examples of the "unsafe and unsound practices" that had provoked one of the greatest financial crises since the Great Depression.

In the 18 months since the North Texas real estate boom went bust, nearly 70 Texas S&Ls have gone broke as depositors withdrew funds faster than the S&Ls could attract new deposits.

Making matters worse, mortgage payments from big developer-borrowers failed to bridge the gap as loan after loan went into default. And foreclosure auctions in many cases have provided no relief, because the properties frequently are worth less than the loan amounts.

In the land deals Green described to Congress, for example, the pastureland in south Fort Worth was worth just $21 million in the opinion of an appraiser hired by the Dallas FHLB. That's $43 million less than had been loaned using the land as collateral, and $64.5 million less than the current owners say the property is worth.

Commenting on the series of sales that so quickly inflated the price of the property, the FHLB's appraisal noted that "several of these title transfers occurred on the same day or within several days of each other and are likely less than 'arm's length' transactions," and "that these might be 'flip' sales" intended to generate "new financing, at dramatically increased amounts . . ."

With one exception, the people involved either would not comment or did not return calls from the Times Herald. Reese, did not return numerous calls made over a period of six weeks.

But the story of what happened to the property on Fort Worth's southern boundary can be found in Tarrant County's real estate deed records. Here's what happened:

Reese

■ Louis G. Reese Inc. bought the property on Oct. 28, 1983, from First City Investments of Vancouver, which financed the transaction with a $17.25 million note, loaning $8,041.51 per acre for what was then a 2,145-acre tract.

■ Reese sold the property the same day to Jerry E. Parsons, who borrowed additional money from State Savings and Loan Association of Lubbock. The mortgage debts on the property totaled $24 million at the end of the day.

■ Parsons sold the land to himself and Reese, from whom he had bought the property only three days before. Their partnership was called the 2138 Joint Venture. No new money was borrowed, so the loan value per acre remained at $11,188.19. But immediately before they sold the property, Reese and Parsons pledged part of it against a $5.3 million loan from Texas American Bank-Fort Worth.

■ Reese and Parsons held the real estate for about 4½ months, selling it to T. Cullen Davis, the Fort Worth oil heir who has filed for bankruptcy; and Richard E. Wensel, a Scottsdale, Ariz., developer. Their partnership, the McCart Tract Venture, borrowed still more money from a subsidiary of Dallas-based Sunbelt Savings, and sold nearly a fourth of the land a few hours later. First

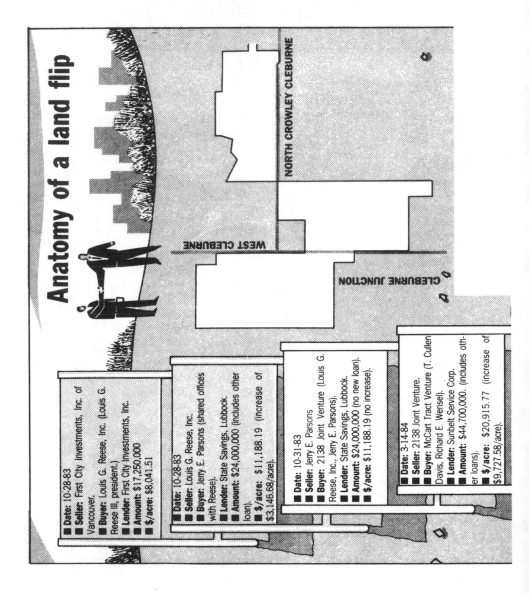

Anatomy of a land flip

Date: 10-28-83
Seller: First City Investments, Inc. of Vancouver.
Buyer: Louis G. Reese, Inc. (Louis G. Reese III, president.)
Lender: First City Investments, Inc.
Amount: $17,250,000
$/acre: $8,041.51

Date: 10-28-83
Seller: Louis G. Reese, Inc.
Buyer: Jerry E. Parsons (shared offices with Reese).
Lender: State Savings, Lubbock.
Amount: $24,000,000 (includes other loan).
$/acre: $11,188.19 (increase of $3,146.68/acre).

Date: 10-31-83
Seller: Jerry E. Parsons
Buyer: 2138 Joint Venture (Louis G. Reese, Inc., Jerry E. Parsons).
Lender: State Savings, Lubbock.
Amount: $24,000,000 (no new loan).
$/acre: $11,188.19 (no increase).

Date: 3-14-84
Seller: 2138 Joint Venture.
Buyer: McCart Tract Venture (T. Cullen Davis, Richard E. Wensel).
Lender: Sunbelt Service Corp.
Amount: $44,700,000. (includes other loans).
$/acre: $20,915.77 (increase of $9,727.58/acre).

NORTH CROWLEY CLEBURNE

WEST CLEBURNE

CLEBURNE JUNCTION

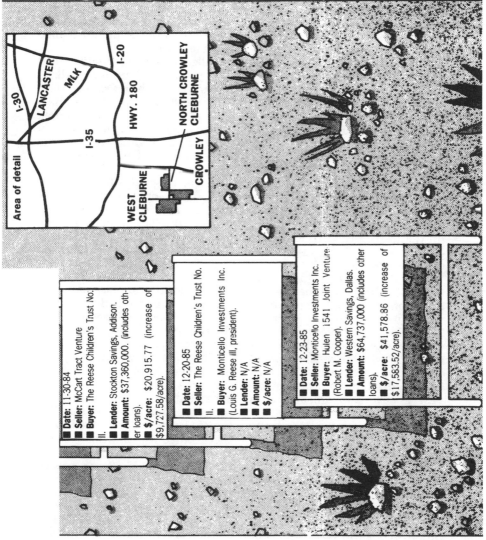

John Green/Dallas Times Herald

City Investments was paid off, but the amount loaned against the property reached a record — $44.7 million. That made the loan value per acre $20,915.77. The loan amount on the property had climbed 160 percent in just 135 days.

■ Davis and Wensel sold what was left of the tract eight months later, and the Reese family name once again was listed on the deed, this time as the Reese Children's Trust No. II. Because Davis and Wensel had sold off some of the land, the loans that funded this purchase were smaller, totaling $37.36 million, but the loan value per acre jumped again, this time to $23,995.34. Sunbelt Savings and State Savings were paid what they were owed, and a new lender, Stockton Savings, joined the pack. The Reese Children's Trust defaulted on its loan from Stockton, which first posted the property for foreclosure, then granted a renewal and extension on the loan Dec. 23 in exchange for payment of $2 million in overdue interest.

■ In documents signed Dec. 20, 1985, three days before the Stockton extension agreement was signed, the Reese Children's Trust No. II sold the property to a corporation, Monticello Investments, of which Reese was president and treasurer. Tarrant County deed records do not reveal a new loan amount, or a new lender.

■ Three days later, Monticello Investments sold the property again. This time the buyer was the Hulen-1541 Joint Venture, which at the time had five partners: Robert M. Cooper, managing venturer, and R. Terrell Reagan, James L. Tarver Jr., Bob R. Smith and Jack Roubinek. The newest and last lender in the chain was Western Savings of Dallas, which was closed by federal regulators in September 1986. According to Cooper, the sales price was $50 million, but Western's loan brought the total indebtedness to $64.737 million — a final loan value of $41,578.86 per acre. The loan value per acre had increased more than five times in 26 months. One consultant to Western has told the now-insolvent S&L that it should write off all of the money loaned to Hulen-1541.

Hulen-1541 Joint Venture filed for protection under federal bankruptcy laws in October 1986. Four partners in the deal — Reagan, Tarver, Smith and Roubinek — have pulled out, leaving only Cooper, according to records filed with the bankruptcy court in Dallas.

In its original filing, Hulen-1541 listed only one asset, the land in Fort Worth, and said it was worth $85.5 million. An appraisal done for Western Savings in November 1985 was cited. But the assessment is contested by lawyers for Stockton Savings, who prefer the appraisal done for the Dallas Federal Home Loan Bank in August 1986, which said the fair market value of the property was only $21 million.

Whatever it's worth, the property could be sold soon, for the first time in almost two years. In a hearing scheduled for Monday morning, the judge in the Hulen-1541 case will be asked to either change its bankruptcy status from reorganization to liquidation, which would allow a trustee to sell the property, or to dismiss the bankruptcy altogether, which would allow the lenders to foreclose and sell the pastureland in south Fort Worth to the highest bidder.

ADDENDUM G: Reprinted with permission from the March 4, 1985 issue of the *Banking Expansion Reporter for the Financial Services Industry*

Administrative Actions Against Banks

By John J. Early and Ira L. Tannenbaum

Mr. Early is currently a Special Consultant to Golembe Associates, Inc. Formerly, he was Director, Division of Bank Supervision, Federal Deposit Insurance Corporation. Mr. Tannenbaum is a Principal of Golembe Associates, Inc.

In 1984, 79 insured banks failed, the most bank failures in the 50-year history of the Federal Deposit Insurance Corporation (FDIC). The 1984 record follows the 48 bank failures in 1983 and 42 in 1982, well above the average of about 10 failures a year in prior years. In only two previous years in the FDIC's history had the number of insured bank failures exceeded 70—77 in 1937 and 74 in 1938.

Over the past year, moreover, the number of banks on the FDIC problem bank list has increased from 642 at the end of 1983 to approximately 894 at the present time—out of the nation's 14,700 insured banks. The FDIC's problem bank list is not limited to the insured nonmember banks the FDIC regularly supervises but also includes national banks and state banks that are members of the Federal Reserve System. The problem bank list is not static and indeed is constantly changing as banks are removed from the list after problems have been corrected and others added to the list as problems develop.

The FDIC problem bank list includes only those banks rated as having the most serious problems, those rated "4" or "5" on a scale ascending from 1 to 5 in accordance with the increasing seriousness of their condition under the CAMEL system used by the Federal bank regulatory agencies to rate insured banks. There are an even larger number of banks rated "3" that have a combination of financial, operational or other problems that require more than normal supervision. If the 3-rated banks were included, some 15 percent of the nation's banks could be subject to formal or informal administrative action by their bank regulator.

The recent increase in the number of bank failures and problem banks has been due to a combination of factors, some of which have reinforced each other in their impact on banks. The recession and subsequent recovery affected various sectors of the economy unevenly and in some sectors problems remain. Agriculture in some sections of the country did not share in the recovery. A combination of low crop prices and declining land values has had a severe impact on the quality of the loan portfolios of many farm banks, particularly in certain parts of the Midwest. International developments, in addition to the well-publicized foreign debt problem, continue to adversely affect activity in the energy and shipping industries. Banks in the Southwest and other energy lenders have been adversely affected by low energy prices and depressed loan collateral values. Real estate loans continue to be troublesome for some banks.

The move toward deregulation in the banking industry coincided with continued high interest rates and exposed the industry to market forces at a not particularly propitious time. A broadening of powers for these financial institutions may also be a potential source of problems for the less able. Internal management problems, such as insider abuse, loan concentrations, and abusive use of brokered deposits, continue to be problems in a number of cases. Under current economic conditions, such problems can further weaken a bank's financial condition.

At the same time, the time between on-site Federal regulatory examinations of banks not considered problems or near-problems has been extended materially, due in part to the increased number of problem banks and bank failures and in part to the belief that well-run banks themselves should be largely responsible for maintenance of a sound financial condition. Greater reliance in the interval between examinations on off-site analysis of computer-based financial information provided to the Federal supervisory agencies by the banks themselves creates the potential for problems to accumulate in some of these banks between examinations, especially if the parameters involved are not statistically quantifiable. When the examiners do arrive, they may find a significant deterioration in a bank's condition or in its operational procedures since the last on-site examination.

Concomitantly with the increase in the number of bank failures and problem banks, there has been a significant increase in the number of administrative actions, both formal and informal, by the Office of the Comptroller of the Currency (OCC) for national banks, by the Federal Reserve Board for state member banks, and by the FDIC for insured nonmember banks. Often, the state bank regulatory agencies will participate in the action with their Federal counterparts in cases involving state-chartered institutions.

The original enabling legislation for each of the banking agencies endowed them with explicit and implicit powers to supervise the institutions under their respective jurisdictions. The Financial Institutions Supervisory Act of 1966 gave them the authority to enter into written agreements with, or issue cease-and-desist orders against, insured banks, bank holding companies, and persons associated with these organizations that engage in unsafe or unsound practices or that violate applicable laws or regulations. The agencies were also authorized to suspend or remove officers, directors, and certain other bank-related individuals.

The Financial Institutions Regulatory and Interest Rate Control Act of 1978 authorized the banking agencies to assess civil money penalties for violations of cease and desist orders or of certain provisions of banking law. More recent legislation, such as the Garn-St Germain Depository Institutions Act of 1982 and the International Lending Supervision Act of 1983, further expanded and strengthened the agencies' enforcement powers.

An accompanying table indicates the recent sharp increase in cease and desist orders and formal agreements to correct unsafe or unsound practices or violations of law or regulations. The bank agencies have also

Federal Bank Regulators—Cease And Desist Orders and Final Agreements, 1981-1984

	1984	1983	1982	1981
Comptroller of the Currency				
Cease and Desist Orders	103	75	34	21
Agreements	337	166	93	64
Federal Deposit Insurance Corporation				
Cease and Desist Orders	125	223*	69	38
Federal Reserve Board				
Cease and Desist Orders	26	40	15	14
Written Agreements	60	33	23	12

* The large number of FDIC cease and desist orders for 1983 was due in part to actions concerning a group of commonly-controlled Tennessee banks.

increased their use of other formal administrative measures. For example, the FDIC initiated 32 termination of deposit insurance proceedings in 1984, compared to 26 in 1983, 18 in 1982, and three in 1981. In these cases, the banks involved usually correct their problems, merge with other banks, or cease operations before insurance coverage is terminated. The OCC has assessed civil money penalties in a number of cases for violations of law as well as violations of final cease and desist orders, as have the other agencies. The Federal Reserve actions involved bank holding companies or their subsidiaries, as well as banks.

The preceding data cover only formal administrative actions. At the same time, the agencies have been increasing their use of informal administrative actions in those cases where a corrective program is desirable but formal administrative action is not considered necessary. In an informal action, the bank and its Federal regulator enter into a Memorandum of Understanding, also known as an MOU. The OCC initiated approximately 500 administrative actions in 1984—formal and informal—compared to 283 in 1983, 175 in 1982, and 128 in 1981.

The Federal Home Loan Bank Board also has increased its use of enforcement actions in recent years, but a discussion of administrative actions against FSLIC-insured institutions is beyond the scope of this article.

This article will now discuss the framework within which problem and near-problem banks are identified and the principal types of administrative actions that can be taken, as well as the banking agencies' enforcement policies for banks so identified. The more common provisions included by the regulators in the administrative actions and some of the options available for dealing with them also will be examined in some detail.

CAMEL

In 1979, the Federal bank regulatory agencies adopted the Uniform Financial Institutions Rating System to provide the framework for a uniform approach to rating financial institutions. The Uniform System has two principal elements. First, an assessment is made of five factors of critical importance to a bank's operations and condition: (1) capital; (2) asset quality; (3) management; (4) earnings; and (5) liquidity; hence, the rating system's acronym "CAMEL." Each of the factors is rated on a scale of 1 through 5, 1 being the most favorable.

The second element of the CAMEL system is the assignment of a composite rating to each bank. Again, the range of ratings is 1 through 5. The composite rating is assigned by the examiner, primarily on the basis of the CAMEL ratings, although other relevant factors are considered when appropriate. The composite rating is not simply an average of the CAMEL ratings but summarizes the examiner's findings and judgment with respect to the bank's condition and operations. Examiner judgment is the key to the rating system.

The composite rating identifies those banks that warrant special supervisory attention. Banks with a composite rating of 1 are sound in almost every respect and are subject to only routine supervision. Banks with a composite rating of 2 have minor correctable weaknesses and are subject to normal supervision. Banks with a composite rating of 3 have a combination of financial, operational or compliance weaknesses that, if not addressed and corrected, could easily result in deterioration of the bank's condition. More than normal supervision is required. Banks with a composite rating of 4 have serious weaknesses and a potential for failure. Close supervision is required together with a definitive plan for correction. A 5-rated bank has a high probability of failure and is subject to continuous and urgent supervisory attention and concern and, if it is to survive, requires aid from stockholders or other financial assistance.

Types of Administrative Agency Actions

As has been indicated, the bank regulatory agencies utilize both formal and informal administrative actions to obtain corrective action. Formal actions in the context of this article are either written agreements or cease and desist orders executed pursuant to the Financial Institutions Supervisory Act of 1966. A high percentage of these actions result in consent agreements, as banks usually choose not to exercise their right to a formal administrative hearing.

A summary of a typical cease and desist order might contain some or all of the following provisions requiring a bank to:

eliminate violations of laws, rules, and regulations and take steps to ensure full compliance in the future; provide qualified management acceptable to the regulatory authorities; charge off losses and reduce the volume of classified assets; cease extending new loans to borrowers already adversely classified; reduce loan volume; establish acceptable written loan (or investment) policies; establish and maintain an adequate reserve for loan losses; obtain new equity capital and maintain a given capital ratio; stop payment of dividends; maintain adequate liquidity; and furnish periodic progress reports.

A typical written agreement would contain many of the same provisions.

The Federal Reserve includes a provision in its written agreements stipulating that the agreements may be enforced in the same manner as a cease and desist order through a court order or assessment of civil money penalties. The OCC's agreements generally are enforceable by a cease and desist action.

In an informal action, the bank's board of directors and the agencies' regional office or Reserve Bank sign a memorandum of understanding. The memorandum is not a written agreement executed pursuant to the Financial Institutions Supervisory Act of 1966, but instead represents an understanding between the bank and its regulator concerning the bank's principal problems and the bank's plans to correct the problems. The bank may be asked to sign the memorandum at the board meeting at which the examiners' evaluation is presented following the conclusion of the examination.

Agency Policies

The bank regulators have found the CAMEL rating system to be an effective administrative vehicle for addressing bank weaknesses and problems. It is OCC policy to take formal administrative action against all banks rated 4 or 5, either through the use of an agreement or a cease and desist order. The OCC will consider formal administrative action with respect to all banks rated 3. If it is concluded that formal action is inappropriate for a 3-rated bank, informal action will be undertaken through the use of a memorandum of understanding.

At the Federal Reserve, 4- and 5-rated banks are presumed to warrant formal action either through the use of a written agreement or a cease and desist order. The Federal Reserve will consider formal action for a 3-rated bank when legal violations are involved or when otherwise warranted, but in most cases will take informal action through the use of a memorandum of understanding.

Whether the OCC or the Federal Reserve will enter into a written agreement or a cease and desist order depends on a number of factors, including the severity of the problems and criticized practices, the presence of significant violations of law, and management's track record.

It is the policy of the FDIC to take formal administrative action against all 4- and 5-rated banks through the use of cease and desist orders. The FDIC does not currently use formal written agreements. As a general rule, and at a minimum, the FDIC considers informal administrative action for all 3-rated banks through the use of memoranda of understanding. The FDIC is the only bank regulatory agency that advises its regulated banks of CAMEL ratings, and it discloses only the composite rating.

Exceptions to these general policies can occur on occasions when there are strong mitigating factors. At the same time, the agencies are not precluded from taking administrative action against a 1- or 2-rated bank where such action is warranted.

Capital

Congress enacted the International Lending Supervision Act of 1983 (ILSA) primarily in response to the international debt problem, but it also addressed the capital adequacy of commercial banks in very specific terms. The legislation did not limit its reach with respect to bank capital just to those relatively few large banks engaged in international lending. As a practical matter, the bank supervisory agencies have always had a good deal of influence on bank capital requirements, although less with large banks. In those instances when a bank has challenged the bank regulator, the courts generally—although not always—have deferred to the bank agency's judgment. ILSA strengthened the bank regulators' hands. In response to these more explicit statutory powers, the FDIC recently adopted final regulations implementing new capital standards. The OCC is expected to adopt similar regulations in the near future, and the Federal Reserve is in the process of developing capital guidelines.

In most administrative actions, there will be a requirement with respect to the bank's capital position. In some instances, a memorandum of understanding may not provide for any specific level of capital, but only require the bank to prepare and submit a capital program covering the next few years. In other cases, a specific amount of additional capital might be required. The capital requirement could be expressed as a dollar amount or as a ratio of capital to assets, or both. A written agreement or order will mandate that the capital requirements be attained within some specific time frame, unless an immediate infusion of capital is urgently needed. In addition, the bank will have to prepare and submit a capital program.

The matter of capital is, in most cases, negotiable, both as to amount and timing. Therefore, it is extremely important to a bank that its capital program be developed with specific goals and strategies spelled out for achieving and maintaining the desired capital position. Assets, liabilities, and earnings must be carefully analyzed. The risk characteristics of the bank's criticized assets must be taken into account, including anticipated loan loss provisions and potential losses and charge-offs. Where asset problems are very severe, consideration might be given to shrinking the bank's assets, if feasible.

Where asset problems are only moderately severe and the bank is not expanding rapidly and is profitable, a bank could try to rely on retained earnings to achieve the desired capital-asset ratio. In such a situation, realistic and detailed earnings projections must be developed since the bank's earnings forecast will not be accepted automatically and uncritically by the bank regulator.

Dividend policy will also have to be reasonable, and dividend payments may require the prior approval of the regulator. If the bank expects to continue to grow while it is dealing with its asset problems or other financial problems, retained earnings alone are unlikely to be sufficient to margin growth, and new capital must be raised.

The amount of capital required by the regulatory authorities will have to be sufficient to bring the bank's capital to asset ratio to a specified level somewhere above the 6 percent capital ratios applicable to those banks that exhibit no material financial weakness. The regulators prefer common stock, but other forms of capital, including preferred stock, mandatory convertible debt, and subordinated notes and debentures may be acceptable to the regulator in appropriate cases, subject to certain limitations and restrictions.

When compliance with a cease and desist order involves the raising of capital through a public distribution of the bank's securities (even when limited to existing shareholders), the FDIC, for example, insists that the order also include a provision requiring the bank to prepare offering materials fully describing the securities being offered, including an accurate description of the financial condition of the bank and the circumstances giving rise to the offering, and any other material disclosures necessary to comply with the Federal securities laws. The plan and materials must be submitted to the FDIC for its prior review and any changes requested by the FDIC incorporated prior to dissemination.

Disclosure of the existence of the order and the factors that brought it about could have an adverse impact on the success of the stock offering and, on occasion, on the deposit stability of certain banks. But the impact could be lessened by the way in which the disclosure is presented. A discussion of the measures already taken and being taken to address the bank's deficiencies, for example, can be helpful. Nevertheless, disclosure issues are often among the most difficult to resolve in connection with compliance with formal agency agreements.

The bank can also consider other strategies to enhance its capital account, including the sale of certain assets, the sale and leaseback of one or more of the bank buildings, and the sale of branches.

Loan Quality

The loan portfolio in most cases involving memoranda, written agreements, or orders will include a large volume of substandard or other criticized loans, perhaps as much as 80 percent or more of the bank's capital. Substandard loans have well-defined weaknesses, either with respect to the borrower's ability to pay or the value of pledged collateral, so that some loss may be incurred if deficiencies are not corrected. In some instances, a memorandum of understanding may require the bank simply to take prompt action to strengthen the loan account and to review—and where necessary revise—loan policies and procedures. A requirement to collect and maintain current and satisfactory credit information and other pertinent documentation on all loans where this information is lacking is commonly included. Strengthening of loan procedures—depending on the individual institution—could involve programs for improving credit analysis and presentation, systematic reviews of loan and credit files, and development or revision of a procedures manual. Establishment of a separate credit department might be considered if the bank does not have one.

In more serious cases, a written agreement or order will require the bank to reduce the level of substandard loans to specific levels within mandated time frames—perhaps one year—with further reductions to bring criticized loans down to an acceptable level in 18 months or some other appropriate period of time. Fairly explicit requirements with respect to credit standards and loan administration and documentation also might be spelled out.

Better implementation of an existing formal loan review program undoubtedly would be part of an agreement involving significant loan problems. If a formal loan review system is not in place, the bank may have to establish one or consider alternative methods, such as periodic reviews of criticized loans and all other large loans, either in-house or with outside assistance. A formal review program helps a bank to identify as soon as possible those loans requiring special attention and thereby assists in reducing loan losses. The loans thus singled out should be reviewed by senior management on a continuing basis and their status reported to the bank's board monthly, detailing the current status of the loan, collection efforts, corrective measures being taken, and other pertinent information. A formal program also presents an opportunity to evaluate on a regular and continuing basis the adequacy of the bank's credit files and to ascertain that the bank's loan policies and procedures comply with banking law and regulations, with the bank's established lending policies, and with general banking practice.

Regulators realize that significant reductions in the volume of substandard loans take time where there is a large volume of such loans. Nevertheless, it is important, in terms of compliance and for the bank's profitability, that these loans be reduced as promptly as possible. In any event, the bank should develop a plan for managing both its troubled loans and its total loan portfolio to prevent recurrence of problems. In addition, the bank may even wish to consider a temporary reduction in loan activity in order to concentrate its efforts on its problem loans and on steps to strengthen its loan account and credit administration process in accordance with the agreement.

Where the bank is extending credit with inadequate diversification of risk, the written agreement or order will include a requirement that such loans to individuals or related interests be reduced to 25 percent or less of the bank's capital within a certain period of time—perhaps six months. Some leeway is usually permitted in situations where the bank's interests need to be protected. The agreement also may require the establishment of guidelines by the bank on risk diversification.

The Loan Loss Reserve

With a large volume of criticized loans, the adequacy of the bank's reserve for loan losses becomes a cause for concern, and both formal and informal agreements will include a requirement that an adequate loan loss reserve be maintained. Provisions for loan losses must be charged to operations and losses charged to the reserve. The reserve should be maintained at a level sufficient to absorb expected loan losses, based upon management's evaluation of the current loan portfolio—an evaluation always subject to review by the bank regulatory authorities. The adequacy of the reserve must be reviewed quarterly, and the results noted in the board minutes. The loan portfolio itself requires constant monitoring by top management. The "watch list" produced by the formal loan review process—the list includes both criticized loans and other loans requiring special attention—provides a basic record for assessment of adequacy of the loan loss reserve.

A certain dollar figure or a specific reserve to loan balance ratio requirement is not likely to be imposed. But any subsequent examiner review will accord great weight to the level of reserves in relation to the kind and volume of criticized loans—and may apply some specific criteria as a measure of adequacy.

Investments

When the quality of a bank's investments has been criticized or other investments considered unsuitable, or there is evidence of other improper investment practices, such as overtrading, the bank will be required to stop the criticized practices. As with other matters, affirmative action may have to be undertaken to correct conditions such as extended maturities, significant portfolio depreciation, and inadequate liquidity. In these instances, the bank's written investment policy will also have to be reviewed and revised.

Liquidity

If, for various reasons, a bank does not have adequate liquidity, its liquidity policies and practices must be reviewed and either modified or a new policy developed. A specific level of liquidity could be required and, in more serious cases, a temporary prohibition placed on the extension of credit. In developing a liquidity policy, management should consider establishing formal asset and liability management policies, even if not specifically required by the agreement. Such a comprehensive policy should take into account not merely anticipated demands on the bank's liquidity position from deposit inflows and outflows and other developments increasing the need for liquidity but should embrace the full gamut of funds management issues, including balance sheet composition, investments, hedging policies if used, the bank's sensitivity to interest rate fluctuations and to other variables, as well as its earnings performance and overall objectives.

Management and Controls

Depending upon the individual circumstances, there may be a number of provisions in any agreement, formal or informal, relating to management—quite apart from suspension or removal of officers and imposition of civil money penalties for violations of statutes or orders that are involved in the more serious cases. At a minimum, management will be required to develop new policies and procedures in all criticized areas. In other cases, the agreement will require the appointment of a new executive officer or some other senior officer, such as a loan officer. If the bank has significant operational problems, there may be a requirement to strengthen that particular area. Appointment of a committee to oversee implementation of any budget requirements or to ensure corrections in various areas has frequently been stipulated. The agreement may also provide that the names of any new officers and their qualifications be submitted to the regulatory agency for review.

If internal audit and controls are found to be weak, the agreement may provide for the appointment of an internal auditor or other actions to address the problem. A bank may be required to review its accounting practices and, where appropriate, republish and refile call reports. Banks have also been required to engage an independent accounting firm to conduct regular or special audits.

Earnings

When a bank is not profitable, it may be required to take steps to enhance earnings. In some cases, all that might be necessary would be adoption of a budget designed to achieve profitability. In other cases, a written agreement or order may be more specific with respect to certain categories of income or expense or certain aspects of the bank's operations.

Violations of Law

All violations of banking laws and regulations must, of course, be corrected as promptly as possible, with compliance by a certain date or within a fixed period of time—perhaps 90 days. Additional time may be granted when the correction cannot be made within the specified time. Violations of legal lending limits or of restrictions on insider and affiliate loans should be given immediate attention.

Public Disclosure

The bank examination report incorporating the results of an examination is confidential, and almost all hearings or meetings on formal or informal administrative actions are private. Nevertheless, when a bank has been the subject of an administrative enforcement action, issues related to public disclosure arise. Banks must comply with applicable securities laws and bank holding companies must meet SEC requirements. Specifically, the issues involve:

(1) Whether to disclose to existing shareholders and prospective investors the existence of cease and desist orders and written agreements;

(2) The specificity of the disclosure concerning the nature of the administrative actions;

(3) The extent to which the material terms of the actions should be disclosed; and

(4) The nature and timing of such disclosures with respect to existing shareholders.

Last year the FDIC and the OCC solicited public comment on general disclosure policy, including the need for additional disclosure of administrative enforcement actions. Recently, the FDIC again solicited comments on a proposed statement of policy which provides for the FDIC to publish and make available to the public the names of all banks and persons participating in their affairs to whom the FDIC has issued notices and final orders in conjunction with statutory enforcement actions.

As mentioned earlier in this article, the FDIC has for some time been including a standard disclosure provision in its cease and desist orders whenever an order involves the raising of capital through a public distribution of the bank's securities. Since late 1984, the FDIC has been including another standard provision in its orders requiring the bank to send to its shareholders or otherwise furnish a description of the order with the bank's next shareholder communication and also with its notice or proxy statement preceding the bank's next shareholder meeting. The description must fully describe the order in all material respects. As in the case of a capital plan, the description and any accompanying communication, statement or notice must be submitted for review by the FDIC and any changes requested by the FDIC made prior to dissemination.

Negotiations

In the discussions and negotiations prior to consenting to a cease and desist order or conclusion of a written agreement, the regulatory authorities usually exhibit flexibility and a willingness to negotiate. The appropriateness of the rating or examination findings can be discussed as well as the terms of the proposed corrective actions. Time limits for compliance and certain dollar provisions are obvious examples. The contents of most memoranda of understanding also are open to negotiation. Any agreement entered into must be acceptable to the regulator and satisfactory to the bank.

Compliance and solutions that can realistically be implemented are in the interest of both the banking agencies and the banks themselves. The bank itself must have a clear concept of what it can and should do toward addressing and correcting its problems as identified in the course of the bank examination and set forth in the agreement. The specific approach may vary from institution to institution, but all should involve a high degree of management cooperation and involvement, constant vigilance in areas of concern, and continuous analysis and review of the progress being made. ■